New Perspectives on Women Entrepreneurs

A volume in
Research in Entrepreneurship and Management
Series Editor: John E. Butler

New Perspectives on Women Entrepreneurs

Edited by

John E. Butler
The Hong Kong Polytechnic University

INFORMATION AGE
PUBLISHING

80 Mason Street • Greenwich, Connecticut 06830 • www.infoagepub.com

Library of Congress Cataloging-in-Publication Data

New perspectives on women entrepreneurs / [edited by] John E. Butler.
  p. cm. – (Research in entrepreneurship and management)
Includes bibliographical references.
  1. Businesswomen. 2. Women executives. 3. Women-owned business enterprises 4. Entrepreneurship. 5. Feminist economics. I. Butler, John E., 1946- II. Series.
  HD6053.N438 2003
  338'.04'082–dc21
                                          2003013602

Copyright © 2003 Information Age Publishing Inc.

All rights reserved. No part of this publication may be reproduced, stored in a retrieval system, or transmitted, in any form or by any means, electronic, mechanical, photocopying, microfilming, recording or otherwise, without written permission from the publisher.

Printed in the United States of America

LIST OF CONTRIBUTORS

Elena Aculai Ministry of Economy of the Republic of Moldova
Chisinau, Moldova
E-mail: eaculai@moldova.md

Leona Achtenhagen Jönköping International Business School
Jönköping, Sweden
E-Mail: Leona.Achtenhagen@ihh.hi.se

Barbara Bird American University
Washington, DC USA
E-mail: bjbird@erols.com

Richard Bliss Babson College
Babson Park, MA USA
E-mail: blissr@babson.edu

Joe Bogue University College Cork,
Cork, Ireland
E-mail:j.bogue@ucc.ie

Candida Brush Boston University
Boston, MA USA
E-mail: cgbrush@acs.bu.edu

Nancy M. Carter University of St. Thomas
Minneapolis, MN USA
Email: nmcarter@stthomas.edu

Sara Carter University of Strathclyde
Glasgow, Scotland, UK
E-mail: s.carter@strath.ac.uk

Richael Connolly	University College Cork Cork, Ireland E-mail: R.Connolly@ucc.ie
Patricia G. Greene	University of Missouri–Kansas City Kansas City, MO USA E-mail: greenep@umkc.edu
Margaret J. Greer	National University Sacramento, CA USA E-mail: mgreer@nu.edu
Colette Henry	Dundalk Institute of Technology Dundalk, Co Louth, Ireland E-mail: Colette.henry@dkit.ie
Nina Isakova	The National Academy of Science Kiev, Ukraine E-mail: nisakova@hotmail.com
Sarah Kennedy	Dundalk Institute of Technology Dundalk, Co Louth, Ireland E-mail: sorcha98@hotmail.com
Nan Langowitz	Babson College Babson Park, MA USA E-mail: Langowitz@babson.edu
Ewa Lisowska	Warsaw School of Economics Warsaw, Poland E-mail: ewael@sgh.waw.pl
Sue Marlow	De Montfort University Leicester, England, UK E-mail: smhum@dmu.ac.uk
Claudia Morgan	Brandeis University Boston, MA USA E-mail: morganite@attbi.com
Catherine W. Ng	The Hong Kong Polytechnic University Hong Kong SAR,China E-mail: mswhng@polyu.edu.hk

Evelyn G.H. Ng	University of Hong Kong Hong Kong, SAR, China E-mail: evelyn-ng-gaikhoon@graduate.hku.hk
Bill O'Gorman	University College Cork Cork, Ireland E-mail: b.ogorman@ucc.ie
Lidija Polutnik	Babson College Babson Park, MA, USA E-mail: polutnik@babson.edu
David Smallbone	Middlesex University The Burroughs, Hendon, UK E-mail: d.smallbone@mdx.ac.uk
Natalja Schakirova	Business Women's Association of Uzbekistan "Tadbirkor Ayol" Tashkent, Uzbekistan E-mail: natalja@uzpak.uz
Friederike Welter	Rhine-Westfalia Institute for Economic Research Essen, Germany E-mail: welter@rwi-essen.de
Mary L. Williams	Widener University Chester, PA USA E-mail: Mary.L.Williams@widener.edu

CONTENTS

NEW PERSPECTIVES ON WOMEN ENTREPRENEURS
An Introduction
John E. Butler — xi

1. **FEMINIST THEORY AND THE STUDY OF ENTREPRENEURSHIP**
   Margaret J. Greer and Patricia G. Greene — 1

2. **COMPARING SOCIAL FEMINISM AND LIBERAL FEMINISM**
   The Case of New Firm Growth
   Nancy M. Carter and Mary L. Williams — 25

3. **EXPLORING LEADERSHIP VISION**
   New Perspectives on Women Entrepreneurs and Executives
   Barbara Bird and Candida Brush — 51

4. **FEMALE ENTREPRENEURSHIP IN GERMANY**
   Context, Development and its Reflection in German Media
   Leona Achtenhagen and Friederike Welter — 71

5. **WOMEN ENTREPRENEURS**
   Breaking Through the Glass Barrier
   Nan S. Langowitz and Claudia Morgan — 101

6. **WOMEN MICRO ENTREPRENEURS IN HONG KONG**
   Balancing the Personal with the Business
   Evelyn G. H. Ng and Catherine W. Ng — 121

7. **ARE THE BARRIERS TO BUSINESS START-UP GREATER FOR FEMALE RECENT GRADUATE ENTREPRENEURS (FRGES) THAN MALE RECENT GRADUATE ENTREPRENEURS (MRGES)?**
   Richael Connolly, Bill O'Gorman, and Joe Bogue — 151

8. **ACCOUNTING FOR CHANGE**
   Professionalism as a Challenge to Gender Disadvantage in Entrepreneurship
   Sara Carter and Sue Marlow — *181*

9. **IN SEARCH OF A NEW CELTIC TIGER**
   Female Entrepreneurship in Ireland
   Colette Henry and Sarah Kennedy — *203*

10. **WOMEN BUSINESS OWNERS AND MANAGERS IN POLAND**
    Richard T. Bliss, Lidija Polutnik and Ewa Lisowska — *225*

11. **FEMALE ENTREPRENEURSHIP IN POST SOVIET COUNTRIES**
    Friederike Welter, David Smallbone, Elena Aculai, Nina Isakova, and Natalja Schakirova — *243*

ABOUT THE CONTRIBUTORS — *271*

NEW PERSPECTIVES ON WOMEN ENTREPRENEURS

An Introduction

John E. Butler

In Chapter 1 Greer and Greene examine entrepreneurship, especially at the business founding stage using three feminist theory perspectives, liberal, Marxist and radical. They highlight how a liberal perspective, which tends to focus on legal or institutional barriers to women, misses some of the factors such as work experience, social networks, and access to initial funding where gender still matters. By focusing too narrowly on trying to make men and women equal in a legal and institutional and legal sense, factors equally important to entrepreneurial behavior are missed.

The Marxist perspective suggests that economic exploitation must be ended before women can achieve economic equality. The authors suggest that there is a body of research that shows that household contributions of women, because they are not calculated and shared equally, may have an impact on entrepreneurial behavior by women. Here they call for more research that compares women entrepreneurs to women working in the private sector, as well as for comparisons between men and women entrepreneurs to determine more precisely the impact of unpaid household work on entrepreneurial opportunities.

The radical feminism perspective views women and men as different and suggests that men have often used these differences to place a higher priority on men's traits and characteristics. Little research exists on programs designed by women and for women, with respect of entrepreneurial behavior. While there are some micro-lending schemes identified, this perspective does suggest an agenda that has been seriously overlooked in the existing research.

When the existing research is mapped onto these feminist perspectives, it becomes more obvious that research needs to expand both the perspectives used to analyze entrepreneurial behavior, as well as the questions addressed and the factors included in the models we use to attempt to more fully uncover entrepreneurial behavior.

In Chapter 2 Carter and Williams use the social feminism and liberal feminism perspective to build a theory that ties resources, initial strategy, initial sales and growth to gender. Feminist theory is used to theorize about the degree to which disadvantages with respect to human capital and resources are likely to affect the formulation of initial strategy, sales and sales growth. The empirical results here, as is true in most early stage research, provide some support for the notion that woman entrepreneurs do exhibit different initial strategies than men. The results also point to the fact that research is needed on developing constructs that can more specifically tie feminist theory to entrepreneurial behavior and success.

Greer and Geene and Carter and Williams both examine the impact that institutional and societal constraints have on women entrepreneurs. It is also likely that these factors also impact on others, in terms of how they view the role of women in the workplace, and even in terms of the types of entrepreneurial ventures or professions that they see as appropriate for women. In Chapters 3, 4, and 5, Bird and Brush, Achtenhagen and Welter, and Langowitz and Morgan make use of the media to identify successful women executives and entrepreneurs in one case (Bird and Brush) while the other two chapters focus on the impact of press images on the nature and form of entrepreneurial behavior by women.

Bird and Brush specifically focus on successful women executives and entrepreneurs, by drawing their sample from individuals identified in the media as successful. These groups are examined in terms of a number of content categories and on various dimensions of vision. This research extends the work on vision by specifically bringing women into the equation. While trait research had tended to find few differences between executives and entrepreneur, the research here suggests that when a managerial perspective such as vision, firm focus, or ways of competing are examined that there may be differences, at least with respect to successful women executives and entrepreneurs.

In Germany entrepreneurial behavior by women has been on the increase, especially in East Germany right after reunification. Achtenhager and Welter focus on the use of discourse in newspapers to examine the socially constructed entrepreneur. Using discourse analysis they show that articles tend to focus on the systemic or economic contributions as well as the substantive (political and cultural) contributions of women entrepreneurs. The newspaper discourses also often focus on factors such as attractiveness and the degree to which women entrepreneurs are still able to fulfill childcare and household duties. In general fulfillment is attributed to women entrepreneurs while men tend to be linked to more tangible financial rewards. The balance between recognizing that higher rates of entrepreneurial behavior by women is good for the economy, and yet also wanting to restrict the degree to which this expanded participation interferes with roles related to home and family appears to blur much of the discourse in Germany.

Langowitz and Morgan directly examine the issue of the woman as a "dire circumstance" business founder, rather than one who starts a business based on their personal desires and the drive to build a successful enterprise. This perspective may act to put a "glass barrier" on women's entrepreneurial ventures, and this paper examines the degree to which profiles of women entrepreneurs in the business press act to reinforce this image. When the profiles of women entrepreneurs are contrasted with those of a representative group of women entrepreneurs, it appears the business press is more inclined to portray women who were down on their luck, got a business idea in a "eureka" fashion, and started relatively small organizations in industries normally associated with women. The fear, of course, is that this will act to channel women into low potential business ventures, rather than into those more representative of women entrepreneurs.

The balance between business and personal goals is picked up in Chapter 6 by Ng and Ng, in their examination of women entrepreneurs in Hong Kong. Their examination of micro-entrepreneurs looks at the degree to which child rearing and household obligations act to limit business growth. Social changes in Hong Kong, which have resulted in large increases in the never married female population have provided a pool from which successful entrepreneurs could, and to some degree are being drawn. Limited access to professional associations, little targeted governmental support, and prevailing attitudes that often channel women entrepreneurs into less promising growth enterprises appear to be acting as constraints on both entrepreneurial behavior at the micro-enterprise level, and movement out of that level.

Normal prescriptions related to entrepreneurship, such as getting work experience and building up a network are difficult for many women entrepreneurs. Connolly, O'Gorman, and Bogue focus on entrepreneurs who deliberately bypass this process, in Chapter 7. They examine a small sample of entrepreneurs who founded their business after graduating and without any post graduation work experience. While this model of entrepreneurship is relatively rare, their research identified a link between part time work experience and the nature of the business started. Gender differences are also identified at the individual, behavioral and environmental perception level. More important, their in-depth qualitative study is used to formulate a model for recent graduate entrepreneurs.

Women have been entering the professions of medicine, law and accountancy in growing numbers in the United Kingdom. Carter and Marlow, in Chapter 8 examine the degree to which women entrepreneurs have been able to establish accounting practices. It appears that women accountants start their own practices at much earlier ages that men do, but the undying reasons may reflect the fact that they see fewer opportunities for promotions in their existing firms. However, there may also be some disadvantages of staring earlier because less experience appears to be associated with a narrower range of business services, which translates to less revenue and less growth in revenue. Most important, this research shows that the revenue gap is not closing.

The final three chapters take a critical look at entrepreneurial behavior in Ireland, Poland, Moldova, Uzbekistan, and the Ukraine. In doing so they highlight the fact that women entrepreneurs in these countries still face some of the very basic institutional and cultural roadblocks that are less visible in some of the other countries where women entrepreneurs have been examined in this volume.

In the European Union, Ireland has the lowest rate of startups by women. In Chapter 9, Henry and Kennedy outline some of the reasons why women make up only 15% of the entrepreneurs in Southern Ireland and 16% in Northern Ireland, and they point out that a recent GEM report suggests that the current rate at which women are becoming entrepreneurs is even lower. Their examination of entrepreneurs in both Northern and Southern Ireland has the goal of developing a model that would facilitate entrepreneurial behavior in Ireland. The authors point out that Ireland's historical legacy as a poor country without a strong entrepreneurial culture, and a tradition that tied women to the role of homemaker may account for some of the lack of women's entrepreneurial behavior.

There appears to be little organized government support to increase the role of women in founding businesses. In their examination Ireland's women entrepreneurs appeared to be focused on service, consultancy and craft industries, with businesses in the North showing more potential than the South. Many of them indicated that frustration with the established workplace, encouragement from family members, or luck was the main force that led them to start their own businesses. In this respect, the research here suggests that the profile of a women entrepreneur as proactive opportunity seekers still needs further development in at least one country in the European Union.

In Chapter 10, Bliss, Polutnik, and Lisowska provide an interesting analysis of the impact of Poland's transition to a market economy on women entrepreneurs and women managers, and examine the differences between these groups. While the state owned enterprises of the socialist era focused on scale and standardization, economic reform brought the opportunity for entrepreneurs to satisfy consumers by offering differentiated products. These authors examine the reasons for women to follow entrepreneurial paths, as well as contrasting them with those choosing managerial careers in larger enterprises. In some cases they are responding to life style choices, as entrepreneurs are more likely to be married and have children, and have less formal education. However, entrepreneurs are three times more likely to be in the highest income bracket than are their women manager counterparts, so it appears likely that women entrepreneurs will continue to emerge at a faster rate in Poland.

In the final chapter Welter, Smallbone, Aculai, Isakova, and Schakirova provide an examination of women entrepreneurs in The Ukraine, Moldova and Uzbekistan. Basic questions related to the distinctive characteristics of women-owned businesses, the position of women in society, and the overall business environment in terms of its support for entrepreneurial behavior by women is examined.

The research here clearly indicates that a multiple lens treatment is needed to understanding entrepreneurial behavior in the new independent countries of the former Soviet Union. Using both surveys and case studies the authors examine women entrepreneurs both in terms of the impact of the impact of life in the Soviet Union, as well as the variety of cultural, religious, family and economic conditions that characterize these three countries.

A reading of the complete set of research papers contained in this volume leads to the conclusion that the research agenda on women entrepreneurs is growing. While developed economies are dealing with issues related to the extension of venture capital and growth, developing economies are still coping with eliminating some of the basic institutional and social factors that inhibit the rate at which women enter the entrepreneurial ranks. Clearly the hope is that this volume has made a contribution to the existing body of research. Hopefully, it will provide some encouragement for academics to continue to engage in research on this important topic.

CHAPTER 1

FEMINIST THEORY AND THE STUDY OF ENTREPRENEURSHIP

Margaret J. Greer and Patricia G. Greene

ABSTRACT

This paper applies three perspectives of feminist theory, Liberal, Marxist, and Radical, to research on entrepreneurial women. The paper discusses each perspective and reviews the appropriate entrepreneurship literature using those perspectives. We then discuss three early examples of feminist theory in entrepreneurship research, the works of Brush (1992), Hurley (1991), and Fisher, Reuber, and Dyke (1993). These studies each represent an important step forward in incorporating gender as an analytic category in the study of entrepreneurship. We contend that future research on women in entrepreneurship would benefit from a thorough grounding in wider sociological scholarship on women's economic activity and in more complete applications of feminist theory.

INTRODUCTION

This paper begins by asking the question, why should we turn to feminist theory to learn about entrepreneurship? Feminist theory is the specific area of social theory that addresses relations of gender. Feminist theory has also supplied a rich tradition of analyzing relations of gender and of class, making it a first choice for researching the economic activity of women and men. The study of women engaging in activities categorized as self-employment, small business ownership or entrepreneurship has grown along with their numbers over the last two decades. However, as other researchers have noted, work in this relatively new field of study often lacks a specific theoretical framework either of feminism or of entrepreneurship (Barrett, 1994; Brush, 1992; Hurley, 1991).

We seek to correct this situation in two ways. The first section of the paper discusses the three major subfields of feminist theory (Liberal, Marxist and Radical) and reexamines existing literature on women entrepreneurs using these theories. The second part of the paper examines several specific efforts to use feminist theory in entrepreneurship research. These works include Brush's (1992) "integrated perspective" which focuses on the woman business owner as embedded in an environment of networked work, family, and society relationships, Hurley's (1991) epistemological review of the collection of entrepreneurial knowledge, and Fisher, Reuber, and Dyke's (1993) use of social feminism to better understand discrimination against women business owners. We have essentially two critiques of these endeavors to date: First: there is a lack of integration between the well-established field of study on women in the labor force and the rapidly expanding body of work concerning women entrepreneurs. Secondly, the applications of feminist theory done so far tend to be piecemeal and do not adequately apply any one focus from feminist theory to the study of women entrepreneurs. The article concludes with some suggestions for a more thorough and effective utilization of feminist theory in the study of entrepreneurship.

FEMINIST THEORY: LIBERAL, MARXIST, RADICAL

As a place to begin a feminist analysis, it is useful to look at categorizations of feminist theory. While there are various sub fields in feminist theory and different ways of classifying them, we will rely on a division of feminist theory into Liberal, Marxist and Radical. We take this approach, in part, because both liberal feminism and Marxist feminist have been widely used within the field of sociology to analyze women's economic activity. The following section outlines the major tenets of these perspectives and reviews research on women entrepreneurs that have drawn on the perspective or to which the perspective is applicable.

Liberal Feminism

The goal of liberal feminism historically has been the elimination of explicit legal and institutional barriers to women's participation in society on an equal basis with men. Liberal feminism regards men and women as equal, autonomous individuals. Thus, the solution to women's lesser achievements is to remove barriers to women's participation, notably in education and employment. The removal of legal barriers allows men and women to be free as individuals, moving ahead based on their talents, skills and willingness to work. The earliest emphases of liberal feminist concerned the citizenship rights of women (Jagger, 1983; Sapiro, 1994). The Married Women's Property Acts of the nineteenth century and the Woman Suffrage Campaign of the nineteenth and twentieth centuries are classic examples of these efforts. More recent liberal feminist reforms continue to focus on barriers in education and employment; 1970s efforts to increase equality in the labor force by removing gender as an explicit job qualification in a wide variety of occupations is clearly both liberal and feminist. Liberal feminism rests on the premise that biological sex should not preclude the equal rights afforded to individuals in a democratic society; thus, men and women can be regarded as essentially the same.

While existing research on women business owners is not consistently organized according to any particular feminist framework, much of this research can be viewed from a feminist perspective. Since the entrepreneurship literature that considers gender often includes both a focus on legal and institutional barriers and recognition that findings from this research rarely support gendered differences in psychological or demographic profiles, this body of work fits well with a liberal feminist view.

The entrepreneurial behavior of women is not now constrained by law. Historically laws existed that prohibited women from owning property, operating a business or borrowing money. However, over time these laws have been repealed and do not directly contribute to limitations on women's business ownership in the United States. We can see the positive effects of liberal legal reforms in terms of entrepreneurship in the fact that more women are choosing to be entrepreneurs. By 2002 the number of women-owned businesses reached a total of 6.2 million majority owned businesses, representing almost 34% of all U.S. businesses. These numbers represent an increase of 16% from the 1992 census data (Center for Women's Business Research, 2001). In addition, the level of revenues generated increased 33% over the same time period. It is estimated that in 2002 women-owned businesses employed 9.2 million people and generated almost $1.15 trillion in sales (Center for Women's Business Research, 2002). However, the legacy of earlier laws restricted the economic behavior of women did contribute to the development of institutional and social practices that continue to constrain entrepreneurial behavior. As a result, the number, size, type and scope of women-owned businesses are still often less than those owned by men. The institutional barriers that contribute to this situation are related to gender differences in: (1) education, (2) work experiences, (3) networks, and (4) access to capital.

The education of women business owners is relevant both to the level and the type of education. The educational background of women business owners has been taken into account in most studies on women entrepreneurs. These studies share the fairly robust conclusion that the female entrepreneur is most often a college graduate (Bowen & Hisrich, 1986; Brush, 1992; Devine, 1994; Hisrich & Brush, 1983, 1987). However, the impact of the education remains in question. An analysis of PUMS data (Public Use Microsample Data) concludes that education and other human capital characteristics such as age and work experience were significant predictors of self-employment status (Carr, 1996). However, previous education does not seem to predict the eventual performance of the business (Allen & Carter, 1996).

The types of educational programs that women select or are placed in are important to their labor market activities. Hisrich (1986) described the educational background of female entrepreneurs as more likely to be in liberal arts, as compared to male entrepreneurs having a degree in business or engineering. Hisrich and Brush (1987, p. 190) also found a preponderance of liberal arts degrees, concluding that for women entrepreneurs "Engineering and science were infrequent areas of study." Indeed, women remain underrepresented in science and engineering related educational programs (Vetter, 1992). However, in 1997 female students in 1998 accounted for approximately 20% of engineering students (Society of Women Engineers, 2002).

This lack of scientific and technological education may make women's entry into technologically sophisticated businesses less likely, and it is these kinds of businesses that may generate the greatest income and profits. Women are more likely to start retail and service oriented businesses that, while they may be successful on other dimensions, do not routinely become as financially lucrative as businesses focused more on development and presentation of technology (Anna, Chandler, Jansen, & Mero, 2000; Brush, 1992, 1999; Brush & Hisrich, 1991; Loscocco & Robinson, 1991; Loscocco, Robinson, & Hall, 1992; Wharton, 1989). In one of the earliest studies on women who start "nontraditional" businesses, Hisrich and O'Brien (1981) found them to be even more highly educated than women owners of gender traditional types of businesses. Overall, however, many questions remain on how educational levels of the population of women business owners vary by industry.

Women's work experiences also shape their entrepreneurial behaviors. Occupational segregation, although slowly decreasing over the last three decades, remains a basic fact of the labor market (Reskin & Padavic, 2002). Women are much more likely to work in retail and service sectors than in manufacturing, construction, and other industrial sectors. This segregation occurs both across and within occupations. For instance, women working in construction will be more likely to work in smaller, less lucrative types of jobs such as wallpapering and interior painting (Loscocco & Robinson, 1991). There is no legal barrier to participation in higher paying trades. However, institutional barriers of custom can be insidiously effective in proscribing certain activities to either gender. For instance, many trade apprentice programs are strongly gendered along traditional lines, with cross-gendered attendance discouraged by family and friends. Hisrich and Brush (1983) found the previous work experience of women entrepreneurs to be primarily in the areas of teaching, middle management, and secretarial and to be highly correlated to the type of business started: 90% service, 7% financial, and only 3% in manufacturing. The educational and occupational choices made by young men and women are enacted into gender related constraints on work experiences that affect the types of businesses women start (Brush, 1992; Bowen & Hisrich, 1986; Robinson & Sexton, 1994).

Not only the type of her work experience but also her vertical placement in the authority structure has a direct effect on a woman's entrepreneurial activity. Women are less likely to hold top management positions in corporate environments. Currently women hold 15.7% of the corporate office positions in the Fortune 500 (Catalyst Census of Women Corporate Officers and Top Earners, 2002).

These are the positions where the general management experience most conducive to learning about running an entire business is gained. The "glass ceiling" remains an institutional limiting factor to gaining the general knowledge and experience that could be leveraged to entrepreneurial success (Moore & Buttner, 1997). Hisrich and Brush (1983) reported that 42% of their sample of entrepreneurial women became involved in the new venture due to job frustration in their previous position. For women, these previous positions are more likely to lead to experience in areas such as human resources where relational competencies, particularly those involved in employer-employee relations, are both an input and outcome of the position (Liou & Aldrich, 1995). These functional areas are often not those that will result in knowledge that will ultimately be helpful in the overarching activities of owning a small business. The long standing occupational segregation of women leads women entrepreneurs to feel particularly deficient in business functions to which they remain less exposed, for example, finance, marketing, and planning (Bowen & Hisrich, 1986; Hisrich & Brush, 1983; Kalleberg & Leicht, 1991).

Social and professional networks are the sources of all types of resources and assistance, both instrumental and expressive, for entrepreneurs. Few differences typically exist between the process of network creation by men and women (Aldrich, Reese, & Dubini, 1989; Brush, 1992). The ongoing discussion has centered largely on the size of the network, gender composition differences between men and women's networks, and the source of those network contacts, whether family or professional (Aldrich, 1989; Aldrich & Reese, 1994; Aldrich et al., 1989; Baines & Wheelcock, 1998; Brush, 1992; Smeltzer & Fann, 1989). Aldrich et al. (1989), studying the personal networks of women entrepreneurs in the United States and in Italy, found that in both places the networks were predominately male.

This research has only begun to deal with issues of relative power and influence differences between men's and women's networks. It is probable that male entrepreneurs share networks with higher status professionals in various fields, such as banking and law, than do women. Network contacts who have higher social and economic power can be of greater assistance during business start-up, as well as important sources of ongoing referrals.

Access to capital also limits women's entrepreneurial behaviors. There are many compounding factors resulting in a shortage of funds available to women for both the establishment and growth of their business. Start-up and business growth, however, are two extremely different types of situations; the capital needs and sources are different for each, and institutional factors at play are different by gender for each as well. These issues are discussed below.

It is unusual for a business start-up to be financed by a commercial bank loan. Most small businesses start with funds borrowed from family and friends. Start-up funds may also be obtained through second mortgages of a home or a personal bank loan. It is under conditions such as these when gender differences become more evident, one reason being that women are less likely to have a home mortgage solely in their name. The question of whether women are less likely to receive such a bank loan than a male business owner is a difficult one. Using a hypothetical business plan, Buttner and Rosen (1989) found no differences in bank funding decisions whether the borrower was male or female, although in an earlier study they found an interaction effect between gender of the entrepreneur, business sex-type (traditional or nontraditional for the gender of the owner), and gender of the funding decision maker (Buttner & Rosen, 1988b). Buttner and Rosen (1988a) also found that women entrepreneurs were perceived by loan officers as less entrepreneurial and less likely to be successful than male entrepreneurs. Riding and Swift (1990) found that many perceived funding decision differences could be accounted for by characteristics of the business. However, after controlling for those business characteristics, Riding and Swift did find that in their sample the collateral requirements for a line of credit were higher for women than for men. However, the original finding of no significant difference in access to debt financing is supported by more recent studies as well (Haynes & Haynes, 1999). Liberal feminist reforms have been very successful in rooting out many kinds of overt gender discrimination at the organizational level. As the above research shows, the kinds of discrimination that remain tend to be more subtle, more difficult to identify, and more complex, but no less effective.

The process of applying for a loan is an indicator of the stereotype of women business owners as less likely to be successful. The institutional structure of many homes and financial institutions still results in the registration of many family assets in a male spouse's name. The wage gap also contributes to the lower loan acceptance rates for women. Women's earnings continue to be significantly less than those of men in similar jobs. This wage differential contributes both to the amount of personal savings that can be accumulated, and to the level of assets that can then be shown on a loan application. Finally, difficulty in acquiring start-up financial capital affects the type of business started. Service businesses, as well as smaller retail businesses, require lower levels of start-up funds than those in manufacturing, construction, mining or agriculture. Thus, difficulties in obtaining start-up credit contribute to the channeling of women into ownership of types of business that are generally of a less financially lucrative nature.

Research shows fewer gender differences for the acquisition of financial capital from banks for existing businesses. A liberal feminist interpretation of this would be that once women have demonstrated their ability to achieve on a par with men, in this case by successfully establishing a new business, they will be treated more equally with men by the institutions of society. The remaining differences in loan acceptance rates are due to lesser collateral and capital accumulation that accrues to the types of business, retail and service, which are more likely to be owned by women (Buttner & Rosen, 1988a, 1988b, 1989, 1992; Greene 1995; Riding & Swift, 1990).

Research on women business owners and equity investments has been almost nonexistent but is beginning to emerge. Over the last 30 years women owned or led businesses received approximately 2.4% of the funds invested as venture capital (Greene, Brush, Hart, & Saparito, 2001). Whereas, 6,362 companies received funds between 1991 and 1996, only 31 of these deals were with women owned firms (Seegull, 1998). However, evidence supports an increasing trend, with 1998 investments in women owned or led firms reported at 4.1% (Greene et al., 1999). The primary reasons given for the gendered difference are similar to those discussed for issues of constrained growth and access to debt, the type of businesses being created, and lack of memberships in relevant networks (Carter, Greene, Brush, Hart, & Gatewood, 2003; Greene et al., 1999).

The liberal feminist analysis of labor market activity is useful for pointing out the persistence of legal and institutional barriers to gender equality. However, the liberal insistence of seeing men and women as equal under the law can also be counterproductive when it obscures ways in which men and women are not the "same" based upon their opportunities and resources. In addition to these kinds of differences, there is another important way in which women and men tend not to be the same, that is, in the balance of work and family labor. The gendered division of labor in the workplace and in the home is highly pertinent to systematic differences in economic achievement between women and men, including entrepreneurial activity. For a feminist analysis of the gendered division of labor in the workplace and in the home, we turn to Marxist feminism.

Marxist Feminism

One of the important contributions of Marxist feminism has been the analysis of women's domestic labor as a kind of productive, though unpaid, work. Marxist feminism has this focus partly in response to the contention from Marx and early Marxists that differences in social class serve as a kind of "master" inequality and that if economic injustice can be eliminated, other kinds of social inequality, such as those of gender and race, also will have been erased. Marxist feminism makes a strong claim that the relationship between a woman's domestic labor and her market labor is a key determinant in understanding the disadvantaged economic position of women compared to men. Today, it is well understood that women still do the majority of housework and childcare in most U.S. families. Though there has been some recent progress in men's participation in domestic labor, at least for some groups, the traditional pattern remains strongly in place (Baca Zinn, & Eitzen, 2002; Coltrane, 2000; Kemp, 1994: Pleck, 1977; Reskin & Padavic, 2002). Marxist feminism suggests two remedies for this inequity. The first is a call for the socialization of housework and child care along with fully equal labor force participation by women resulting in a union with men in the development of a working-class consciousness.

Another strategy offered is the demand that wages should be paid to homemakers in order to recognize the long ignored economic contribution of women's domestic labor to capitalism (Sokoloff, 1981; Tong, 1989). The importance of recognizing household labor as part of the output of nations receives more mainstream attention from a source far removed from Marxist feminism. Gary S. Becker, 1992 Nobel laureate and professor at the University of Chicago authored an Economic Viewpoint in *Business*

Week magazine (Oct. 16, 1995) in which he stated, "ignoring household labor distorts growth statistics and robs those who stay at home—mostly women—of self-esteem." Together, the strategies proposed under Marxist feminism are meant to achieve a two-pronged goal: radically altering the terms under which women's labor is analyzed and squarely planting the work of women in the analysis of capital.

The relationship between patriarchy and capitalism is the central theme of much of the later Marxist feminist analysis. Hartmann (1976, p.138) defines patriarchy as "a set of social relations which has a material base and in which there are hierarchical relations between men, and solidarity among them, which enable them to control women." The understanding of this shared material base, the ideological bases of patriarchy and capitalism, as well as the mutually reinforcing nature of the two systems, leads to a more complete understanding of women's labor force positions (Sokoloff, 1981). Both the gender system of male domination and the class system of economic domination require the subordination of women in the labor market and their unpaid domestic labor in the home.

A Marxist-Feminist approach to studying female business owners raises different types of questions than those suggested by Liberal Feminism. Carrying forward the key relationship between paid labor and domestic labor leads us to compare women to women and women to men. Is the typical "double day" of the female employee the same for female entrepreneurs? Do female entrepreneurs have different ways of coping with the double day? And secondly, are the typical differences in the distribution of domestic and market labor between female and male entrepreneurs the same as they are for wage and salary workers? Or does entrepreneurship affect the gendered division of labor in the home in somewhat different ways than other kinds of employment?

The greater need of women to balance work and family commitments may make entrepreneurship more appealing than wage and salary work to some women. Though self-employment often requires long workweeks, it also can offer the possibility for greater flexibility in structuring the workday. Some studies of wage and salary workers show that it is the scheduling of work hours rather than the total number of hours worked that causes the most stress for people combining work life and family life (Eichardus, & Glorieux, 1994; Longstreth, Stafford, & Mauldin, 1987; Voydanoff, 1987). The entrepreneurial intention, or state of mind directing entrepreneurial behavior, may combine with other beliefs, habits, values, and goals to be oriented toward control over work and family issues (Anna & Chandler, 2000; Bird, 1992).

Only a few studies in entrepreneurship explicitly address these questions. Some make the claim that entrepreneurship should break down the patriarchal home-workplace relationships common to employed women.

One study in particular, though not Marxist scholarship, focuses on issues germane to the perspective. Goffee and Scase (1983) recognize the potential for business ownership to reproduce an oppressive system of dependent patriarchal relationships as opposed to providing a path for women's economic liberation. They contend that material and ideological effects of entrepreneurship are gendered, resulting in women business owners increasingly questioning the structure of societal gender relationships.

Specific differences between entrepreneurial women and wage and salary women have been examined less than the posited differences between entrepreneurial men and women. Women who report themselves as self-employed are more likely to be married and have children than the average woman who works for a wage or salary (Devine, 1994; Greene & Johnson, 1995). This suggests that self-employed women are more likely to be combining work and family labor and facing the conflicts such combinations often entail. Research on the balance of domestic and market labor among self-employed women has been done by Longstreth et al. (1987). These authors analyzed the amount of time spent in domestic labor per week, the number of hours spent in market labor per week, as well as the level of assistance received from a spouse, children, or domestic hired help. This study compared part-time to full-time self-employed women and found few differences in their likelihood to have help at home whether from husbands or others.

Stoner, Hartman, and Arora (1990) more specifically examined the conflict between the domestic and market spheres for female business owners, questioning whether self-employment, with a perceived nature of autonomy or control over working conditions, allows the self-employed to limit work-home role conflicts. These authors find significant levels of work-home role conflict for women business owners, regardless of marital or parental status.

The influence of domestic attachments upon the entrepreneurial behavior of women and men has been explored in the entrepreneurship literature through studies of the effect of being married, of having a working spouse in the household, and of having preschool children in the household. Again, while these questions were not posed in the setting of a Marxist Feminist framework, the findings of these studies can be examined within this framework. Brush (1992), in her comprehensive study of research on female entrepreneurs, reports findings that male entrepreneurs are slightly more likely to be married than female entrepreneurs (Stevenson, 1986). Male entrepreneurs are also more likely to have a spouse who does not work outside the home (Honig-Haftel & Martin, 1986). Another study found that being married has a negative impact on the earnings of self-employed women, whereas they had positive impacts on the earnings of self-employed men (Clain, 2000). These findings suggest that male entrepreneurs are indeed less involved in domestic labor than female entrepreneurs. Brush (1992) also cites evidence to suggest that for women a desire for a work situation that provides flexibility for family and work responsibility contributes to their decision to become business owners (Chaganti, 1986; Goffee & Scase, 1983; Scott, 1986).

Radical Feminism

This area of feminist theory covers a group of approaches united by the common theme that women and men are essentially different. Differences are innate, psychological, emotional, and typically attributed at least to some degree to basic distinctions in reproduction of the species. Women's bodily experiences in conception, pregnancy, birth and lactation are thought to induce a variety of characteristics such as a connectedness with others and with nature, nurturance and a lack of aggression, while men's more removed reproductive role leads them to be more separated from others, to see themselves as atomized individuals. Radical feminism does not look at these essential differences as benign but rather as central to the oppression of women by men (Daly, 1984; Firestone, 1972; Millett, 1970; Tong, 1989). Male dominance is maintained, then, by systematically ranking the difference between women and men in such a way that men have more power (socially, economically, politically, occupationally, symbolically) and women have less. The practical implications of radical feminism range from the need for separatist communities, to the call for equal male participation in childrearing, to the contrary demands for technological means that would liberate women from the necessity of childbearing on one hand, as well as a ban to reproductive technologies on the other.

Radical feminist has not been widely used to analyze economic activity. However, the assumption of innate difference, rather than sameness, between women and men typically underlies research than compares women and men entrepreneurs. Behavioral differences and outcomes, however, remain difficult to separate from outcomes resultant from inherent traits, those developing from a woman's socialization, and those, the most likely case, which develop from a combination of many inputs. A final question to address is whether separatist economic activities play a role in the phenomena of entrepreneurial women. While again, although it is difficult to separate the impact of these organizations by outcome, the role of gender separatist organizations must be considered.

One recent work more directly exemplifies the type of approach that may be taken under the radical feminist approach. Bird and Dreyfus (1995) develop a model of the organization creatrix, emphasizing the need for more "feminine" metaphors than had previously been used to describe entrepreneurial activities. The research questions driving the paper are not unique: "How do women founders architect their ventures differently than their male peers? What effect do these differences play in venture outcomes?" (p. 3). However, the authors draw from Jungian psychology to propose that biological, natural, and possibly divine sources are the basis for differences in masculine and feminine experiences and attributes. These differences have the potential for explaining subsequent entrepreneurial differences, including motivation, structure, and strategic plans and goals.

The question of gender separatist entrepreneurial activities is one that is essentially untouched within this body of literature. In the United States, and increasingly in other countries as well, there are programs that are strictly for women, for example training programs, funding sources, business incubators. These programs almost never operate with a complete lack of male involvement. However, the separatist ideology plays strong in that the intent of the program design is to function in a significantly different way from the already existing masculine derived models. The use of the term feminine is not to connote weak or lesser, but to recognize and emphasize the unique strengths of women that can contribute to their business success. Johnson (1995) examined the trend toward microlending organizations in the United States that supported only women business owners. These mutual aid organizations were created to fill the funding gap left by banks and venture capital groups to whom the size and type of the women's businesses were not attractive.

The practice of lending only to women for self-employment activities has also received much attention through the activities of the Women's World Banking (WWB) program (Cuff, 1990; Gorman, 1990). WWB is a not-for-profit financial institution. Inaugurated in 1979, WWB operates as a global network of local organizations with activities in more than fifty countries. WWB describes itself as an embodiment of a key paradigm for the 1990s, "showing that low-income women entrepreneurs are restructuring the global economy" (WWB, 1992, p. 1). The WWB justifies its focus on women business owners by saying, "...A dollar or rupee or peso in the hands of a woman gets into the mouths, medicine, and schoolbooks of her children. Once empowered economically, women are courageous change agents in and beyond their local communities" (WWB, 1992, p. 2). While the WWB does not go on to posit what happens to a dollar, rupee, or peso in the hands of a man, the language and practices of the program correspond with the tenets of the radical feminist perspective, women as connected with others, demonstrating a priority placed on nurturing activities.

Programs targeting women and equity investments are also increasing. Springboard 2000 is actually a series of events being held across the United States to match women led businesses with equity capital providers, largely venture capitalists. This program is in partnership with groups such as the National Women's Business Council and the Forum for Women Entrepreneurs. The stated intent is to serve as a "national initiative designed to increase investment channels and facilitate deal flow for women led high-tech and life sciences companies" (Business Wire, 2000).

The approach to questions regarding economic advancement evident in the behaviors of entrepreneurial women is tightly confounded in the ideological approach to the phenomena. Who determines the desired outcome toward which we are measuring progress? As discussed earlier, a founding assumption of the liberal feminist approach is that men and women should be regarded as essentially the same and equally free to progress based on talents, skills, and willingness to work. While this does not explicitly assume that male defined and modeled economic behaviors are the ideal, the question of, "Progress toward what?" is too seldom raised. The theme found throughout most of the entrepreneurship literature measures female business owners according to their differences from male business owners and uses measures derived from studies often consisting predominately or even entirely of males (Barrett, 1994; Brush, 1992; Stevenson, 1990).

THE INTERSECTION OF GENDER, RACE, AND SOCIAL CLASS

One of the most important foci of current feminist work is how gender, social class and race or ethnicity operate at the structural level to affect individual lives (Collins, 1989; Feiner, 1994; Gonzalez, 1987; Hartsook, 1997; Hooks, 1984, 1994; Rothenberg, 1995). There is a long established pursuit in the study of the sociology of entrepreneurship that is highly relevant to the race, gender and class concentration in feminist study. That is the tradition of empirical and theoretical study of the economic behavior of minority groups (Waldinger, Aldrich, Ward, & Associates, 1990). This research can be traced from the writings of Weber (1989 [1904]) and Sombart (1914) on religion to more contemporary work by Bonacich and Modell (1980), Butler (1991); Portes and Bach (1985), Light (1980), Zhou (1992), and Sanders and Nee (1987, 1992, 1996) on race and ethnicity. These works develop the concepts of middleman minority theory and/or ethnic enclave theory or apply frameworks derived from those theories. The theoretical explanations are grounded in a situation of a minority population turning to certain types of self-employment activities in order to avoid falling to the bottom of the economic barrel. The retail and service industries are the primary sectors of economic activities for these populations.

Few of the works on ethnic entrepreneurship deal in any systematic way with issues of gender. One of the first exceptions to this is the work of

Phizacklea (1988) who analyzes the intersection of race and ethnicity with gender in her study of economic behavior of immigrant women. Phizacklea (1988, p. 22) describes ethnic business as predominately male controlled, achieving success due to "social structures that give easier access to female labor subordinated to patriarchal control mechanisms." However, the intersection between race or ethnicity and gender and entrepreneurship is just beginning to receive any research attention.

Alcorso (1993) and Carr (1993) furthered this work by illustrating the strong effect of patriarchal systems within family businesses owned by members of minority groups. Discussing such topics as overlapping family and business roles for women, business divisions of labor (Alcorso, 1993), decision making, and payment arrangement (Carr, 1993), these authors recognize the confounding nature of group memberships and the effect of those memberships on economic behaviors. And finally, Dallalfar (1994) emphasizes gender as a definitive factor in determining entrepreneurial behavior given differential access to ethnic community resources. Based on two case studies within the Los Angeles Iranian community, Dallalfar finds that the merging of the public and private spheres of the Iranian entrepreneurial women is of significant import to their businesses. One example of this is that the business setting is often in the home, making the home a site of convergence of domestic and market activity. All the literature to date suggests that for ethnic groups with strong patriarchal structures, entrepreneurial women work in an environment strongly characterized by the connection between their domestic and market labor.

This body of literature has recently been expanded to include the early findings of the Panel Study for Entrepreneurial Dynamics (PSED) (Reynolds, 2000). The PSED focused upon the identification and analysis of nascent entrepreneurs, those individuals actually in the process of starting their business. The findings of the PSED are notable as to differences found regarding entrepreneurial activity by gender, race or ethnicity, and age (Reynolds, Carter, Gartner, Greene, & Cox, 2002).

USING FEMINIST SCHOLARSHIP IN THE STUDY OF ENTREPRENEURSHIP

Feminist theoretical ideas are not completely missing from the study of entrepreneurship; however, there are two unusual characteristics in this body of work. There are no really thorough applications of any one complete theory to entrepreneurship research. The practical applications that do exist often borrow ideas from a range of scholarship on gender, applying various degrees of theoretical vigor, while at the same time proffering newly named theories for use within their own discipline based on these eclectic borrowings. In this section we address three of the most comprehensive efforts in this area to date (Brush, 1992; Fischer et al., 1993; Hurley, 1991).

Brush (1992) summarizes fifty-seven works concerning women entrepreneurs to conclude that there are few gender-based differences between women and men entrepreneurs in regard to psychological traits and motivations linked to entrepreneurial success, as well as to most business skills, types of problems encountered, planning, and outside financing. However, Brush reports significant differences in reasons that women and men give for business start-up or acquisition, for the timing and circumstances of start-up, in type of educational background, work experience, and some business skills. Additionally, gender differences are apparent in business goals, management styles, business characteristics and growth rates. Theoretically, Brush advances an "integrated perspective" based on theories of social interaction and psychological studies (Berger & Luckman, 1967; Gilligan, 1982). Though incomplete from the point of view of feminist analysis of women's economic activity, Brush's perspective represents significant progress toward an adequate inclusion of gender in the study of entrepreneurship.

The development of the integrated perspective is a reaction to traditional entrepreneurship research which "has explored business creation and performance based on the assumption that the venture is viewed as a separate economic entity designed primarily to achieve profit through competitive advantage and the creator of the business is assumed to follow a logical sequence of steps" (Brush, 1992, p. 17). Brush describes the integrated perspective approach to studying women business owners as based on the conception of businesses as a cooperative network of relationships rather than emphasizing profit-making motives for the creation of businesses. While Brush does not explicitly frame the integrated perspective in terms of feminist theory, the guiding assumptions of the perspective suggest it. Brush's emphasis is on women's different way of defining and conducting business, one in which business, family, social and personal relationships are mingled into a network of relationships. Brush explicitly suggests that reasoning through the integrated perspective contributes to a better understanding of differences between male and female owned businesses. Brush is not alone in recognizing that entrepreneurship research has been based on models of male economic activity (Barrett, 1994; Stevenson, 1986).

The integrated perspective offers an explanation for how women business owners take both paid, economic labor and unpaid, domestic labor into account in structuring their lives. Drawing out its connections to the Marxist feminist analysis of women's labor could enrich this analysis. The integrated perspective takes for granted the relationship between patriarchy and capitalism without elucidating it. One assumption of the integrated perspective seems to be that women taking on new business ventures would continue to be solely or primarily responsible for family labor. No attention is given to the possible disruption of gendered domestic, as well as economic, arrangements which starting a business might precipitate for women and their families. Brush generates an important list of future research questions to explore the integrated perspective, only one of which refers to male perspectives on domestic life. Brush's integrated perspective implies that it is plausible to continue the separation of domestic and economic activity at least as far as men are concerned. This is a good point at which to reflect that the gender system applies to the labor of both men and women. The integrated perspective is limited by suggesting that the relationship between domestic and economic activity affects only women and that it is legitimate to continue to analyze men's economic activity as if it is completely separated from family labor.

Hurley's (1991) approach to the application of feminist theory to entrepreneurship is largely epistemological. She sets forth the goals of feminist theory as reappraising what counts as knowledge, what knowledge is produced and the methods used in the production of knowledge. Drawing heavily from Calas and Smircich (1992), she approaches the existing body of literature through steps of "revising," identifying where women have been absent as researchers and as subjects; "reelection," a constant consideration of how knowledge is constructed; and "rewriting," a deconstruction and reconstruction of writings in organization theory clearly recognizing patriarchal assumptions. Hurley brings out several relevant points about historical entrepreneurship research, explicitly establishing the male biased foundation of this area of study. She illustrates a conceptual development based on the material labor and ideology of men. This development basically ignores similar economic activities of women since these are often integrated with a woman's domestic environment. Like Brush, Hurley considers the importance of gender-based realities, based on different social frames and values. She recognizes patriarchy as a form of male dominant gender relations and suggests the desirability of changing the patriarchal system.

Hurley's framework of sociological entrepreneurship research is based on how the environment affects entrepreneurship, beginning with McClelland's (1961) work on the need for achievement. The environment is defined to include effects on founding rates, political factors and state policies, cultures, and spatial location. In addition, a particularly interesting point is to question how business schools train nascent entrepreneurs for a male, profit-oriented, growth-oriented economic entity. Hurley continues with a critique of existing work in this field. However, while her suggestions for future research are anchored in feminist methods, she stops short of analyzing the theoretical explanations and/or implications of future research in entrepreneurship.

Fischer et al. (1993) make one of the most noted efforts to date to apply feminist theory to women's entrepreneurial activity. Using a liberal feminist perspective, they examine the effects of discrimination against women business owners. They also examine the effects of gender socialization, drawing on a theoretical perspective called "social feminism" which was put forward by Black (1989). While liberal feminism does provide one kind of framework for viewing the operations of the labor market, we argue that social feminism is a limited theoretical categorization with two central weaknesses: (1) It is not really a distinct theory but is assembled from too many divergent sources. (2) Pursuing this particular set of ideas does not lead to greater knowledge or clarity regarding movement toward change.

Social feminism is a combination of ideas about gender socialization pieced together with elements of psychological and philosophical theory about innate differences between men and women in personality makeup or moral development. While this echoes a central claim of radical feminism, Black's (1989) original formulation did not include radical feminism as a source. Women and men are conceptualized as essentially different, with the proviso that this inherent difference does not mean that one gender is superior and the other inferior. Rather, they have differing experiences and modes of rationality that are "equally valid." In our view a major weakness of the social feminism focus on the different but equally valid natures of men and women is that it ignores very real material inequalities between men and women. Fischer et al. (1993) offer social feminism as a major school of feminist theoretical thought, along with liberal feminism. The contrasting idea between the two seems to grow from the distinction about whether men and women are the "same" or whether they are "different." The debate about whether and to what degree an irreducible gender difference exists in human nature is an ongoing one in feminist theory. At the same time, the arguments about sameness or difference have been called a blind alley when it comes to reducing the disadvantages of women relative to men (MacKinnon, 1987). A key problem with both sameness and difference arguments is that both are judged in relation to a male-defined standard; both conceal the guiding principles of man as the measure of all things.

Even if we leave aside this important idea at the heart of differing theoretical perspectives, there is another problem that comes from the lack of theoretical distinction in social feminism. That is, the study of socialization does not stand in contrast to liberal feminism. In fact, ideas about gender role socialization coexist quite nicely within the framework of liberal feminism. Socialization explains how human beings internalize the values and learn the expected behaviors of their society, and how they develop a sense of self. These explanations are widely used in sociology and psychology to describe the microsocial, interpersonal processes by which we come to accept as necessary and natural the use of knives and forks as well as the subordinate status of women and the superordinate status of men. Socialization can be seen as both reflecting and perpetuating discrimination. In fact, liberal feminism implies that if socialization were simply more egalitarian, for example, if boys were taught to be more sensitive and girls to be more aggressive, this would result eventually in the reduction of economic inequality between men and women.

A third shortcoming in the conceptualization of socialization in social feminism is that socialization appears to be a process that takes place and is concluded early in life. One of the elementary ideas about socialization is that socialization is a lifelong process, and its effects are cumulative. This makes attributing differences in the economic activity of adults to socialization an untidy undertaking. For example, studies show that women entrepreneurs have less supervisory experience than men. The subsequent question is how do we account for the effects of early socialization that may have contributed to the lesser supervision in the first place, and the effects of workplace socialization of women to be supervised rather than supervisors?

IMPLICATIONS FOR FUTURE RESEARCH

We propose that the study of women entrepreneurs needs to begin with the understanding that gender does not apply only to women. The U.S. labor force is still highly gender segregated and gender stratified; it is essential to understand how the entrepreneurial activity of both men and women is gendered. As many of the earlier works cited show, this perspective is gaining ground in organizational and entrepreneurial research. Calas and Smircich (1992, p. 229) use feminist theory with organization theory to "rethink our field." They describe earlier, still rampant, literature on women in management which equates the following: "gender = sex = women = problem" with a resulting focus on how to solve the problem.

Gender is not a problem to be fixed or eliminated; like social class and race, gender is a basic element of human social interaction and, importantly, stratification. This article is another step away from seeing gender as a problem that has to be fixed and toward a more inclusive view of gender in entrepreneurial research. For instance, we know that women owned businesses typically are smaller and earn less money than those owned by men. A traditional approach to entrepreneurship would focus on how to assist women business owners with growth and income generation, two areas where they typically lag behind. A more feminist and sociological approach recognizes the additional validity of a low growth, less aggressive approach to earnings, along with the importance of business survival as a criterion of business success.

In our view, the greatest omission in the application of feminist theory to entrepreneurship is in the area of Marxist feminism. All feminist theories have a political goal—the elimination of oppression. Marxist theory is the most developed theory explaining the links between patriarchy and capitalism. Capitalism is a system built on a structure of dominance and subordination that maintains privileges for some groups over others. From this perspective it matters little whether women and men are presumed to be different or to be the same; either ideological position can be used to justify inequality. Our economy depends on what has been referred to elsewhere as the "work-family role system" which reinforces the traditional, gender division of labor in both the workplace and the home (Pleck, 1977). Marxist feminism posits this division as the primary mechanism that keeps inequality in place. We cannot separate the outcomes of economic endeavors from domestic realities. This seems a rich possibility for exploring the origins and meanings of gender differences in entrepreneurial activities. For example, are women entrepreneurs purposely limiting business size in an attempt to keep a viable balance between work and family obligations? Or are they held back from business expansion by family obligations and expectations? How do entrepreneurial men deal with the balance of work and family obligations and family expectations? Marxist feminism also suggests that one pertinent focus for this study should be how entrepreneurial activity reinforces or disrupts the gendered division of labor in twenty-first century capitalist patriarchy.

ACKNOWLEDGMENT

The authors wish to thank Howard Aldrich, Mary Barrett, Barbara Bird, Candida Brush, Margaret Johnson and Pat Seitz for their insightful comments and suggestions.

REFERENCES

Alcorso, C. (1993, Fall). And I'd like to thank my wife: Gender dynamics and the ethnic family business. *Australian Feminist Studies, 17,* 93–108.

Aldrich, H. (1989). Networking among women entrepreneurs. In O. Hagen, C. Rivchun, & D. Sexton (Eds.), *Women-owned businesses* (pp.103–122). New York: Praeger.

Aldrich, H., & Reese, P.Y. (1994, March 9–11). *Gender gap, gender myth: Does women's networking behavior differ significantly from men's?* Paper presented at the 1994 Global Conference on Entrepreneurship, INSEAD, Fontainebleau, France.

Aldrich, H., Reese, P.R., & Dubini, P. (1989). Women on the verge of a breakthrough: Networking among entrepreneurs in the United States and Italy. *Entrepreneurship & Regional Development, 1,* 339–356.

Allen, K.R., & Carter, N.M. (1996). Women entrepreneurs: Profile differences across high and low performing adolescent firms. In P.D. Reynolds, S. Birley, J.E. Butler, W.D. Bygrave, P. Davidsson, W.B. Gartner, & P.P. McDougall (Eds.), *Frontiers of entrepreneurship research* (pp. 98–99). Wellesley, MA, Babson College.

Anna, A.L., G.N. Chandler, G.N., Jansen, E., & Marco, N. (2000). Women business owners in traditional and non-traditional industries. *Journal of Business Venturing 15*(3), 279–303.

Baca Zinn, M., & Eitzen. D.S. (2002). *Diversity in families* (6th ed.). New York: Harper Collins College Publishers.

Baines, S., & Wheelcock, J. (1998). Working for each other: Gender, the household and micro-business survival and growth. *International Small Business Journal, 17*(1), 16.

Barrett, M. (1994). Feminism and entrepreneurship: Reflections on theory and an Australian study. In *International Council for Small Business: Proceedings of the 39th World Conference: Small Business and its Contribution to Regional and International Development.* Strasbourg.

Becker, G.S. (1995, Oct. 16). Economic viewpoint. *Business Week.*

Berger, P.L., & Luckman, T. (1967). *The social construction of reality.* New York: Anchor Press.

Bird, B.J. (1992). The operation of intentions in time: The emergence of the new venture. *Entrepreneurship Theory and Practice, 17*(1), 11–20.

Bird, B., & Dreyfus, C. (1995). *Organization creatrix* (Working paper). Washington, DC: The American University.

Black, N. (1989). *Social feminism.* Ithaca, NY: Cornell University Press.

Bonacich, E., & Modell, J. (1980). *The economic basis of ethnic solidarity: Small business in the Japanese-American community.* Berkeley: University of California Press.

Bowen, D.D., & Hisrich, R.D. (1986). The female entrepreneur: A career development perspective. *Academy of Management Review, 11,* 393–407.

Brush, C. (1999). Women's entrepreneurship. *Proceedings, The Second ILO Enterprise Forum.* International Small Enterprise Programme. International Labour Office.

Brush, C. (1992). Research on women business owners: Past trends, a new perspective and future directions. *Entrepreneurship Theory and Practice, 16*(4), 5–30.

Brush, C.G., & Hisrich, R.D. (1991). Antecedent influences on women-owned businesses. *Journal of Managerial Psychology, 6,* 9–16.

Butler, J.S. (1991). *Entrepreneurship and self-help among Black Americans: A reconsideration of race and economics.* Albany: SUNY Press.

Business Wire. (2000, Jan. 24). *Springboard 2000.* Redwood City, CA: Author.

Buttner, E.H., & Rosen, B. (1988a). Bank loan officers' perceptions of the characteristics of men, women, and successful entrepreneurs. *Journal of Business Venturing, 3,* 249–258.

Buttner, E.H., & Rosen, B. (1988b). The Influence of entrepreneur's gender and type of business on decisions to provide venture capital. *Proceedings*, Southern Management Association, Atlanta.

Buttner, E.H., & Rosen, B. (1989). Funding new business ventures: Are decision makers biased against women entrepreneurs? *Journal of Business Venturing, 4*, 249–261.

Buttner, E.H., & Rosen, B. (1992). Rejection in the loan application process: Male and female entrepreneurs' perceptions and subsequent intentions. *Journal of Small Business Management, 30*(1), 58–65.

Calas, M.B., & Smircich, L. (1992). Re-writing gender into organization theorizing: Directions from feminist perspectives. In M. Reed & M. Hughes (Eds.), *Rethinking organization* (pp. 227–253). London: Sage Publications.

Carr, D. (1996). Two paths to self-employment? *Work & Occupations, 23*(1), 26.

Carr, J. (1993). Negotiating patriarchy: Gender and ethnic patterns of small business ownership. *Australian Feminist Studies, 17*,109–126.

Carter, N., Greene, P.G., Brush, C.G., Hart, M.M., & Gatewood, E. (2003). Women entrepreneurs breaking through to equity markets: The influence of human, social, and financial capital. *Venture Capital, 5*(1).

Catalyst. (2002). *The 1998 census of women corporate officers and top earners of the fortune 500.*

Center for Women's Business Research. (2001). *Breaking the boundaries: The continued progress and achievement of women owned businesses.* Washington, DC: CWBR.

Center for Women's Business Research. (2002, August 27). New analysis documents employment and revenue distribution of women-owned firms in 2002. www.womensbusinessresearch.org.

Chaganti, R. (1986). Management in women-owned enterprises. *Journal of Small Business Management, 24*,18–29.

Clain, S.H. (2000). Gender differences in full-time self-employment. *Journal of Economics and Business, 52*(6), 499–513.

Collins, P.H. (1989). The social construction of black feminist thought. *Signs, 14*, 4.

Coltrane, S. (2000). Modeling and measuring the social embeddedness of routine family labor. *Journal of Marriage and the Family, 62*.

Cuff, D.F. (1990, November 13). Helping women abroad get started in business *The New York Times.*

Dallalfar, A. (1994). Iranian women as immigrant entrepreneurs. *Gender and Society, 8*(4), 541–561.

Daly, M. (1984). *Pure lust: Elemental feminist philosophy.* Boston: Beacon Press.

Eichardus, M., & Glorieux, I. (1994). The search for the invisible hours: The gendered use of time in a society with a high labour force participation of women. *Time and Society, 3*, 5–27.

Feiner, S.F. (1994). *Race and gender in the American economy.* Englewood Cliffs, NJ: Prentice-Hall.

Fischer, E.M., Reuber, A.R. & Dyke, L.S. (1993). A theoretical overview and extension of research on sex, gender and entrepreneurship. *Journal of Business Venturing, 8*, 151–68.

Firestone, S. (1972). *The dialectic of sex.* London: Paladin.

Gilligan, C. (1982). *In a different voice.* Cambridge, MA: Harvard University Press.

Goffee, R., & Scase, R. (1983). Business ownership and women's subordination: A preliminary study of female proprietors. *Sociological Review, 31*, 625–647.

Gonzalez, R.M. (1987). Distinctions in western women's experience: Ethnicity, class and social change. In S. Armitage & E. Jameson (Eds.), *The women's west*. Norman: University of Oklahoma Press.

Gorman, C. (1990, June 4). Women start taking credit. *Time, 135*(23).

Greene, P.G. (1995, March). *Women entrepreneurs: A consideration of capital types*. Paper presented at the IC^2 Conference. Immigrant and Minority Entrepreneurship: Building American Communities, University of Texas at Austin.

Greene, P., Brush, C., Hart, M., & Saparito, P. (2001). Patterns of venture capital funding: Is gender a factor? *Venture Finance, 3*(1), 63–83.

Greene, P.G., & Johnson, M.A. (1995). Social learning and middleman minority Theory: Explanations for self-employed women. *National Journal of Sociology, 9*, 59–84.

Hartmann, H. (1976). Capitalism, patriarchy and job segregation by sex. *Signs, 1*(3), 137–169.

Hartsook, N.C.M. (1997). *Money, sex and power: Toward a feminist historical materialism*. Northwest University Press.

Haynes, G.W., & Haynes, D.C. (1999). The debt structure of Small businesses owned by women in 1987 and 1999. *Journal of Small Business Management, 37*(2), 1–19.

Hisrich, R.D., & Brush, C.G. (1983). The woman Entrepreneur: Implications of family, educational, and occupational experience. In J. Hornaday, J.A. Timmons, & K.H Vesper (Eds.), *Frontiers of entrepreneurship research* (pp. 255–270). Wellesley, MA: Babson College.

Hisrich, R.D., & Brush, C.G. (1987). Woman entrepreneurs: A longitudinal study. In N.C. Churchill, J.A. Hornaday, B.A. Kirchhoff, O.J. Krasner, & K.H. Vesper (Eds.), *Frontiers of entrepreneurship research* (pp. 187–199). Wellesley, MA: Babson College.

Hisrich, R.D., & O'Brien, M. (1981). The woman entrepreneur from a business and sociological perspective. In K.H. Vesper (Ed.), *Frontiers of entrepreneurship research* (pp. 21–39). Wellesley, MA: Babson College.

Hooks, B. (1984). *Feminist theory from margin to center*. Boston: South End Press.

Hooks, B. (1994). *Teaching to transgress*. New York: Routledge.

Hurley, A.E. (1991, August). *Incorporating feminist theories into sociological theories of entrepreneurship*. Paper presented at the Annual Meetings of the Academy of Management, Miami, FL.

Jagger, A.M. (1983). *Feminist politics and human nature*. NJ: Rowan and Allenheld.

Johnson, M.A. (1995). *Women entrepreneurs in the United States: Explaining gendered trends and nontraditional business financing*. Paper presented at the IC^2 Conference, Immigrant and Minority Entrepreneurship: Building American communities, University of Texas at Austin.

Kalleberg, A.I., & Leicht, K.T. (1991). Gender and organizational performance: Determinants of small business survival and success. *Academy of Management Journal, 34*, 136–161.

Kemp, A.A. (1994). *Women's work*. Englewood Cliffs, NJ: Prentice-Hall.

Light, I. (1980). Asian enterprise in America: Chinese, Japanese and Koreans in small business. In S. Cummings (Ed.), *Self-help in urban America: Patterns of minority economic development* (pp. 33–57). Port Washington, NY: Kennikat Press.

Liou, N., & Aldrich, H.E. (1995, August). Women entrepreneurs: Is there a gender-based relational competence? Paper presented at the American Sociological Association meetings, Washington, DC.

Longstreth, M., Stafford, K., & Mauldin, T. (1987). Self-employed women and their families: Time use and socioeconomic characteristics. *Journal of Small Business Management, 25*, 30–37.

Loscocco, K.A., & Robinson, J. (1991). Barriers to women's small business success in the United States. *Gender and Society, 5*, 511–533.

Loscocco, K.A., Robinson, J., & Hall, R.H. (1991). Gender and small business success: An inquiry into women's relative disadvantage. *Social Forces, 70*, 65–86.

MacKinnon, C. (1987). *Feminism unmodified*. Cambridge, MA: Harvard University Press.

McClelland, D.C. (1961). *The achieving society*. Princeton, NJ: D. Van Nostrand.

Millett, K. (1970). *Sexual politics*. Garden City, NY: Doubleday.

Moore, D.P., & Buttner, E.H. (1997). *Women entrepreneurs: Moving beyond the glass ceiling*. Thousand Oaks, CA: Sage.

Phizacklea, A. (1988). Entrepreneurship, ethnicity and gender. In S. Westwood & P. Bhachu (Eds.), *Enterprising women* (pp. 21–33). New York: Routledge.

Pleck, J.H. (1977). The work-family role system. *Social Problems, 24*, 417–427.

Portes, A., & Bach, R.L. (1985). *Latin journey*. Berkeley: University of California Press.

Reskin, B.F., & Padavic, I. (2002). *Women and men at work* (2nd ed.). Thousand Oaks, CA: Pine Forge Press.

Reynolds, P.D. (2000). National panel study of U.S. business startups: Background and methodology. In J.A. Katz (Ed.), *Advances in entrepreneurship, firm emergence, and growth* (Vol. 4, pp. 153–227). Stamford, CT: JAI Press.

Reynolds, P.D., Carter, N.M., Gartner, W., Greene, P.G., & Cox, L. (2002). *The entrepreneur next door*. Kansas City, MO: Kauffman Center for Entrepreneurial Leadership.

Riding, A.L., & Swift, C.S. (1990). Women business owners and terms of credit: Some empirical findings of the Canadian experience. *Journal of Business Venturing, 5*, 327–340.

Robinson, P.B., & Sexton, E.A. (1994). The effect of education and experience on self-employment success. *Journal of Business Venturing, 9*(2), 141–156.

Rothenberg, P.S. (1995). *Race, class and gender in the United States*. New York: St. Martin's Press.

Sanders, J.M., & Nee, V. (1996). Social capital, human capital, and immigrant self employment. *American Sociological Review, 61*, 231–249.

Sanders, J.M., & Nee, V. (1992). Problems in resolving the enclave economy debate. *American Sociological Review, 57*, 415–418.

Sanders, J.M., & Nee, V. (1987). Limits of ethnic solidarity in the enclave economy. *American Sociological Review, 52*, 745–773.

Sapiro, V. (1994). *Women in American society*. Mountain View, CA: Mayfield Publishing Company.

Scott, C.E. (1986, October). Why more women are becoming entrepreneurs. *Journal of Small Business Management, 24,* 37–44.

Seegull, F. (1998). *Female entrepreneurs' access to equity capital.* Cambridge, MA: Harvard Business School Working Paper.

Smeltzer, L.R., & Fann, G.L. (1989). Gender differences in external networks of small business owner/managers. *Journal of Small Business Management, 28*(2), 25–32.

Sokoloff, N.J. (1981). *Between money and love.* New York: Praeger Press.

Society of Women Engineers. (2002). Based upon statistics from the National Science Foundation and the Bureau of the Census. (www.swe.org)

Sombart, W. (1914). *The Jews and modern capitalism* (Trans. by M. Epstein). New York: E.P. Dutton.

Stevenson, L. (1990). Some methodological problems associated with researching women entrepreneurs. *Journal of Business Ethics, 9,* 440–446.

Stevenson, L.A. (1986). Against all odds: The entrepreneurship of women. *Journal of Small Business Management, 24,* 30–36.

Stoner, C.R., Hartman, R.I., & Arora, R. (1990, Jan.). Work-home role conflict in female owners of small businesses: An exploratory study. *Journal of Small Business Management,* pp. 30–38.

Tong, R. (1989). *Feminist thought.* Boulder, CO: Westview Press.

Vetter, B.M. (1992). *What is holding up the glass ceiling? Barriers to women in the science and engineering workforce* (Occasional Paper 92-3). Washington, DC: Commission on Professionals in Science and Technology.

Voydanoff, P. (1987). *Work and family life.* Beverly Hills, CA: Sage.

Waldinger, R., Aldrich, H., Ward, R., & Associates. (1990). *Ethnic entrepreneurs.* Newbury Park, CA: Sage.

Weber, M. (1989/1904). *The Protestant ethic and the spirit of capitalism.* London: Unwin Hyman.

Wharton, A.S. (1989). Gender segregation in private-sector, public sector, and self-employed cccupations, 1950–1981. *Social Science Quarterly, 70,* 923–940.

Zhou, M. (1992). *Chinatown: The socioeconomic potential of an urban enclave.* Philadelphia: Temple University Press.

CHAPTER 2

COMPARING SOCIAL FEMINISM AND LIBERAL FEMINISM

The Case of New Firm Growth

Nancy M. Carter and Mary L. Williams

ABSTRACT

The linkage between gender and the growth of new businesses has been the subject of several recent investigations. Educational backgrounds, access to capital, age and size of business have been used as covariates. In this research we extend previous analyses to examine the importance of the firm's founding strategy in business growth. We use feminist theory to examine whether the strategy women-owned businesses adopt can compensate for discrimination or systemic barriers women may have faced in their socialization patterns. The interaction between strategy type and gender is analyzed using multinomial logit and linear regression analysis. As expected, women-owned firms are most apt to pursue a narrow differentiation, or "specialist" strategy. This selection, however, does not increase their odds of having a high growth rate in the first year or over time. Women-owned businesses have lower sales in the first year and over time. The entry strategy selection of women-owned businesses does nothing to alter their initial sales or ensuing growth.

INTRODUCTION

Women owned businesses are growing at a faster rate then the economy as a whole in many countries around the world. The 2001 Global Entrepreneurship Monitor (GEM) reports the total entrepreneurial activity (TEA) rate for the 29 countries surveyed ranged from 4.8 of every 100 adults in Belgium, to about 18 of every 100 adults in Mexico (Zacharakis, Neck, Bygrave & Cox, 2001). Across all GEM countries, women represent about 33% of those attempting to start a business, with the ratio of men to women being highest in Italy (1:1) and lowest in Israel (1:3.6). By the end of 2002, there is expected to be an estimated 6.2 million majority women-owned privately-held businesses in the United States, employing more than 9.2 million people and generating more than 1.15 trillion in sales (NFWBO, 2001). Between 1997 and 2002, the number of women-owned firms is expected to increase by 37%, four times the growth rate of all firms. Despite this increase, the number of firms owned by women still lags behind that of men, and the sales and income of women-owned firms are significantly lower than those of men-owned firms (U.S. Small Business Administration, 2001). The discrepancy between the number of firms owned by women and men and their economic success has been a popular theme among researchers. Some have suggested that performance differentials result from women having fewer resources or assets with which to create a firm (Caputo & Dolinsky, 1998; Carter & Rosa, 1998; Cromie & Birley, 1991; Verheul & Thurik, 2001), less access to opportunities, different managerial styles and intentions (Brush, 1992; Kaplan, 1988; Muhktar, 2002), and less beneficial social networks to assist the start-up process (Aldrich & Reese, 1997). However, other researchers have found few differences between the needs and experiences of men and women entrepreneurs that would explain differences in firm performance (Buttner & Rosen, 1988; Kalleberg & Leicht, 1991; Sexton & Bowman-Upton, 1990; Sonfield et al., 2001).

Inconsistencies in the empirical findings have lead to calls for theory-driven research from which a more systematic knowledge base can be developed. Fischer, Reuber, and Dyke (1993) responded to this challenge by demonstrating how liberal feminist and social feminist theories can be used to reconcile discrepancies in previous findings. They applied liberal feminist theory to studies that posited sex-based discrimination as the difference between the experience of women and men entrepreneurs. Social feminism was used to categorize studies that viewed inherent differences as accounting for the divergent outcomes.

In addition to the theories' capacity to organize and interpret past research, Fischer et al. (1993) view them as useful for investigating understudied sources of performance differences. As an example, they cite the possibility that women's socialization may lead them to manage their firms in ways that offset sex-based discrimination or systematic bias.

One aspect of management that could be used to counter deficiencies in the resources women possess is the founding strategy they adopt. Research establishes the linkage between strategy and new ventures' performance and survival rates (Keeley & Roure, 1990; McDougall & Robinson, 1990; Romanelli, 1989; Sandberg & Hofer, 1987; Stearns et al., 1995). Implicit in these studies is the argument that an effective strategy maintains satisfactory alignment between opportunities and risks in the firm's external environment and the organization's capabilities and resources. In other words, a firm's strategy should match what the firm might do given the external threats and opportunities, with what the business can do given the internal strengths and weaknesses.

For new ventures, the entrepreneur's human and financial capital are major sources of the firm's internal capabilities and performance (Hitt et al., 2001). If women-owned firms have fewer resources at start-up, the question becomes whether or not the "primary strategy" (Bourgeois, 1980) they adopt allow them to exploit their inherent capabilities such that they compensate for resource deficiencies. If so, the overall market performance of women-owned firms should not differ from that of men-owned firms, albeit the strategies of the two sup-populations may vary.

In this study we extend the work of Fischer et al. (1993) by using liberal feminist and social feminist theories to examine the role that initial resources, founding strategy, and gender play in predicting initial sales and new firm growth. Data for the study come from new ventures in the retail industry. We chose retail for two reasons. First, new ventures founded by women are very prevalent in retail (Zellner et al., 1994; U.S. Small Business Administration, 2001), providing us with a sufficient number of women-owned firms to compare with those founded by men. Second, we limit our sample to one industry since research has shown that significant strategy-industry interactions exist in predicting new firm performance and survival (Keeley & Roure, 1990; Sandberg & Hofer, 1987; Stearns et al., 1995).

FEMINIST THEORIES AND NEW FIRM PERFORMANCE DIFFERENCES

Liberal Feminist Theory

Research based on the assumption that discriminatory practices have denied women access to the critical resources necessary to establish and run new ventures is consistent with the liberal feminist perspective. Liberal feminist theory (hereafter referred to as LF) is an outgrowth of political thinking about equality, entitlement and individual rights. Sometimes termed "mainstream feminism," LF assumes that society can be properly reformed to maximize individual autonomy if everyone has equality of opportunity.

The fundamental thesis of LF was articulated by Mary Wollstonecraft in 1792 (c.f. Jagger & Rothenberg, 1984). She argued that rationality, not physical sex, was the proper basis for individual rights. Claiming that women's capacity to reason was equal with that of men, she contended that any inferiority on the part of women could be attributed to unequal opportunities for developing their full intellectual capacity. Contemporary liberal feminists continue to maintain that nonphysical differences between men and women are consequences of historical inequalities in education and access to opportunities. In order for the relative depravation to be eliminated, both legal discrimination and systematic bias must be eradicated.

A key supposition in entrepreneurship research is that a firm's resources at start-up are critical determinants of its eventual success. Research has focused on two sets of resources: those assets individuals bring with them to the entrepreneurial process in the form of human capital, and the entrepreneur's ability to access resources in the environment (e.g., financial capital, supplies, start-up team members, customers). Research consistent with LF has implicitly argued that women have had restricted access to both sets of resources, rendering their firms more vulnerable to failure than those started by men.

Human Capital—Human capital derives from individuals' choices to invest in themselves by developing their innate capabilities through education (formal and occupational experiences) and training. The more specific the human capital to the nature of the new start-up, the higher the likelihood of success. For example, research has found a positive relationship between entrepreneurs' prior experience in the industry and the success of the new firm (Carter et al., 1994; Van de Ven, Hudson, & Schroeder, 1984). In orthodox economic theory, the acquisition of human capital is viewed as almost entirely under the individual's control. LF challenges this assumption and views systematic barriers arising from social, cultural and work structures as impeding women from acquiring adequate levels of human capital. Research supporting this challenge finds that in comparison with men, women entrepreneurs: are less likely to have experience gained from owning prior businesses or working in private firms (Cromie & Birley, 1991); are more likely to have pursued undergraduate studies in liberal arts rather than in technical disciplines such as business or engineering (Brush, 1992; Honing-Haftel & Martin, 1986); have careers that are more frequently interrupted (Kaplan, 1988); and are less likely to be part of start-up teams for high-growth new firms (Reynolds, 1993). Jones and Tullous (2002) find that Hispanic women needed more help in the area of finance and accounting than male Hispanics in the pre-venture stage.

To the extent that deficiencies in human capital render new firms vulnerable, those begun by women would seem more likely to have a lower growth rate than those started by men.

Access to Resources—In contrast to systemic barriers, overt discrimination has been viewed as restricting women's access to critical opportunity structures and resources in the external environment. Access to capital markets has been regarded as among the most important resources denied women. Tigges and Green (1994) suggested three reasons why women may be disadvantaged in capital markets: (1) they tend to have less experience and equity in their businesses than men; (2) they may be discriminated against by resource lenders on the basis of outmoded gender role beliefs; and (3) their belief that they will receive differential treatment may reduce the rate of lending applications among women business owners.

Empirical studies that have tested these assumptions present mixed findings. Some researchers have found women entrepreneurs to have access to less external financing, weaker collateral possessions, and the belief that they have been discriminated against or received unequal treatment by financing institutions or other resource providers (Carter & Rosa, 1998; Coleman, 2000; Fay & Williams, 1993; Olm, Carsrud, & Alvey, 1988). Others, however, have found little evidence of obvious discrimination against women (Buttner & Rosen, 1989). Coleman (2000) found no evidence of overt lender discrimination in the decision to lend/not lend on the basis of gender. But other results of that study showed that women-owned firms paid higher interest rates than men-owned firms and that women-owned service firms were more likely to put up collateral than men-owned service firms. Particularly when samples of men and women have been matched on key variables like business age, firm size and growth rate, few differences in resource access have been identified (Haines, Orser, & Riding, 1999; Riding & Swift, 1990). Taken as a whole these studies suggest that speculations regarding overt discrimination may be overstated. However, the contradiction in the findings indicates that the topic merits further review.

In summary, the research findings consistent with LF lead to predictions that:

H_1: *Women entrepreneurs will bring a lower stock of human capital to their new ventures.*

H_2: *Women-owned firms are less likely to have access to financial capital.*

Social Feminist Theory

The central assumption of social feminist theory (hereafter referred to as SF) is that women and men have different experiential backgrounds and different ways of thinking. These differences result from variation in socialization patterns and neither form is a less valid representation of human experience (Calas & Smircich, 1992). Burrell (1992, p. 72) captured the essence of SF in his argument that, "Sexuality is not a given; it is a social construction." From birth, women and men encounter differing social experiences that shape the way they view the world. Black (1989) argued that women's bundle of beliefs arise from situations they share, especially their universal involvement with domestic activities and their relative lack of public power and authority.

The emphasis SF places on socialization underscores the distinction between sex and gender. Sex is regarded as the physiological differences between women and men. Gender refers to culturally specific patterns of behavior that can be ascribed to the sexes, including societal orientation, values and roles (Oakley, 1972).

Because SF views experiences as culturally embedded, it rejects liberal feminists' belief that it is possible to have genuine equality of opportunity. Whereas liberal feminist thinking is essentially assimilationist, social feminist theory is separatist. The goal of liberal feminism is for women and men to be indistinguishable (androgynous) in terms of public policy. Social feminists seek to acquire a proper recognition and appreciation for women's achievements and values. Fundamentally, SF views the genders as "different but equal."

Entrepreneurship research consistent with SF has focused on distinguishing traits as the explanation for differences in women's and men's entrepreneurial behaviors or performance. Although some differences have been found between women and men, current thinking tends to downplay the notion that an enduring set of personal traits can distinguish women and men entrepreneurs. Instead, researchers have concluded that there are more similarities than differences. Hurley (1992) challenged this conclusion arguing that failure to detect gender differences may be a product of the measures researchers employed. She contended that studies of women business owners have been based on male derived psychological traits and focus on business issues as they affect male populations. Hurley's (1992) argument parallels criticism raised by researchers who promote the need to "gender" organizational analysis by placing both women and men at the center of explanatory frameworks (Mills & Tancred, 1992). Examples of such analyses would include an expanded conceptualization of women's lives from a holistic perspective rather than viewing their lives as compartmentalized into rigid and unrelated spheres (Calas & Smircich, 1992).

Brush's (1992) argument that women's motives for establishing and managing a new firm may differ from men's conforms to this call for "gendering" analysis. She contended that men often establish new businesses out of a desire to be entrepreneurs or to not work for someone else. Women's rationale includes the desire to create employment where they can balance work and family. The difference in these motives signals a divergence in the basic definition of a business. Instead of as an economic entity designed to achieve profit through competitive advantage, Brush contends that women perceive their businesses as "cooperative networks of relationships" where business relationships are integrated with rather than separated from family, societal and personal relationships.

Founding Strategy—One area where differences resulting from variations in women's and men's socialization patterns may be evident is in the strategy entrepreneurs adopt for their businesses. Research on information-processing theories from social psychology argues that strategic choice is limited by individual's belief structures, or cognitive maps (Walsh & Fahey, 1986). Belief structures are shaped by the experiences to which individuals have been subjected. Since SF posits that the experiential backgrounds of women and men are fundamentally different, it follows that their belief structures and resulting strategic choices also will be different. Furthermore, acceptance of SF's tenet that women and men are "different but equal" leads to the expectation that in making strategic choices, women will exploit their unique strengths. Consequently, performance of their firms should not differ from that of men-owned firms, even though the strategies of the two sub-populations may vary.

Predicting precisely how the founding strategy adopted by women will differ from that of men requires speculation. Few empirical studies have related gender and strategy to new firm performance. To formulate hypotheses consistent with SF we relate literature that has sought to identity attributes women derive from their socialization patterns to research on the strategy of small or new ventures in general. Finally, we seek support from findings regarding the influence of gender on strategy and performance.

Over the past two decades a considerable body of feminist research has addressed women's segregation in the workplace. Increasingly, interests concerned with determining women's "relative worth" within organizations have turned to identifying the styles of leading and managing exhibited by women, and why those styles are particularly useful at this time in history (Astin & Leland, 1991). Sheppard's (1992) work on how women in management view themselves as women and as organizational members is representative of this trend. Studying a small, but purposive sample, Sheppard found that women mangers and professionals view themselves as "humanistic" and "personal-oriented" as opposed to "cost-oriented." Their management style was described as service-oriented with an emphasis on persuasion, appeasement and maintaining good relations. Sheppard characterized women's decision-making as having a strong "relational" component and as embedded within a particular context. She found that in career planning, women portray their expertise as within a particular area, whereas men see themselves as generalists.

Although the women Sheppard studied were not entrepreneurs, the attributes she identified relate to the "specialist/generalist" distinction that researchers have used to predict appropriate strategies for new ventures. The "specialist" perspective maintains that new businesses should seek a "niche" in the marketplace where they can avoid direct competition with larger, more established firms. According to this perspective, new firms lack adequate resources for effective organizational learning, and this "liability of newness" (Stinchcombe, 1965) limits the firm's ability to compete on the basis of price (Deeks, 1976; Stegall, Steinmetz, & Kline, 1976). Advocates of this perspective caution that new ventures should become "specialists" by targeting narrow market segments that have been overlooked by larger firms and serve those customers through specially designed, high quality products or services (Broom & Longenecker, 1971; Chon & Lindberg, 1974; Hosmer, 1957).

Alternatively, other researchers have argued that broad strategies will lead to better survival and growth potential for new ventures. Biggadike (1976) contended that entrepreneurs must adopt an aggressive posture when entering markets, and match the broad appeal offered by competitors. Researchers concurring with this "generalist" perspective have argued that new ventures penalize themselves unless they compete head-to-head with the market leaders, including competing on the basis of price (Cooper, Willard, & Woo, 1986; MacMillan & Day, 1987; Miller & Camp, 1985). To successfully implement a pricing strategy requires the knowledge to achieve efficiencies and cost savings across the entire value chain of the firm's operation. Typically, the firm must keep its per unit costs low, minimize spending on unnecessary operating expenses and have sufficient resources for broad-scale marketing (Porter, 1985).

A broad interpretation of the "specialist" versus "generalist" perspective is that new ventures with few or constrained initial resources should adopt differentiation or "specialist" strategies. Those with more diverse capabilities are better equipped to pursue broad strategies, which may include an emphasis on pricing. Extrapolating from Sheppard's (1992) findings noted above, this interpretation leads to the expectation that women-owned businesses are better advised to adopt a "specialist" strategy rather than a "generalist" approach. If the management style of women entrepreneurs is similar to that of the women mangers studied by Sheppard, strategies that reflect a service orientation, emphasize a particular area of expertise or specialty, and target a narrow segment of the market where they can integrate their "cooperative network of relationships" as noted by Brush (1992) will best "fit" the capabilities arising from women's socialization processes. By adopting such strategies, women entrepreneurs should be able to compensate for resource deficiencies and increase the likelihood of their business's success. Men-owned new ventures, on the other hand, are more likely to benefit from generalist strategies. The socialization pattern of men are apt to have included more opportunities to acquire business related experiences. This background better positions men entrepreneurs to emphasize multiple strategic foci simultaneously. Similarly, their more diverse business experiences provide knowledge regarding how to achieve the cost-efficiencies necessary for executing successful pricing strategies.

Research by Kalleberg and Leicht (1991) offers some support for these speculations regarding gender and founding strategies. In an extensive study of small business owners, Kalleberg and Leicht found that men were more likely to build a strategy around offering a wide range of products and services whereas women were more likely to feel that emphasizing quality gave their businesses a competitive advantage. Although these results substantiate the expectations consistent with SF, further tests intended to link these gender-strategy differences to firm performance provide less conclusive confirmation. Women's businesses that adopted a quality emphasis in their strategy were significantly more successful, but the corresponding coefficient for men was in the same direction, although not statistically significant. Kalleberg and Leicht found businesses headed by men were no more likely to be successful than those headed by women.

The mixed support provided by the findings of Kalleberg and Leicht (1991) raises two caveats for the present study. First, Kalleberg and Leicht reasoned that their failure to detect significant gender interactions may have been due to a lack of statistical power. They concluded that their data collection strategy resulted in successful, viable businesses being over represented in the sample. Second, the firms Kalleberg and Leicht studied were not necessarily new ventures, our interest in the present study. The average company age was 13.19 years. It is unclear whether the strategy differences they detected arose from variations in the firm's initial founding strategy or from strategic adaptations entrepreneurs made over time.

Collectively, the literature reviewed provides insight for formulating the following hypotheses consistent with SF:

H_3: *Women will choose different entry strategies than men.*

H_4: *Women led firms with lower levels of human and financial capital will adopt narrow entry strategies.*

H_5: *The overall growth rate among new ventures founded by women does not differ from those founded by men.*

H_6: *Women-owned firms that pursue a "specialist" strategy will have higher growth rates than women-owned firms that adopt a "generalist" strategy.*

METHODS

Sources of Data

Data for addressing characteristics of new ventures were collected via a longitudinal survey of new firms in the states of Minnesota and Pennsylvania beginning in 1986 (Reynolds & Freeman, 1987; Reynolds & Miller, 1988). A follow up study of the firms was concluded in 1994. All regions of these states were represented. The initial sample was based on firms listed in the Dun's Market Identifier (DMI) files as between one and six years old just prior to the survey. Phone call verification excluded all listings that were not new, autonomous, and active; about half of the listings qualified. Each eligible new firm was sent a mail questionnaire three times, with a reminder postcard between the first and second mailings. Instructions included with the questionnaire asked that the survey be completed by a person that had the major responsibility for starting the firm and is active in the management of the firm. Any of the founders could qualify. Phone interviews were completed with about half of those who had not returned the mail questionnaire. The final response rate was 69%. The data were developed for more than 2,500 new firms representing all industry sectors. We limit our analysis in the present study to the retail firms in the sample.

Measures

Growth Rates—Growth is a crucial factor of new firm performance. Early growth (within the first year) can explain later growth and longer periods of survival. Following several studies on new firm performance (Cooper, Gimeno-Gascon, & Woo, 1994; Stuart & Abetti, 1987; Vivarelli & Audretsch, 1994) this study uses changes in sales as the measure of growth. We utilize two growth measures and a recursive model. Initial growth is measured as the change in sales during the first year of operation. Both LF and SF hypotheses are tested in an attempt to explain the new venture's initial sales growth during the first year. We then test the LF and SF hypotheses in a model of sales growth over time using initial growth, and age of the firm as control variables.

Gender Composition of the Founding Team—New ventures may be founded by individual entrepreneurs or by teams of entrepreneurs. Thus, the "gender designation" of the founders must take into account the fact that a team of founders may be composed of women and men. Those ventures in which the majority (greater than half) of team members were women, and those started by a single woman are classified as "women-owned." Those ventures in which the majority (greater than half) of team members were men and those started by a single man are classified as "men-owned." Of the 95 businesses in the analysis, 13 were started by one woman, 3 were founded by a majority-women team, 36 were started by one man, 7 were founded by a majority-men team and 36 were started by teams with equal number of men and women. When women-led and men-led teams were compared, those with equal numbers of men and women were dropped from the analysis, leaving a sample size of 59. When gender was included as an explanatory variable, the percent of women on the start-up team was included in the analysis.

Firm Age—The year in which the owner of the new firm first made a resource commitment to the firm also was included in the second level of analysis as control. All firms in the sample were six years or less in age when the first wave of data was collected in 1986. We assumed that firms that were one year of age would have differential rates of growth than firms that were six years of age in 1986. If our assumption is true, we would expect age to be significant and positive (e.g., older firms in the 1986 would have higher rates of growth by 1985). By using firm age as a covariate, we partial out the effect of age at the time the firm enters into the risk set. Age was measured as the number of months since founding, and was transformed to a logarithm of age to normalize the age distribution.

Financial Resources—There were two measures of access to financial resources used in the analysis. First, we measured whether or not the businesses used formal external sources to provide capital for start-up to proxy their access to formal loans. This variable does not measure access to credit markets since the sample only includes entrepreneurs who succeeded in establishing businesses. Those denied access to credit sources may not be in the sample. Instead, the variable measures whether or not the businesses rely on formal sources for capital as opposed to financing start-up from other sources (e.g., personal equity stakes). Responses are coded 1 if loans were obtained from banks or other formal lending institution and 0 if these formal sources did not provide any of the capital infusion. Second, we included the dollar amount (in thousands) of personal savings used in the business prior to obtaining formal outside financial support. In the case of new venture formation by a team, the aggregate of the team's personal savings was utilized.

Human Capital—Three indicators of human capital were used to test the hypotheses. Since the unit of analysis is the business, the indicators are again aggregate values when the firm is founded by a group, or team. The first indicator is the extent to which members of the founding team have prior experience starting new ventures. The variable was calculated as the percent of the founding team that had helped start at least one other new firm prior to the current venture. The second indicator is the extent to which team members have experience working in the same industry as that of the new venture. Industry experience was measured as the total number of years team members had worked in the retail industry and was transformed as the square root of this number to normalize that distribution. The third measure was the size of the start-up team. The ability to put a team together, take advantage of social networks, or be invited by others to join a start-up team is an indication of one's perceived entrepreneurial ability.

Strategy—The questionnaire method of data collection relies on key informants to indicate the focus of the firm's competitive strategy. As architects of the founding strategies, the survey respondents are uniquely qualified to assess strategic intentions. Respondents to the survey questionnaire were asked to indicate on a four-point scale ranging from critical (1) to insignificant (4) the importance of thirteen attributes of competitive strategy to their firm's strategic focus. These items were chosen for their correspondence to previously identified strategy attributes and their appropriateness to new ventures.

In previous analyses (Carter et al., 1994) these 13 measures were shown to be associated with six strategic attributes: market sensitivity, technology, product distinctiveness, site appeal, service, and price. Appendix 1 displays the items from the questionnaire sorted by their factor loadings and the Cronbach alpha reliability coefficients associated with each factor. Because strategy likely consists of a composite or bundle of actions rather than an emphasis on one dimension, Carter, et al. subjected the strategic attributes from the factor analysis to a cluster analysis to discern strategy archetypes. These procedures are consistent with the prevailing conceptualization in the literature that firm strategy is a multidimensional construct. The six strategy archetypes as defined by the extent to which they emphasize the strategy attributes are described in Appendix 2.

Results from the original six cluster solution determined by Carter et al. (1994) were used to classify the retail firms in the present study into one of the six strategy archetypes. The cluster centroid means for each strategy dimension from the original analysis (see Carter et al., 1994, p. 32) were used as initial starting values in an iterative partitioning analysis. This procedure sorts each retail firm in the sample according to its emphasis on the six strategy attributes and assigns it to the closest centroid vector of the original six cluster solution. This approach assumes that the original structure identified by Carter, et al. adequately represent the strategy archetypes used by new ventures across industries and avoids the construction of a typology unique to the retail industry. In related research, Stearns et al. (1995) ranked the six strategy archetypes from broadest to narrowest in scope depending on the number of strategy dimensions emphasized in each archetype. Appendix 2 presents the strategies from broadest to narrowest in scope according to the number of dimensions emphasized.

In retail, few businesses adopt the technology value or equivocator strategies. Since only two of the businesses headed by women pursued these strategies, they were eliminated from the sample. Since strategy is a categorical variable, it was included as a dummy variable with the broadest strategy (super achiever) selected as the omitted category. The results therefore measure the effect of a certain strategy relative to the omitted, or broadest strategy.

RESULTS

Descriptive Analysis

Descriptive statistics appear in Table 2.1.

There were no statistical differences in the length of time women- and men-owned firms had been in operation. On average the firms had been operating for four years. Growth rates in sales during the first year were significantly greater for the men-owned firms, but sales growth over time was not significantly different between the groups.

The mean comparisons reported in Table 2.1 provide mixed support for expectations consistent with LF. The expectation that women-owned firms posses a lower stock of human capital received some support. As predicted, businesses headed by women have significantly fewer years of experience working in the retail industry, and their teams were significantly smaller. However, there was no significant difference between the groups as far as the number of other new ventures started. On average, 44% of the founding

Table 2.1. Descriptive Statistics of the Sample

	Men		Women		
	Mean	S.D.	Mean	S.D.	T-Value
Firm Age	47.89	20.06	48.80	18.15	0.16
Sales First Year[a]	4.86	1.53	3.79	1.86	−2.22***
Sales Most Recent Year[a]	1.73	0.34	1.68	0.24	−0.53
Human Capital					
Start Others	0.40	0.50	0.44	0.51	0.22
Industry Experience[b]	1.89	1.82	0.93	1.09	−1.97**
Team Size	2.12	1.06	1.56	0.63	−1.96**
Financial Resources					
Savings[b]	3.99	3.01	2.92	3.62	−1.15
Loan	0.73	1.81	0.14	1.78	−1.12
Strategy					
Super Achievers	0.36	0.48	0.19	0.40	−1.24
Quality Proponents	0.12	0.33	0.13	0.34	0.06
Price Competitors	0.12	0.33	0.25	0.45	1.23
Niche Purveyors	0.40	0.50	0.44	0.51	0.22

Notes:
* = significant at the 10% level, **= significant at the 5% level, *** = significant at the 1% level
[a] Variable measured as logarithm
[b] Variable measured as square root

team in women-owned firms had experience in starting previous businesses, while 40% of the entrepreneurs in men-owned firms had such background. Contrary to our expectations, women-owned firms exhibited no significant differences in the financial resources they brought to the business. Although men-owned firms were more likely to rely on credit from formal sources—73% for men versus 14% for women—the results were not significantly different in a statistical sense due to the high variance in this variable. In addition, there was no significant difference in the average amount of personal savings utilized by the teams. Support for SF would indicate there would be gender differences in the strategies selected by the new venture teams. We expected to note significant differences in the percentage of men and women-owned firms regarding their choice of an entry strategy. Using a comparison of mean percentage, the results in Table 2.1 show no differences in the percentage of men and women-owned teams that chose the broad or narrow strategies.

Multinomial Logit Analysis

To further analyze strategy choice, a multinomial logit model was estimated.[1] Of interest here is the effect of human and financial resource allocations on the strategy choices of the start-up teams. Do teams with more females try to compensate for a lower stock of human and financial capital by pursuing a niche strategy? To answer that question, the four categories of strategy were included in a multinomial logit model. The probability that team (a) would choose strategy "j" is the probability that strategy "j" is more beneficial than other potential strategies. Let X_a be a vector of variables describing the team, B_j be vectors of parameters, and ε_{aj} be unobservable random error terms. To employ maximum likelihood logit analysis, the random error terms are assumed to be independent with density function: $f(\varepsilon) = \exp(-\varepsilon) \{\exp[-\exp(-\varepsilon)]\}$.

Since the benefit to the team of choosing a strategy can be considered the "utility" of the decision, linear functions can approximate these indirect utility functions. Thus for team "a," the indirect utility associated with strategy "j" is $U_{aj} = X_a B_j + \varepsilon_{aj}$. The utility U_{aj} depends on the characteristics and backgrounds of the team. For example, having a greater percentage of women on the team may influence the start-up strategy. Furthermore, the effects of women on the team may differ depending on the stock of human and financial capital available to the team. Price, Niche, and Quality were included in the multinomial dependent variable, with the broadest strategy (Super Achiever) as the left-out category. The results of each equation in a set would be interpreted relative to the broadest category. In this model, the independent gender variable included was the female percentage of the start-up team.

Results of the Multinomial Logit Analysis

The results of the multinomial model appear in Table 2.2.

In the first column of Table 2.2, the gender variable was included with the covariates for human and financial capital. The variable—start others—was included as a dummy variable for ease of interpretation, as there was no difference in results whether it was included as a continuous or dummy variable. The dependent variable was a categorical strategy variable with

1 = Niche
2 = Price
3 = Quality
4 = Super Achiever (reference category)

As indicated earlier, Super Achiever was considered the broadest strategy.

Table 2.2. Multinomial Logit Results

		Without Interaction			With Interaction
Intercept	1	–1.344			–0.814
	2	0.266			–0.101
	3	0.906			3.149***
% Female	1	0.021***			–0.004
	2	0.018**			0.005
	3	0.003			–0.140***
Start Others	1	0.300			0.978**
	2	–1.672***			–3.292***
	3	–0.981*			–1.338
Team Size	1	0.236			–0.010
	2	–0.483			–0.109
	3	–0.706*			–2.770***
Experience[a]	1	0.078	% female	1	–0.0002
	2	–0.040	Start Others	2	0.0003**
	3	–0.071		3	0.0003*
Savings[a]	1	0.079	% female	1	0.018**
	2	–0.007	Team Size	2	0.003
	3	–0.069		3	0.081***
Loan	1	0.155			
	2	–0.202			
	3	–0.029			
		$n = 95$			$n = 95$

Notes:
* = significant at the 10% level, ** = significant at the 5% level, *** = significant at the 1% level
[a] Variable measured as square root

The CATMOD procedure of SAS was used to estimate the equation. The dependent variable is the log of the odds of choosing one strategy over another. In this particular context, the dependent variable [(ln (Pa/Pb))] is the log of the ratio of the probability of selecting strategy "a" relative to the probability of selecting a Super Achiever strategy. The estimation was performed using weights provided to compensate for potential bias due to oversampling in some geographical areas.

When covariates are included in the analysis, we find support for H_3 (SF); women choose different entry strategies than men. As the percentage of females on the starting team increased, the odds of choosing a narrow strategy (Niche and Price) relative to the broad strategy significantly increased.

Probability of selecting a Niche strategy relative to Super Achiever strategy is statistically significant at the 1% level, and the probability of selecting a Price strategy relative to Super Achiever is significant at the 5% level. Although the coefficients here are statistically significant, there is little economic significance. The log of the odds of choosing these strategies goes up only about two tenth of 1% for every 1% increase in the percentage of females on the team.

In this analysis, those with experience starting other ventures were significantly less likely to choose the narrow strategies (Price and Quality) relative to the broadest strategy. The other significant result was for team size, as the team grew in size, they were less likely to choose a narrow strategy (Quality) relative to Super Achiever.

In order to test H_4, interaction terms were included in the multinomial logit model. These results are reported in the second column of Table 2.2. Since only start-up experience and team size had been significant covariates in column 1, these were the only two variables included in the interaction with percentage female. For those teams that had start-up experience, as the percentage of females on the team increased, the teams were significantly more likely to choose narrow strategies (Price and Quality) relative to the broadest strategy. This result was significant, at the 1% level even though the coefficient of 0.0003 was extremely small. This indicates that it was not a lack of start-up experience that influenced women to select a narrow strategy. In fact, women with start-up experience were more likely to choose these strategies. In addition, for those teams that were larger in size, as the percentage of females increased, teams were significantly more likely to choose narrow strategies (Niche and Quality) relative to Super Achiever.

The above results do not support H_4, but instead indicate that increased female representation on start-up teams moves the teams toward the choice of a narrow entry strategy regardless of their human capital.

Regression Analysis

To determine: (1) whether gender differences in the characteristics of business account for differing growth rates; and (2) whether founding strategy can compensate for such gender differences and affect growth, we use

OLS regression analysis to test the hypotheses. Entry strategy was included as a dummy variable with Super Achiever again the left-out category.

Table 2.3 reports results of the analyses using sales growth as the dependent variable.

Table 2.3. Regression Analyses

	Sales First Year[a]	Sales First Year[a]	Sales Most Recent Year	Sales Most Recent Year
Intercept	4.111***	5.107***	1.814***	1.876***
% Female	−0.006	−0.017**	−0.001	0.002
Start Others	0.460		−0.035	
Team Size	0.156		0.007	
Experience	0.001		0.001	
Savings	0.137		0.019	
Loan	0.213**	0.255***	0.020	
Niche	−0.098	−0.406	0.003	0.019
Price	−0.840	−0.514	0.094	0.214
Quality	−0.104	−0.648	−0.026	0.109
% Fem*Niche		0.012		−0.002
%Fem*Price		0.001		−0.005*
%Fem*Quality		0.014		−0.006*
Age			−0.004**	−0.005***
R[b]	0.24	0.19	0.12	0.12

Notes:
* = significant at the 10% level, ** = significant at the 5% level, *** = significant at the 1% level
[a] Variable measured as logarithm
[b] Variable measured as square root

The first two columns in Table 2.3 report the results for sales growth in the first year of business. The first column includes all the covariates. In this version, the gender variable had no affect on sales in the first year, supporting H_5. There was no difference between men and women. The only covariate that significantly affected sales was the access to formal financing.

When interaction terms were included, the percentage female became statistically significant and negative. As the female participation on the team increased, sales in the first year declined. Although statistically significant, the effect is economically insignificant. For teams that chose a niche strategy, as the percentage of women on a start-up team increased 1%, sales were approximately $1.00 less in the first year.

In columns 3 and 4, sales in the most recent year was modeled as the dependent variable. In these regressions, age of the firm was included to avoid confounding the effect that age has on the growth in sales. Strategy interacting with gender was added in column 4 to test the SF hypotheses.

Looking at strategy in column 3, we find age of the firm the only significant variable, with the gender and strategy terms insignificant. When analyzing the interaction terms (column 4) we find that two are significant, and the signs are opposite of that expected. Teams with a greater percentage of women that chose a narrow Price strategy grow slower relative to firms choosing the omitted broad category. This is also true for teams that chose a narrow quality strategy. We have no support for H_6.

Hypotheses Three and Four derived from SF assume that women will choose different entry strategies and that narrow entry strategies will more likely be chosen by women with lower levels of human and financial capital. There was limited support for these hypotheses. Women are more likely to choose narrow entry strategies. Yet, when the interaction terms are included, we find that these choices are not a result of some lack of human or financial capital. Women with higher levels of start-up experience and larger teams were more likely to choose the narrower entry strategies.

Hypotheses 5 and 6 assume that growth rates in the sales of firms will not differ due to gender because of the entry strategies, and that among women, narrow strategies will generate higher growth. We find no support for entry strategies by themselves affecting the growth in sales for the first year or for the most recent sales. The findings indicate that the availability of formal financing was the only variable that significantly affected sales growth.

The addition of the strategy interaction terms indicated the opposite of our expectations. When the gender interaction terms are included, we find that teams with the higher percentage of females that choose a narrow strategy of Price or Quality show lower sales growth in the most recent year, although again, the coefficients are so small as to be economically insignificant.

DISCUSSION

Liberal feminist and social feminist theories were used in the present study to examine the role that initial resources, founding strategy, and gender play in predicting new firm growth. Hypotheses consistent with LF received limited support. Our analysis supports the work of Cromie and Birley (1991) in that we find women have significantly less industry experience than do men. Mixed support for the LF and SF perspectives found in the present study may reflect the variable chosen to operationalize discrimination and systematic barriers. Alternative measures of the access of financial resources may reveal more support for the theory. Additionally, other forms of human capital like skills needed to interface effectively with critical stakeholders such as customers and suppliers may better represent the theory.

Founding strategy was portrayed as representing differences in women's and men's belief structures that derived from variations in their socialization patterns. The hypotheses derived from SF assumed that women could compensate for resource deficiencies by choosing a founding strategy that fit their particular competencies. The results do not support this supposition. Women-owned firms that chose narrow strategies relative to the broad have significantly lower growth rates. The hypothesis that the narrow, "specialist" strategy would best fit women's competencies, was not supported. Women-owned businesses that adopt a "generalist" strategy significantly increased the growth rates of their new ventures over time.

CONCLUSIONS

This study adds to the knowledge pool about the effects of gender on organization performance. The use of feminist theory extends previous research and provides an explanation for contradictions in the literature.

While the findings offer limited support for the liberal feminist perspective it would be premature to conclude that discrimination and systematic barriers do not affect the founding and operation of women's businesses. Future examinations based on LF theory should respond to challenges that measures traditionally employed in research reflect male derived measures. Greater attention should be given to the development of measures that appropriately represent both genders.

ACKNOWLEDGMENT

The initial data collection in Pennsylvania was sponsored by the Appalachia Regional Commission and the Pennsylvania Department of Commerce. The initial data collection in Minnesota was sponsored by 10 states, regional, and local agencies in Minnesota. The follow-up data collection was a joint effort of the Marquette University Center for the Study of Entrepreneurship, University of Minnesota Carlson Entrepreneurial Center, University of Pennsylvania Snider Entrepreneurial Center, and Widener University School of Business Administration.

NOTE

1. See Amemiya (1981, pp. 1416–1418). According to multinomial logit analysis, if there are five categories, X is a 1xk vector of determinants, and bj is a kx1 vector of parameters (j=1,...4), then the probability of status m ($1 < m < 4$) is

$$Pm = \frac{\exp(X\beta_m)}{\sum_{j=1}^{4} \exp(X\beta_j)}$$

The set of β's is estimated by a set of b's such that

$$\sum_{j=1}^{4} bj = 0.$$

If there are six characteristics, the estimated log of odds of status 1 relative to status 4 is

$$\ln[(P_1)/(P_4)] = (b_{10} - b_{40}) + (b_{11} - b_{41})X_1 + (b_{12} - b_{42})X_2 + (b_{13} - b_{43})X_3 + \ldots + (b_{16} - b_{46})X_6.$$

So, a unit increase in X_1 causes the estimated log of the odds of status 1 relative to status 4 to increase by $b_{11} - b_{41}$. Differences in b's are estimated using a maximum likelihood technique. In this paper, Super Achiever was chosen as the reference category (status 4).

In estimating a multinomial logit model, one assumes independence of irrelevant alternatives (IIA). With IIA, the odds between any two statuses are assumed unaffected by the existence of other statuses. The assumption can be problematic, especially in applications where some categories are very similar and some very dissimilar. One such problematic case is McFadden's famous transportation example (cited in Amemiya, 1981, p. 1417), in which there are three options: a car, a blue bus, and a red bus. Does violation of the IIA assumption affect the accuracy of the model estimated in the current analysis? The categories in this analysis were deliberately chosen in order to separate independent alternatives. Thus, the IIA assumption is not likely to create a problem.

APPENDIX 1

Factor Analysis of New Firm Competitive Strategy Associated with Factor Dimensions

Competitive aspects emphasized	Descriptive
Factor 1 alpha = .63	**Market Sensitivity**
Fast response to changes in markets (.81) Serve those missed by others (.69) More effective marketing/advertising (.68)	Knowledge of the market emphasized reach and respond quickly to key customer needs
Factor 2 alpha = .81	**Technology**
Develop new/advanced technology (.92) Utilize new/advanced technology (.87)	Emphasize process or product technology by developing or using new or advanced
Factor 3 alpha = .61	**Product Distinction**
More contemporary, attractive products (.76) Distinctive goods/services (.71) More choices (.64)	Seek to distinguish the firm from others in the market place by providing unique products or services.
Factor 4 alpha = .71	**Site Appeal**
Superior location/customer convenience (.84) Better, more attractive facilities (.83)	Attractiveness and convenience of facilities and location emphasized.
Factor 5 alpha = .68	**Service**
Better Service (.86) Quality products/services (.81)	Provide a higher level of service than competitors.
Factor 6	**Price**
Lower prices (.93)	Sell products or services at a lower price than competitors.

APPENDIX 2

Strategy Archetype Descriptions

1. **Super Achievers**—Firms pursuing this strategy strive to promote multiple strategic attributes simultaneously. New ventures adopting this strategy attempt to be all things to all people. They seek a flexible and responsive position in the market by emphasizing characteristics of their site location, exploiting advanced technology, and by emphasizing the quality of their distinctive products and services relative to the price charged. This strategy is broad based in its effort to exploit a diverse set of resources.
2. **Quality Proponents**—Firms adopting this strategy also have a penchant for a broad market. Quality Proponents are much like Super Achievers except they do not emphasize price as an integral strategic focus.

3. **Equivocators**—Firms adopting this strategy fail to emphasize any particular strategy focus. This strategy may be analogous to Michael Porter's (1985) description of firms "stuck in the middle." At best ambivalent, uncertainty seemingly characterized strategy formation in these new ventures. Because a distinct strategic emphasis is absent, this strategy can be considered neither broad nor narrow.
4. **Price Competitors**—This strategy reflects new ventures' attempts to rely on a combination of marketing/advertising and low price to attract customers. This strategy appears to be the most flexible since pricing and advertising can be changed quickly in response to competitor actions.
5. **Niche Purveyors**—These firms emphasize site qualities. Attractive facilities at superior, convenient locations are seen as creating customer value. By coupling convenience with exceptional or unique products at competitive prices, firms pursuing this strategy narrow their scope and attempt to secure a distinctive foothold in the competitive landscape by focusing on a narrow segment of the population.
6. **Technology Value**—Firms adopting this strategy pursue a narrow differentiation approach. They attempt to distinguish themselves by making price-competitive products through the use and/or development of new technology. This strategy is narrow-based as technology products and services limit the market segment they seek to serve.

REFERENCES

Aldrich, H., Elam, A.B., & Reese, P.R. (1996). Strong ties, weak ties, and strangers: Do women business owners differ from men in their use of networking to obtain assistance? In S. Birley & I.C. MacMillan (Eds.), *Entrepreneurship in a global context (International business & the world economy,* pp. 1–25). London: Routledge.

Amemiya, T. (1981). Qualitative response models: A survey. *Journal of Economic Literature, 19*, 1483–1536.

Astin, H.S., & Leland C. (1991). *Women of influence, women of vision.* San Francisco: Jossey-Bass.

Biggadike, R.E. (1976). *Corporate diversification: Entry, strategy and performance.* Boston: Harvard University Press.

Black, N. (1989). *Social feminism.* Ithaca, NY: Cornell University Press.

Bourgeois, L.J., III. (1980). Strategy and environment: A conceptual integration. *Academy of Management Journal, 5*(1), 25–39.

Broom, H., & Longenecker, J.G. (1971). *Small business management* (3rd ed). Cincinnati, OH: South Western.

Brush, C. (1992). Research on women business owners: Past trends, a new perspective and future directions. *Entrepreneurship Theory and Practice, 16*(2), 5–30.

Burrell, G. (1992). Sex and organizational analysis. In A.J. Mills & P. Tancred (Eds.), *Gendering organizational analysis* (pp. 71–92). Newbury Park, CA: Sage.

Buttner, E.H., & Rosen, B. (1988). Bank loan officers' perceptions of the characteristic of men, women and successful entrepreneurs. *Journal of Business Venturing,* 3(3), 249–258.

Buttner, E.H., & Rosen, B. (1989). Funding new business ventures: Are decision makers biased against women entrepreneurs. *Journal of Business Venturing,* 4(4), 249–261.

Calas, M.B., & Smircich, L. (1992). Using the "F: word: Feminist theories and the social consequences of organizational research. In A.J. Mills & P. Tancred (Eds.), *Gendering organizational analysis* (pp. 222–234). Newbury Park, CA: Sage.

Caputo, R.K., & Dolinsky, A.L. (1998). Women's choice to pursue self-employment: The role of financial and human capital of household members. *Journal of Small Business Management,* 36(3), 8–17.

Carter, N.M., Stearns, T.M., Reynolds P.D. ,& Miller, B. (1994). New venture strategies: Theory development with an empirical base. *Strategic Management Journal,* 15(1), 21–41.

Carter, P., & Rosa P. (1998). The financing of male and female owned-business. *Entrepreneurship and Regional Development,* 10(3), 225–241.

Chon, T., & Lindberg, R.A. (1974). *Survival and growth: Management strategies for the small firm.* New York: AMACOM.

Coleman, S. (2000). Access to capital and terms of credit: A comparison of men- and women-owned small businesses. *Journal of Small Business Management,* 38(3), 37–52.

Cooper, A.C., Willard, G.E., & Woo C.Y. (1986). Strategies of high performing new and small firms: A reexamination of the niche concept. *Journal of Business Venturing,* 1(3), 247–260.

Cooper A.C., Gimeno-Gascon, F.J., & Woo C.Y. (1994). Initial human and financial capital as predictor of new venture performance. *Journal of Business Venturing,* 9(5), 371–395.

Cromie, S., & Birley, S. (1991). Networking by female business owners in Northern Ireland. *Journal of Business Venturing,* 7(3), 237–251.

Deeks, J. (1976). *The small firm owner-manager.* New York: Praeger.

Fay, M., & Williams, L. (1993). Gender bias and the availability of business loans. *Journal of Business Venturing,* 8(4), 363–376.

Fischer, E.M., Reuber, R.R., & Dyke, L.S. (1993). A theoretical overview and extension of research on sex, gender, and entrepreneurship. *Journal of Business Venturing,* 8(2), 151–168.

Haines, G.H., Orser, B.J., & Riding, A.L. (1999). Myths and realities: An empirical study of banks and the gender of small business clients. *Canadian Journal of Administrative Sciences Review,* 16(4), 291–307.

Hitt, M.A., Bierman, L., Shimizu K., & Kochlar, R. (2001). Direct and moderating effects of human capital on strategy and performance in professional service firms: A resource-based perspective. *Academy of Management Journal,* 44(1): 13–28.

Honing-Haftel, S., & Martin, L. (1986). Is the female entrepreneur at a disadvantage? *Thrust: The Journal for Employment and Training Professionals, 7*, 49–64.

Hosmer, L.T. (1957). Small manufacturing enterprises. *Harvard Business Review, 35*(6), 111–122.

Hurley, A. (1992, August). *Incorporating feminist theories into sociological theories of entrepreneurship.* Presented at the Annual Academy of Management Meeting, Miami, FL.

Jagger, A.M., & Rothenberg, P.S. (1984). *Feminist frameworks.* New York: McGraw-Hill.

Jones, K., & Tullous, R. (2002). Behaviors of pre-venture entrepreneurs and perceptions of their financial needs. *Journal of Small Business Management, 40*(3), 233–249.

Kalleberg, A., & Leicht. K. (1991). Gender and organizational performance: Determinants of small business survival and success. *Academy of Management Journal, 34*(1), 136–161.

Kaplan, E. (1988). Women entrepreneurs: Constructing a framework to examine venture success and business failures. In B.A. Kirchoff, W.A. Long, W.E. McMullan, K.H. Vesper, & W.E. Wetzel, Jr. (Eds.), *Frontiers of entrepreneurship research* (pp. 643–653). Wellesly, MA: Babson College.

Keeley, R., & Roure. J. (1990). Management, strategy, and industry structure as influences on the success of new firms: A structural model. *Management Science, 36*(10), 1256–1267.

MacMillan, I.C., & Day, D.L. (1987). Corporate ventures into industrial markets: Dynamics of aggressive entry. *Journal of Business Venturing, 2*(1), 29–40.

McDougall, P., & Robinson, R.B. Jr. (1990). New venture strategies: An empirical identification of eight "archetypes" of competitive strategies for entry. *Strategic Management Journal, 11*(6), 447–467.

Miller, A., & Camp, B. (1985). Exploring determinants of success in corporate ventures. *Journal of Business Venturing, 1*(1), 87–105.

Mills, A., & Tancred, P. (1992). *Gendering organizational analysis.* Newbury Park, CA: Sage.

Mukhtar, S.M. (2002). Differences in male and female management characteristics: A study of owner-manager businesses. *Small Business Economics, 18*(4), 289–311.

NFWBO, National Foundation for Women Business Owners. (2001). *Key facts: U.S. women-owned businesses.* Silver Spring, MD: NFWBO.

Oakley, A. (1972). *Sex, gender and society.* London: Temple Smith.

Olm, D., Carsrud, L., & Alvey, L. (1988). The role of networks in new venture funding for the female entrepreneur: A continuing analysis. In B.A. Kirchoff, W.A. Long, W.E. EcMullan, K.H. Vesper, & W.E. Wetzel, Jr. (Eds.), *Frontiers of entrepreneurship research* (pp. 658–689). Wellesy, MA: Babson College.

Porter, M. E. (1985). *Competitive advantage.* New York: Free Press.

Reynolds, P.D. (1993). *High performance entrepreneurship: What makes a difference* (Working paper). Milwaukee, WI: Marquette University.

Reynolds, P.D., & Freeman, S. (1987). *1986 Pennsylvania new firm survey.* Washington, DC: Appalachia Regional Commission.

Reynolds, P.D., & Miller, B. (1988). *1987 Minnesota new firm survey.* Minneapolis: University of Minnesota Center for Urban and Regional Affairs.

Riding, A., & Swift, C. (1990). Women business owners and terms of credit: Some empirical findings of the Canadian experience. *Journal of Business Venturing,* 5(5), 327–340.

Romanelli, E. (1989). Organization birth and population variety: A community perspective on origins. In L.L. Cummings & B.M. Staw (Eds.), *Research in organizational behavior* (Vol. 11, pp. 211–246). Greenwich, CT: JAI Press.

Sandberg, W.R., & Hofer, C.W. (1987). Improving new venture performance: The role of strategy, industry structure, and the entrepreneur. *Journal of Business Venturing,* 2(1), 5–28.

Sexton, D.L., & Bowman-Upton, N. (1990). Female and male entrepreneurs: Psychological characteristics and their role in gender-related discrimination. *Journal of Business Venturing,* 5(1), 29–36.

Sheppard, D. (1992). Women manger's perceptions of gender and organizational life. In A.J. Mills & P. Tancred (Eds.), *Gendering organizational analysis* (pp. 151:166). Newbury Park, CA: Sage.

Sonfield, M., Lussier, R.N., Corman, J., & McKinney, M. (2001). Gender comparisons in strategic decision-making: An empirical analysis of the entrepreneurial strategy mix. *Journal of Small Business Management,* 39(2), 165–173.

Stearns, T.M., Carter, N.M., Reynolds, P.D., & Williams, M.L. (1995). New firm survival: Industry, strategy and location. *Journal of Business Venturing,* 10(1), 23–42.

Stegall, D.P., Steinmetz, L.L., & Kline, J.B. (1976). *Managing the small business.* Homewood, IL: Irwin.

Stinchcombe, A. (1965). Social structure and organizations. In J.G. March (Ed.), *Handbook of organizations* (pp. 142–193). Chicago: Rand McNally.

Stuart, R.T., & Abetti, P.A. (1987). Start-up ventures: towards the prediction of initial success. *Journal of Business Venturing,* 52(3), 215–230.

Tigges, L.M., & Green, G.P. (1994). Small business success among men- and women-owned firms in rural areas. *Rural Sociology,* 59(2), 289–310.

U.S. Small Business Administration. (2001). *Women in business.* Office of Advocacy, APEC Women Entrepreneurs Report: United States.

Van de Ven, A., Hudson, R., & Schroeder, D. (1984). Designing new business start-ups: Entrepreneurial, organizational, and ecological considerations. *Journal of Management,* 10(1), 87–107.

Verheul, I., & Thurik, R. (2001). Start-up capital: Does gender matter? *Small Business Economics,* 16(4), 329–345.

Vivarelli, M., & Audretsch, D. (1994). *The link between the entry decision and post-entry performance* (Working paper). CNR Project Internationalization.

Walsh, J.P., & Fahey, L. (1986). The role of negotiated belief structures in strategy making. *Journal of Management,* 12(3), 325–338.

Zacharakis, A.L., Neck, H.M., Bygrave, W.D., & Cox, L.W. (2001). *Global Entrepreneurship Monitor: National Entrepreneurship Assessment-United States, 2001 Executive Report.* Kansas City, MO: Kauffman Center for Entrepreneurial Leadership at the Ewing Marion Kauffman Foundation. See, http://www.entreworld.org/Bookstore/Product.cfm?DID=6&Product_ID=77&CATID=22

Zellner, W., King, R.W., Byrd, V.N. , DeGeorge, G., & Birnbaum J. (1994, April 18). Women entrepreneurs. *Business Week,* pp. 104–110.

CHAPTER 3

EXPLORING LEADERSHIP VISION

New Perspectives on Women Entrepreneurs and Executives

Barbara Bird and Candida Brush

ABSTRACT

Extending earlier empirical and conceptual studies of leadership vision, this chapter focuses on the content of vision statements of women entrepreneurs and executives. The study uses criterion-based and open content analysis to surface vision themes. It then links these themes to previously developed quantitative measures of vision as well as vision implementation measures. Results suggest women executives and entrepreneurs have different foci for their vision and employ somewhat different implementation measures. The implications include the use of qualitative methods for the study of vision, the extension of visualized outcomes beyond growth, and suggestions on measuring implementation of vision.

INTRODUCTION

Entrepreneurial and leadership vision, shared with key organizational stakeholders, sets the direction of an enterprise, focuses activities and resources, energizes effort, and determines the values sought and served. Leaders and teams of top managers of existing organizations who seek change and improvement in their organization's performance usually craft this vision; entrepreneurs and their partners craft the vision for new and closely-held ventures. Effective vision is thought to be feasible, desirable, actionable, and clearly articulated (Nutt & Backoff, 1997). If implemented effectively, it produces organizational change or creation, which can include growth in any key metric.

Vision can be characterized as a form of mental model, with two core components: values and imagery (Bird & Brush, 2002a; Collins & Porras, 1994). Vision begins as a mental activity that links current conditions to "future perfect enactments" (Weick, 1979) and which inspires and directs participants toward a particular future. The image of the future is often visual in nature—seen by the inner eye. The image of the future serves to demonstrate to the "seer" a possible future where currently held values or unmet needs are fulfilled.

While there is considerable attention to leadership vision (Bennis & Nanus, 1985; Conger, 1992, Nutt & Backoff, 1997; Tichy & Devanna, 1996) there has been less attention to entrepreneurship vision. Bird and Brush (2002a) distinguish entrepreneurial vision as operating in a unique context. Entrepreneurs face fewer constraints in terms of the possible futures and values to be enacted since they begin without an existing organization. Executives are more constrained by their organization's history, strategy, structure, and stakeholders. Likewise, entrepreneurs directly and personally affect the implementation of their vision whereas executives operate through systems and established employment and resource contracts.

Our study extends the earlier studies of Larwood, Kriger, and Falbe (1993), Larwood and Falbe (1994), Larwood, Falbe, Kriger, and Miesing (1995) and that of Baum, Locke, and Kirkpartick (1998) and Baum (1995) by measuring vision content using a qualitative method and asking deeper questions on implementation. We compare leaders in two role contexts (entrepreneurs in organizations they created or purchased and executives in organizations which employ them) while using the (Larwood et al., 1995) measure of vision dimensions and multidimensional qualitative vision content. In addition, we examine implementation within the firm as well as outside the firm and include both communication and policy measures.

Perhaps what is most important, our study also extends previous work by examining leadership vision in women entrepreneurs and executives. Gender was not identified in either the Larwood or Baum studies. It is highly likely that these samples were predominantly male given the sampling proportions of women in prior studies. The Larwood studies sampled business school deans, entrepreneurs and CEOs of Fortune 1000 firms, which were 95% male (Falbe, personal communication). The Baum study was in a construction-related (and male dominated) industry.

It is possible that by omitting women from previous studies, some aspects of vision content may be less visible. For example, vision content could include more dimensions than growth (the only content studied previously), since growth is suspect as a masculine variable (Bird & Brush, 2002b; Brush, 1992; Gilligan, 1982). Further, the concept of reality may be more interconnected, shared and reflect a slower and present oriented time horizon (Bird & Brush, 2002b). We might expect other vision content to be found in businesswomen, even among entrepreneurs where new venture growth is in some ways easier. For example, vision might include greater attention to developing employees and educating customers. Thus, our study is unique in its entirely female sample.

BACKGROUND

Leadership scholars define vision as a transcendent ideal or mental model representing shared values that are ideological in nature, and having moral overtones (House, 1977; House & Shamir, 1993). It is an ideal to which the organization should aspire, or a mental image of the products, services and organization that the business leader(s) wants to achieve (Bennis & Nanus, 1985). Vision is used to inspire others to perform well (Bass, 1985; Bennis & Nanus, 1985; Conger & Kanungo, 1987) and provides personal motivation or "temporal tension" for entrepreneurs (Bird, 1989). Effective vision arouses followers' needs and values (House, 1977), is discrepant from status quo, challenges followers (Conger & Kanugo, 1987), and generally directs action toward a desired outcome (Kouzes & Posner, 2002).

In general terms, mental models are tacit and explicit understandings of how conditions, actions, and resources are interrelated across time and space (Senge, 1990) and include schemata (Marks, 1990). A mental model may be as simple as an image embedded in a set of relationships showing some causality or consequence, (i.e., the picture of an "if... then relationship), a picture or diagram of critical interdependencies in a system being formed or changed (Jenkins & Johnson, 1997), or a mental motion picture of a chain of events (i.e., mental rehearsal; Rockey, 1986). It may be as complex and abstract as a theory-in-use (Argyris & Schon, 1996). Like all mental models, a business vision is an incomplete map, yet vision is instrumental in motivating and directing one's own and others' thoughts and mental models as well as behavior.

In practice, organizational vision is often synonymous with executive vision. Here vision is derived from an organization-wide involvement of many people, sifted through layers of decision makers, and fed back to the organization. This process obscures the impact of the leader's personal values through aggregation and normative processes. In other cases individual leaders set the vision for the organization. This is particularly true in entrepreneurial ventures, not only start ups but also to some degree acquisitions, international subsidiaries, and new corporate ventures. As Nutt and Backoff (1997) point out, organizations likely to formulate successful visions need to be susceptible to change, which they define as the absence of bureaucratic formalization, centralization, and stratification. New organizations are by definition, changing the arrangement of resources and highly susceptible to internal change inherent in identified liabilities of newness and smallness. Because they are new and not bureaucratic, that vision is most likely to begin with the leaders' personal values rather than a normative process. A new venture is in the process of unfolding, boundaries are unclear, cultural norms are being formed, and strategic commitments evolving (Gartner, Bird, & Starr, 1992; Katz & Gartner, 1988). Hence it is reasonable to expect that the processes and content of vision would be quite different for entrepreneurs and executives. At the start, the entrepreneur's vision for the new venture reflects the values held by the founder and her earliest partners and is simpler than the executive's vision of her larger, older enterprise whose multiple stakeholders may contribute different and even conflicting values.

Generally, vision processes include formulating, articulating, and implementing the vision and vision content comprises values, images, purpose and a pattern for an organization's future. Larwood et al. (1993) and Falbe and Larwood (1995) measured leadership perceptions of vision and found a consistent pattern of dimensions among business people. Across samples, three reliable subscales emerge: vision formulation (five items, with emphasis on strategic planning), implementation (three items, with emphasis on communication and buy-in), and innovative realism (ten items, a mix of innovation, action, and flexibility). One of these studies (Falbe & Larwood, 1995), examined leadership role (executive or entrepreneur) as a variable in the articulation of leadership vision and found that entrepreneurs score lower than executives in formulation of their organizational visions and higher than executives in innovative realism as well as single items of risk and detail. No differences were found between entrepreneurs and executives in vision implementation or in the importance of the vision to top management, the extent to which it is shared, the length of time it is held, and the length of time into the future that the vision is cast.

The studies by Larwood and her colleagues (1993, 1995) are limited by the exclusion of vision content, implementation activities other than communication, and organizational impact. As discussed earlier, vision content would theoretically reflect organizationally specific values and images. Implementation would extend beyond communication to include retention by others as well as enactment through organizational policies and practices. For example, the use of vision terminology among stakeholders might show the extent to which the vision is embedded in the organization. Likewise, employee benefits and organizational policies might be ways that some leadership visions are manifested in the firm.

Baum et al. (1998) is one study that looked at vision attributes, content, communication, and organizational growth in owner-managed woodworking firms. The authors coded vision statements for "attributes" of brevity, clarity, abstractness, challenge, future orientation, stability, and desirability. Their content measure was defined as the degree to which growth was included in the vision statements on their questionnaire. Implementation was defined as communication and restricted to two nominal variables reflecting the presence of a written vision statement and whether the CEO talked about the vision. Venture growth (sales, employment, and profits) was the performance measure. In the study of 127 CEO-employee pairs, Baum et al. (1998) found vision attributes, content and communication had a significant impact on venture growth. However, their study is limited by the narrow definitions of vision content and implementation and the male sample.

This study attempts to fill the gaps in prior literature on entrepreneurial vision by comparing female executive and entrepreneurial leaders and to elaborating the relationship between entrepreneurial vision and its implementation. Specifically we address the following research questions as they pertain to women's role in an existing or entrepreneurial organization:

1. What is the content of leadership vision and how does vision content vary by leader's role?
2. What is the relationship between the content of leadership vision and the dimensions of vision and how does this relationship vary by leader's role?
3. How is vision implementation related to differences in vision content and how does this vary by leader's role?

METHOD AND SAMPLE

A sample of 227 successful women entrepreneurs and 160 successful women executives were identified from publicly available sources. "Success" was defined as an appearance on a media listing such as *Working Women Magazine's* "Top 50 Women Entrepreneurs," or local publications such as *Dallas Business Journal's* top women business owners. We utilized both national and city publications to insure geographic representation. Our four-page questionnaire was pretested on 3 women entrepreneurs and 4 faculty experts.

From the entrepreneurs' list, 65 were discontinued or bad addresses, bringing the total sample to 154. We received 61 responses, an effective response rate of 38%. For the executives, 44 were either no longer in the company or bad addresses, bringing the total sample to 122. We received 46 responses for an effective response rate of 36%. In addition, we interviewed twelve women leaders who also completed the survey (seven entrepreneurs and five executives) for a total sample of 119 successful women entrepreneurs and executive business leaders.

Variables

Two measures of vision were used, first, an open question asking respondents to *"Please describe your personal vision for your organization,"* and second, the same 26-item scale used previously by Larwood et al. (1995). The vision scale includes a variety of items to be rated on a 5-point scale, anchored by "very little" (1) and "very much" (5). For our sample, this scale yielded a reliability of alpha .81. Subscales derived from Larwood et al. (1995) were based on items that had unique or strongest factor loadings of the vision dimension scale. These include vision formulation (five items, α = .78), implementation (three items, α = .78), and innovative realism (ten items, α = .83). The other Lawood et al. (1995) subscales had fewer than two unique items and low reliabilities and are not included in this study.

Measures of personal and organizational characteristics were similar to those used by Larwood and her colleagues, including questions regarding work experience and size and structure of company. Sales or revenues in 1994 ranged from $13,000 to $18.3 billion, with a median of $10 million; 1994 employment ranged from 1 to 118,00, with median of 71. In addition to the Larwood et al. (1995) scale, implementation was also measured by nominal variables of whether or not the leader used the following as indicators of the integration of vision within the company, division, or business unit: (1) managers use vision vocabulary in communication, (2) employees use vision vocabulary in communication, and (3) people outside the organization use vision vocabulary in communication. Other measures of implementation of vision include company spending on employee benefits, the percentage of women in the top management group, and the extent of environmental practices (a nominal variable).

Table 3.1. Sample Characteristics

	Mean/sd		Median		n =		
	Exec	Entre	Exec	Entre	Exec	Entre	Signif
Personal Characteristics							
Age	45.4 5.3	50.0 9.3	48	50	48	66	.002
Tenure with firm	12.4	14.7	11	14	47	68	.09
Tenure in position	4.8	11.6	4	10	47	65	.001
Length of time held vision	5.8 10.5	9.3 11.5	7	10	41	63	ns
Vision view into future	6.4 7.4	11.5 15.1	5	5	47	64	.04
Company Characteristics							
Age	67.8 50.0	24.7 19.6	64	20	43	72	.001
Number of management levels below leader	4.8 3.8	3.3 1.8	5	3	45	70	.005
Number of people reporting to leader	11.7	12.2	7	5	46	67	ns
Total on top management team	17.4 23.3	5.3 5.0	10	4	45	67	.001
Revenue growth	$.563 B $1.340 B	$7.98 M $11M	$56 M	$2.9 M	20	40	.01
% revenue growth	97% 143%	192% 362%	37%	100%	20	40	ns
Employment growth	−3,679 11,632	22 73	0	11	27	35	.05
% employment growth	35% 100%	66% 90%	0	41%	27	35	ns

RESULTS

As might be expected there were some significant differences between executives and entrepreneurs in demographic variables. Executives were younger, held their position for less time than entrepreneurs, and had shorter future horizons. Executives have older firms with more levels of management and bigger top management teams. Firms run by executives show greater revenue growth and less employment growth than those run by entrepreneurs although the rate of growth in revenues and employees is not significantly different.

Vision Content

Ninety-eight of the respondents wrote a vision statement. These statements were then content analyzed using two methods. First, we applied the Boyatizis (1998) method of criterion coding to a sub-sample determine whether any content discriminated between the women executives and entrepreneurs. This method, applied empirically rather than derived from theorized differences, resulted in seven possible content areas. In addition, the sub-sample of vision statements was content analyzed without criterion, to find relevant themes. These themes are listed in Table 3.2 and Table 3.3 along with criterion for subsequent coding of the entire set of vision statements. All vision statements were then coded independently by two trained coders. The coders compared coding categories and interrater reliabilities were determined. For the discriminating codes, reliability is .78; for the thematic codes, reliability is .81. Following the initial comparison, the raters discussed differences and arrived at consensus codings for each vision statement.

Table 3.2. Content Themes Hypothesized to Discriminate

Externally focused (more entrepreneurial)
- vision focuses primarily on external environment of the firm
- mentions customers, suppliers, marketplace, competition, *and does not* mention internal players (employees or self)
- Example: "Adding value to services in order to compete successfully against big firms."

Firm focused (more entrepreneurial)
- vision focuses primarily on internal environment of firm and/or well-being of the firm and its employees
- mentions profit or growth goals, corporate culture, employees, management, internal structures *and does not* mention customers, markets, suppliers, competition
- Example: "A caring, fun place to work."

Externally and firm focused (more entrepreneurial)
- vision focuses equally on internal and external environments of firm
- mentions customers, suppliers, marketplace, competition and profit or growth goals, corporate culture, employees, management, internal structures
- Example: "Having fun as a team of creative engineers and managers and collectively creating new products that knock the socks off our competition"

Table 3.2. Content Themes Hypothesized to Discriminate (Cont.)

Traditional employer role (more executive)
- vision includes an orientation toward job creation and/or rewards for employees
- mentions providing jobs, rewards, compensation for employees
- Example: "…a provides jobs for women and minorities." "…generous benefits"

Post modern employer role (more executive)
- vision includes an orientation is toward employability, training and/or personal growth & development of employees
- mentions providing growth opportunities, career development for employees
- Example: "provide training to staff to sustain cutting edge"

Creatively competitive (more executive)
- creative orientation is toward competition and marketplace
- mentions product or service innovation, and becoming standard or leader or achieving comparative advantage
- Example: "innovates new products that allow us to achieve recognition and financial return"

Creatively supportive (more entrepreneurial)
- creative orientation is toward internal culture and/or external community with certain values implicit or explicit *other than economic values*
- mentions self-fulfillment or personal growth in customers, employees, or self, organizational culture with general or specific values embedded
- Example: "products that enhance the self-esteem of the handicapped" "an organization that is fun and excited about our products"

While not theoretically derived, these themes suggest post hoc, that entrepreneurs might have a more holistic view of their firm and its environment. That is, based on the code development, entrepreneurial vision is expected to be external and internal in focus, broad in scope and creatively supportive of employees. In contrast, executive vision is expected to be traditional (job, reward) and/or post-modern (training and employee growth) and creatively competitive, emphasizing competitors rather than community.

Theoretically, all non-criterion content themes can be present in firms of any size or ownership status since they are generally held as positive values by the marketplace, employees, business advisors, and educators. However, these themes may show distinct relationships with each other, with implementation of vision, and organizational outcomes and these relationships may vary between executives and entrepreneurs.

Table 3.3. Content Themes

Quality orientation

- vision addresses improvements, innovations or quality in product or service
- mentions quality, improvement, excellence, and synonyms for quality
- Example: "…deliver quality products" "continuous improvement in customer satisfaction"

Firm as leader

- vision is to establish firm as the leader in a market or niche
- statements use the superlative (most, best, largest, number 1, top)
- statements use the concept of leading as applied to the firm and its market
- statements refer to setting standards for the industry or marketplace
- Example: "become a household name," "top provider of health care services," "highest quality home furnishings"

Competitive orientation

- vision is oriented toward competitive advantage in the marketplace
- use of comparatives with other firms (better than, different from), *excludes internal comparisons* (e.g., improvements)
- statements use competitive terminology.
- with reference to markets, expanding share
- Example: "to compete with the best of them" "move ahead of the pack" "become a player in our market" *excludes "better than we were last year"*

Growth orientation

- vision is oriented toward the growth of the firm
- statements include references to organizational growth in size, employment, market share, expansion geographically, diversification
- Example: "to achieve 20% growth in sales" "diversify into new markets" "open an international operation by 2000"

Profit orientation

- vision is oriented toward profitability of the firm
- statements refers to profits or its surrogates such as margins, returns
- Example: "maintain a profitable operation while increasing customer satisfaction"

Change orientation

- vision indicates a change from current conditions, status, position or role as agent of change (leader)
- statements use verbs such as build, create, establish, foster, grow (*other than organizational size*), develop
- Example: "open a European office" "enter the xyz market" (which is new to the firm) "foster the growth of our staff" "maintain a profitable operation while increasing customer satisfaction"

Table 3.3. Content Themes (Cont.)

Maintenance oriented

- vision indicates a continuity of current conditions, status, position, or stable role
- statements use verbs such as maintain, keep, limit, remain, continue
- Example: "continue to provide above average benefits" "maintain a profitable operation while increasing customer satisfaction"

Dummy variables were created for each category and added to the data analysis. Table 3.4 shows the frequency with which the category was present in the total sample. Among all leaders, vision with an external and firm focus, quality orientation, and establishing the firm as a leader were the most frequent themes. The least common themes were the post modern and traditional employer roles, firm focus, and profit orientation. To check on the validity of criterion codes, a Chi-square analysis was performed for the presence/absence of the theme among entrepreneurs and executives. Only firm focus showed significance with entrepreneurs showing this theme more often than executives. Thus, the criterion categories were generally not useful in differentiating the leadership role of the respondent.

Table 3.4. Frequencies of Content Categories

Theme	Percentage of statements with theme			Difference between groups
	Total sample	Executives	Entrepreneurs	
External focus	36.7	40.5	33.9	ns
Firm focus	12.2	4.8	83.3	.05
External and firm focus	47.9	50.0	46.4	ns
Traditional employer role	11.2	9.5	12.5	ns
Post modern employer role	9.2	7.1	10.7	ns
Creatively competitive	29.6	28.6	30.4	ns
Creatively supportive	27.5	26.2	28.6	ns
Quality orientation	41.8	42.9	41.1	ns
Firm as leader	40.8	38.1	42.9	ns
Competitive orientation	22.4	11.9	30.4	.03
Growth orientation	27.6	26.2	28.6	ns
Profit orientation	17.3	14.3	19.6	ns
Change orientation	34.7	40.5	30.4	ns
Maintenance orientation	29.6	19.0	37.5	.04

While not expected to discriminate between leadership groups, two general content themes did. Entrepreneurs more than executives articulated visions with a competitive and a maintenance orientation. These differences may be linked to the firm focus, which was expected and found to be more indicative of entrepreneurs concerns. The firm focus was internal, concerned with firm and its employees rather than external concerns of the marketplace. Entrepreneurs, who have primary or even sole ownership and/or decision-making control over the entire firm, would certainly be expected to care strongly about the internal qualities of the firm. In this same manner, entrepreneurs could be expected to value the firm's continuity and ability to survive over the years as reflected in the maintenance orientation. Likewise, it may be the personal sense of responsibility (rather than corporate) and ownership (rather than as agent) that brings the competitive theme more strongly into entrepreneurs' visions.

When the Larwood et al. (1995) scales were analyzed, all leaders showed a strong preference for describing their vision in innovative terms and as a process of formulation as shown in Table 3.5. There were no differences between executives and entrepreneurs on any of the Larwood et al. (1995) scales.

Table 3.5. Vision Dimensions ANOVA

Scale	Total	Executive	Entrepreneur	Difference
	Mean Mean/n of items sd	Mean Mean/n of items sd	Mean Mean/n of items sd	
Vision formulation	19.5	19.9	19.3	ns
	3.9	4.0	3.9	
	3.4	3.3	4.4	
Vision implementation	11.3	11.4	11.5	ns
	3.8	3.8	3.8	
	2.2	2.5	2.2	
Vision innovative realism	40.0	39.8	40.1	ns
	4.0	4.0	4.0	
	5.9	5.5	6.3	

To test relationships between vision content and the Larwood et al. (1995) dimensions of vision, a set of Spearman correlations was performed for the entire sample. Table 3.6 shows these correlations. Innovative realism is the only dimension of the Larwood instrument which shows a statistically significant relationship to the content areas, and these are restricted to quality orientation and profit orientation. This suggests that content of vision may be relatively independent of the descriptions in the Larwood measure with the exception of innovativeness. We also tested the entrepreneurs and executives separately for the relationships between firm focus, competitive orientation, and maintenance orientation and the Larwood scales. These tests showed that for entrepreneurs, the vision formulation scale is marginally and negatively related to the maintenance orientation. This may suggest that entrepreneurial organizations with the vision of sustaining current levels may not engage in planned or strategic visioning processes.

Table 3.6. Correlations Between Vision Content and Articulation Dimensions (n = 89)

	Articulation Dimensions		
Content Dimensions	Vision formulation	Vision implementation	Vision innovative realism
External focus	.06	−.04	−.04
Firm focus	.07	−.03	.11
Executives	.15	−.18	−.03
Entrepreneurs	.00	.04	.10
External + internal focus	−.06	.09	−.01
Traditional employer	−.13	.04	.05
Post modern employer	.06	.05	−.01
Creatively competitive	.08	−.04	.14
Creatively supportive	.02	−.02	−.14
Quality orientation	.02	.08	.25*
Firm as leader	.07	.12	.00
Competitive orientation	.00	.02	.11
Executives	−.18	−.09	−.05
Entrepreneurs	.08	.08	.13
Growth orientation	.06	.01	.17
Profit orientation	.17	.17	.25*
Change orientation	.05	−.19	−.15
Maintenance orientation	−.20**	−.09	−.12
Executives	.01	−.10	−.20
Entrepreneurs	−.23*	−.05	−.08

Notes:
*Spearman's rho $p < .05$; ** Spearman's rho $< .06$

Vision Implementation

There are five measures of vision implementation. Three were nominal communication variables measuring whether or not employees and managers used vision vocabulary in communicating with each other, and whether or not outsiders used vision vocabulary in communications with the firm. In addition, we examined policies and practices, which might follow from vision, including the average cost of employee benefits, the percent of women in the top management team, and an index of the number of environmental practices in the firm.

First we explored the use of vision vocabulary. Both executives and entrepreneurs see manager (82%) and employee (77%) use of vision vocabulary as indicators that the vision has been integrated into the organization or business unit. However, Chi-square analysis shows that more executives than entrepreneurs see manager and employee use of vision vocabulary as an indicator. Both executives and entrepreneurs are less likely to see outsider use of vision vocabulary as an indicator of the vision's implementation, with only about half of the respondents in each sub-sample using this indicator. We next explored the interrelationship among these indicators, using Chi-square analysis for the total sample as shown in Table 3.8. There is a strong relationship among the use of indicators of vision being integrated in the firm, when a leader looks to subordinate manager's buy in through vocabulary, she is more likely to also look to employees and outsiders. Finally, we created and index of implementation based on the use of vision vocabulary by summing the indicators used. Chi-square analysis shows that entrepreneurs use more total indicators than executives with 30% relying on two or more indicators compared to 9% of executives ($p < .01$).

Table 3.7. Use of Indicators in Vision Implementation

Indicator	Total sample Using N	%	% Executives Using	Not Using	% Entrepreneurs Using	Not Using	Chi-Square	(significance)
Managers use vision vocabulary	92	82	91.3	8.7	76.1	23.9	4.3	$p < .05$
Employees use vision vocabulary	83	74	89.1	10.9	62.7	37.3	9.9	$p < .002$
People outside use vision	64	57	53.3	46.7	59.7	40.3	0.45	ns

Table 3.8. Interaction of Implementation Measures

	Employee use	Outsider use
Manager use	52.1*	5.1**
Employee use		6.2**

* Chi Square $p < .001$

There were no differences between groups in benefits cost. The proportion of women on the top management team did significantly differ, with entrepreneurs having an average of nearly 50% compared to executives with 23% ($t = -4.6$, $p < .001$). The environmental practices measure included the use of recycling, water conservation, paperless office, and preference for green products among others. These were summed and eight respondents indicated that all eight practices were in place in their firms. The median number of practices was six and the measure was recoded as high and low environmental sensitivity by a median split. There were no significant differences between subgroups in a Chi-square test.

Next we looked at the interrelationship among the implementation measures, including the scale of vision implementation from Larwood et al. (1995), shown in Table 3.9. Spearman's rho correlations for the relationship between benefits cost, proportion of women in top team, the vision implementation scale (interval data) and the nominal variables (environmental intensity and the integration index) resulted in a significant negative relationship between average benefits and the integration index. This suggests that firms with the greatest benefits package are less likely to use manger, employee and outsider behavior (speaking) as an indicator of vision being embedded in the firm. The vision implementation scale (which includes aspects of communication and understanding) was also significantly and negatively related to the integration index. Environmental sensitivity and proportion of women in top management showed no relationship to either integration index or the vision implementation measure (Larwood et al., 1995). There was however, a marginally significant relationship between environmental sensitivity and using outsiders as a measure of vision integration (Chi-square 3.17, $p < .06$). Other implementation measures were not significantly related to each other.

Table 3.9. Significant Relationships Among Implementation Measures

Measures[a]	Vision Implementation	Benefits Cost	Percent Women	Environmental Intensity (Hi Lo)
Indicators Index	−.28*	−.22**	.15	3.5
	$p < .004$	$p < .05$	ns	ns
Vision Implementation		.06	.01	−.05
		ns	ns	ns
Benefits Cost			−.08	−.07
			ns	ns

Note:
[a] Pearson correlation between scaled/continuous variables, Spearman's rho between scaled/continuous and nominal variables, Chi Square between nominal variables.

Relationship Between Vision Content and Vision Implementation

The relationship between these implementation measures and the vision content showed only two marginally significant relationships. If the leader's vision had a firm or maintenance focus, she was more likely to use multiple indicators for the vision integration (Chi-square $p < .09$). As shown earlier in Table 3.6, there was no relationship between vision content and the vision implementation scale from the Larwood et al. (1995) study. Likewise there were no significant relationships between vision contents and benefits cost. However, there was a negative relationship between the post-modern employer theme and the proportion of women (Spearman's rho $-.21$, $p < .05$), that is those leaders whose firms have more top women avoid visions that suggest values of helping staff remain employable through development. There were positive relationships between visions which are creatively competitive and profit oriented with the proportion of women at the top (Spearman's rho .24, $p < .02$, .22, $p < .04$ respectively). This suggests that women who lead top management teams with more women on the team are likely to have visions of competing on innovation and profitability (and these leaders are more likely to be entrepreneurs). There was only one significant relationship between themes and environmental intensity (median split). Leaders whose vision is externally focused are more likely to have high environmental intensity (Chi-square 7.1, $p < .01$).

CONCLUSIONS

The premise of this paper was to extend current work on vision formulation and implementation and to examine these in a sample of women. Our intention was not to compare men and women, rather to explore possible differences between two groups of successful women leaders, executives and entrepreneurs. A previous study found no differences between entrepreneurs and executives on descriptive dimensions of importance, extent to which vision is shared, time held, or length of time vision extends into the future. In our sample, we find, similarly, that there is no difference in length of time held, but that entrepreneurs are more likely to have a longer time horizon for their vision. Some theory suggests that older individuals will have a longer time perspective, and in our sample, the women entrepreneurs averaged about 5 years older. Further, the entrepreneurs' tenure in the firm was longer than executives and this too has been shown to influence length of time horizon (Larwood et al., 1995). With regard to the Larwood et al. (1995) vision dimensions, they found that entrepreneurs scored lower on formulation but higher on innovative realism and risk, with no differences between executives and entrepreneurs on implementation. In contrast, we found no significant differences between women executives and entrepreneurs.

A major purpose of this paper was to examine aspects of vision not previously studied; the content and dissemination practices. We did not narrow our coding examination of content to "growth" but rather asked an open question intended to capture the entirety of the leaders' vision. We find that entrepreneurs tend to express visions that are more holistic, include internal and external dimensions, and are creatively supportive, whereas executives emphasize traditional job/rewards, training and growth. Unexpectedly, the criterion categories that we developed did not distinguish between entrepreneurs and executives.

Yet, we did find differences between entrepreneurs and executives in other content themes. Entrepreneurs reflected a firm focus, and a competitive and maintenance orientation. Considering that the entrepreneurs had fewer levels of top management and a smaller top management team with more women represented, it is possible the vision reflects a stronger personal concern to maintaining the commitment of employees to the organization. A next step would be to examine the relationship between vision content and organizational strategy to see if the competitive orientation is related to particular strategies (i.e., low cost, or differentiation).

Our total sample analysis of the content themes to the vision dimensions produced few significant results. The only significant relationships were the correlation between quality orientation and innovative realism. The other significant relationship was innovative realism and profit orientation. In examining subgroups, there was one significant difference—vision statements of entrepreneurs with a maintenance orientation in content were marginally less often associated with vision formulation (generally strategic planning variables).

With regard to vision implementation, in contrast to Larwood and Falbe (1994) who found no differences between entrepreneurs and executives, we found that executives were more likely to measure successful implementation by the use vision vocabulary of managers and employees.

There were no differences in practices and policies. However, when we considered the total vision implementation indicator (both the scale and practices), we found that entrepreneurs were more likely to use more indicators and rely on vision vocabulary being used internally. A possible interpretation might be market scope-executives typically ran companies of large size and scale, whereas the entrepreneur's firms were smaller. An examination of the product/market strategy as this relates to implementation is a next step.

This paper extends current empirical work on vision, its content and implementation, by examining similarities and differences between women entrepreneurs and executives. We show that vision content does differ by role (entrepreneur/executive) and how vision implementation is indicated. Our findings thus far suggest that differences in vision of entrepreneurs and executives might be further defined by level of complexity, dependent on size and development of organization, and by values which in new ventures rest more directly on the personal experience, and goals of the entrepreneur.

REFERENCES

Argyris, C., & Schon, D. (1996). *Organizational learning II: Theory, method and practice.* Reading, MA: Addison-Wesley.

Bass, B.M. (1985). *Leadership and performance beyond expectations.* New York: Free Press.

Baum, J. (1995). The relation of traits, competencies, motivation, strategy and structure to venture growth. In W. Bygrave, B. Bird, S. Birley, N. Churchill, M. Hay, R. Keeley, & W. Wetzel (Eds.), *Frontiers of entrepreneurship research* (pp. 547–561).

Baum, R., Locke, E., & Kirkpatrick, S. (1998). A longitudinal study of the relation of vision and vision communication to venture growth in entrepreneurial firms. *Journal of Applied Psychology. 83*(1), 43–54.

Bennis, W. (1989). *On becoming a leader.* New York: Addison-Wesley.

Bennis, W., & Nanus. B. (1985). *Leaders: The strategies for taking charge.* New York: Harper & Row.

Bird, B. (1989). *Entrepreneurial behavior.* Glenview, IL: Scott Foresman.

Bird, B.J., & Brush, C.G. (2002a). What is entrepreneurial vision and how does it work? Under review at *Academy of Management Review.*

Bird, B.J., & Brush, C.G. (2002b). A gendered perspective on organizational creation. *Entrepreneurship Theory and Practice. 26*(3), 41–66.

Brush, C.G. (1992). Research on women business owners: Past trends, a new perspective and future directions. *Entrepreneurship Theory and Practice. 16*(4), 5–30.

Collins, J., & Porras, J. (1994). Organizational vision and visionary organizations. *California Management Review, 34,* 30–52.

Conger, J. (1992). *Learning to lead: The art of transforming managers into leaders.* San Francisco: Jossey Bass.

Conger, J., & Kanungo, R. (1987). Toward a behavioral theory of charismatic leadership in organizational settings. *Academy of Management Review, 12,* 637–647.

Falbe, C., & Larwood, L. (1995). The context of entrepreneurial vision. In W. Bygrave, B. Bird, S. Birley, N. Churchill, M. Hay, R. Keeley, & W. Wetzel (Eds.), *Frontiers of entrepreneurship research* (pp. 187–202). Babson Park, MA: Center for Entrepreneurial Studies, Babson College.

Gartner, W., Bird, B., & Starr, J. (1992). Acting as if: Differentiating entrepreneurial from organizational behavior. *Entrepreneurship Theory and Practice, 16,* 13–30.

Gilligan, C. (1982). *In a different voice.* Cambridge, MA: Harvard University Press.

House, R. (1977). A 1976 theory of charismatic leadership. In G. Hunt, & L. Lawson (Eds.), *Leadership on the cutting edge*. Carbondale: University of Illinois Press.

House, R., & Shamir, B. (1993). Toward the integration of transformational, charismatic and visionary theories of leadership. In M. Chemers, & R. Ayman (Eds.), *Leadership theory and research: Perspectives and directions* (pp. 81–107). San Francisco: Academic Press.

Jenkins, M., & Johnson, G. (1997). Entrepreneurial intentions and outcomes: A comparative causal mapping study. *Journal of Management Studies, 34*(6), 895–952.

Katz, J., & Gartner, W. (1988). Properties of emerging organizations. *Academy of Management Review, 13*, 429–441.

Kouzes, J., & Posner, B. (2002). *Leadership challenge* (3rd ed.). San Francisco: Jossey-Bass.

Larwood, L. Kriger, M., & Falbe. C. (1993). Organizational vision: An investigation of the vision construct-in-use of the AACSB business school deans. *Group and Organization Management, 18*, 214–236.

Larwood, L., & Falbe, C. (1994, August). *Strategic vision among entrepreneurs: Similarities and differences with other top executives*. Paper presented at the Academy of Management Meetings.

Larwood, L., Falbe, C., Kriger, M., & Miesing, P. (1995). Structure and meaning of organizational vision. *Academy of Management Journal, 38*, 740–769.

Marks, D. (1990). On the relationship between imagery, body and mind. In P. Hampton, D. Marks, & J. Richardson (Eds.), *Imagery: Current developments*. New York: Routledge.

Nutt, P., & Backoff, (1997). Crafting vision. *Journal of Management Inquiry, 6*(4), 308–328.

Rockey, H. (1986). Envisioning new business: How entrepreneurs perceive the benefits of visualization. In R. Ronstadt, J. Hornaday, R. Peterson, & K. Vesper (Eds.), *Frontiers of entrepreneurship research* (pp. 344–360). Wellesley, MA: Babson College.

Senge, P. (1990, Fall). The leader's new work. *Sloan Management Review*.

Tichy, N., & Devanna, M. (1986). *The transformational leader*. New York: Wiley.

Weick, K. (1979). *The social psychology of organizing*. Reading, MA: Addison-Wesley.

CHAPTER 4

FEMALE ENTREPRENEURSHIP IN GERMANY

Context, Development and its Reflection in German Media

Leona Achtenhagen and Friederike Welter

ABSTRACT

In Germany, fostering female entrepreneurship is viewed as one of the solutions to fulfill the aim of increasing the overall level of entrepreneurship. As in many other countries, it is believed that a higher level of entrepreneurship would reduce the level of unemployment. In this context, the discourse on female entrepreneurship plays an important role in structuring our perception of entrepreneurial reality and in transmitting female entrepreneurship as something desired by society. Newspapers are an important means to transmit cultural values and ideas. Therefore, we conduct a discourse analysis of newspaper texts to investigate how female entrepreneurship is reflected in the German media. We analyze the discourse around the concept of "female entrepreneur" (*Unternehmerin*) as presented in two prominent German newspapers, the *Welt*, a conservative paper and the *Süddeutsche Zeitung*, a more leftist paper, between 1995 and 2001. We link the discourse to the overall entrepreneurship environment and its developments in the same time frame. The discourse is strongly embedded not only as an economic topic, but also as a cultural topic. An increasing prominence of female entrepreneurs in the articles reflects the growing public interest in the topic of female entrepreneurship. This also is apparent in the strong focus on positive role models of successful female entrepreneurs, although here the language used often reinforces more traditional roles. Our findings might have implications for policy makers as they point to gaps between discourse and policy objectives.

INTRODUCTION

In recent years, many politicians and public institutions have proclaimed the fostering of female entrepreneurship as one of the solutions to increase the overall level of entrepreneurship in Germany, which has been considered too low for many years. Currently, official data show that only 6% of all employed women, but nearly 13% of men, are classified as entrepreneurs. A similar gender gap also is apparent when looking at the rate of potential entrepreneurs: 15.9% of all men, compared to only 7.4% of women, are generally interested in starting their own business, while 3.6% of all women and 8% of all men mentioned detailed entrepreneurial ideas, and the rate for female entrepreneurs amounts to only 1.3% of the German population, compared to 2.4% for men (Welter, 2001).

Over the last years, the German government and the federal states have initiated a number of programs to promote entrepreneurship. In the same vein, female entrepreneurs have been discovered as an untapped resource. Female entrepreneurship would not only reduce unemployment, but also create a work environment in which job and family could be combined—considered an important step in the goal to achieve equal opportunities in Germany. Consequently, the focus on fostering female entrepreneurship has gained importance in an attempt to enhance the overall level of entrepreneurship.

Around 80% of the German population ascribes a high or very high level of influence to the media on politics and political decision-making (Gleich, 1998). Even though empirical studies do not always verify this cause-and-effect relationship, the public perception of this influence is of importance in itself. There is little doubt about the role of media in setting the agenda of (political) topics discussed in the public sphere (Gleich, 1998) as well as in interpersonal communication networks (Schmitt-Beck, 1994). Among the different media, newspapers are an important way to transmit cultural values and ideas, as well as sociopolitical ideologies (Soothly & Grover, 1997). Stevenson (1995) argues that newspaper analysis would be crucial to understand cultural issues.

Thus, newspapers play an important role in influencing female entrepreneurship in Germany, by creating a discourse that transmits the ideas constituting the valuation of such a career choice. Newspapers are an especially powerful producer and reproducer, as well as circulator, of the public discourse on (female) entrepreneurship, as they persuade "our consent to ways of talking about reality that are often regarded as normal and acceptable beyond the confines of media" (Macdonald, 1995, p. 3). The aim of this chapter is to analyze the discourse on female entrepreneurship as created by the influential medium newspaper, linked to its context. We are interested in how female entrepreneurship and the discourse around it develop over time, as well as how this is related to overall economic activities and infrastructural settings.

METHODOLOGY AND RESEARCH STRATEGY

Our analysis is based on two prominent German newspapers, the *Welt* and the *Süddeutsche Zeitung* (SZ). The *Welt* reaches 860,000 readers per day, and is thus one of the large national newspapers. In its political orientation the *Welt* is classified as very conservative while the *SZ*, which is read daily by 1,150,000 readers, is considered a progressive and more leftist newspaper (cf. Media-Analyse, 2002).

Both newspapers' online archives were searched for articles covering the female entrepreneur ("Unternehmerin"), female business founder ("Gründerin"), woman AND business-owner ("Frau" UND "selbständig"/"selbstständig"[1]), as well as female AND business-owner ("weiblich" UND "selbständig"/"selbstständig") between 01/01/1995 and 12/31/2001. This includes the period before, during, and after the Internet hype, covering a period of major changes in the entrepreneurship policy context. Table 4.1 presents the number of articles for the different concepts extracted from both newspapers for the analyzed time frame. The significant increase in the number of articles referring to female entrepreneurship and related key terms already hints at the growing importance publicly attributed to this topic.

Because of the large number of articles found (2,676), we concentrated the analysis in this chapter on one key concept, the "female entrepreneur." The analyzed numbers of articles per year are depicted in Table 4.2. We chose the concept of female entrepreneur, as it was considered most relevant for the focus of this chapter.

All 539 articles identified for this topic were downloaded, no matter in which section they appeared. No preselection along topics was conducted, as we wished to gain a picture of all instances in which female entrepreneurs were considered noteworthy in these newspapers. Relevant text passages

Table 4.1. Articles Mentioning Female Entrepreneurship and Related Key Terms

	1995	1996	1997	1998	1999	2000	2001	Sum
				Süddeutsche Zeitung				
Female entrepreneur	41	39	26	44	58	50	78	336
Female business founder	33	43	40	57	54	54	70	351
Woman AND business-owner	116	134	145	153	139	179	213	1079
Female AND business-owner	4	4	5	6	4	2	6	31
Sum	195	222	219	263	256	287	367	1797
				Welt				
Female entrepreneur	2	7	5	9	33	48	99	203
Female business founder	1	3	1	4	20	55	80	164
Woman AND business-owner	3	16	19	38	69	110	172	427
Female AND business-owner	0	1	1	7	9	25	42	85
Sum	6	27	26	58	131	238	393	879

Note: Compiled by authors.

Table 4.2. Number of Analyzed Articles in this Chapter

Female entrepreneur	1995	1996	1997	1998	1999	2000	2001	Sum
Welt	2	7	5	9	33	48	99	203
Süddeutsche Zeitung	41	39	26	44	58	50	78	336
Sum	43	46	31	53	91	98	177	539

Note: Compiled by authors.

were converted into an Excel-file, allowing us to identify the topics discussed around female entrepreneurship as well as the characteristics attributed to it. Also, this file allowed us to conduct bivariate statistical operations. All entries into the Excel-file were double-checked by both authors for content and consistency of categorizing the text, referring to the original newspaper articles, to increase the robustness of this study.

In order to ground the discourse analysis in its context, we additionally describe and analyze the environment for (female) entrepreneurship in Germany. Here, we present both the development of business start-ups and entrepreneurship as well as the relevant trends in entrepreneurship-related policies and support for women entrepreneurs in the years 1991–2001. The analysis of new venture creation and entrepreneurship in the analyzed period mainly relies on one official statistic, i.e., the micro census. The "business register" (Gewerbemeldungen) that could be used as a proxy for business start-ups and business closures does not allow for a gender-specific analysis. The micro census is a yearly 1% representative sample of the German population, which collects longitudinal data on entrepreneurs, thus allowing us to compare the development of female entrepreneurship across regions. The category "self-employment" (Selbst[st]ändige), which includes the gender of the entrepreneurs, refers to persons who (co-)own and manage an enterprise or who work as self-employed. It also includes home-based entrepreneurs. In this context, one needs to take into account that the micro census does not fully capture the dynamism of entrepreneurship because it does not register inflows and outflows.

This chapter is structured as follows. First, we introduce the topic of discourse analysis and relate it to female entrepreneurship. To depict the context of the discourse, we then present the development of female entrepreneurship in Germany in statistical terms, as well as characterize the supporting policies and infrastructure for female entrepreneurship. The presentation, analysis, and discussion of the discourse on female entrepreneurship as created by newspaper texts follow, leading lastly to conclusions.

A DISCOURSE ANALYSIS OF FEMALE ENTREPRENEURSHIP

According to Berger and Luckmann (1969) knowledge is socially constructed, meaning that knowledge is not developed based on observations alone. Rather, understanding is created in social context, implying that each person constructs knowledge and acts based on her/his perceptions and experiences. In this way, social constructivism implicitly draws attention to the cognitive process connected with entrepreneurial activities featured prominently in theories of opportunity recognition (c.g., Beattie, 1999; Kirzner, 1979).

The choice of social constructivism in analyzing female entrepreneurship refers to the way human beings relate to reality and how they generate knowledge about reality. Social constructivism assumes that reality is produced in social processes. In consequence, meanings are produced by the interaction of people. Based on these interactions, we perceive reality through meaning and, consequently, construct different versions of reality, which steer our knowledge claims. Thus, what we perceive as truth and facts is also socially negotiated, implying that our understanding of reality is historically and culturally specific. Our understanding then depends on the "particular social and economic arrangements prevailing in that culture at that time" (Burr, 1995, p. 4). Language offers a system of categories to structure and make sense of our experience. Thus, language serves as an important mediator for constructing reality.

The social construction of the discourse on female entrepreneurship creates and recreates the perceived entrepreneurial reality. Entrepreneurship takes place in an "enacted" environment, based on these perceptions (cf. Weick, 1995, 1998). Here lies the potential contribution of discourse analysis: it permits the exploration of the processes of socially constructing entrepreneurship, more specifically female entrepreneurship, and its economic/societal implications (cf. Ainsworth, 2001).

What is discourse analysis? Building on Foucault (1972), different scholars in the field of management studies have conceptualized discourse as power/knowledge relations, which are linguistically communicated, historically located, and embedded in social practice (Heracleous & Barrett, 2001, p. 757). Discourses are seen as deeply politically implicated or "mediated through socially constructed hegemonic practices" (Boje, 1991, p. 107). Du Gay (1996, p. 43) defines discourse as "a group of statements which provide a language for talking about a topic and a way of producing a particular kind of knowledge about a topic. Here, the term refers both to the production of knowledge through language and representation and the way that knowledge is institutionalized, shaping social practices and setting new practices into play." This has important implications for female entrepreneurship: The discourse on female entrepreneurship then influences not only the *perception* of female entrepreneurship in society, but also the *nature and extent* of the entrepreneurial activities by women.

A multitude of different approaches to discourse analysis can be found. Yet, they share a number of common characteristics, such as the use of text or talk as data, attention to the structuring effects of language, a focus on the context of discourse, a focus on discourse as a social practice, attention to how social members interpret, categorize, and construct their social experience and the use of interpretive and reflexive analysis styles (Ainsworth, 2001, p. 3). The impact of discourses on our perception of reality can be very subtle. Discourses work in structuring our understanding of reality, also implicitly, as they are often taken for granted (Ahl, 2002, p. 65). The textual construction of entrepreneurship and female entrepreneurship requires this theory and method that direct our attention to the production of meaning and a critical examination of it. As female entrepreneurship is seen as a socially constructed, discursive phenomenon, our interest lies in interpreting how the concept is constructed and reconstructed. The newspaper articles recognize the existence of a cultural phenomenon called female entrepreneurship by addressing it.

Discourse analysis approaches have often been criticized for their inadequate attention to context and temporality (Cicourel, 1981; Fairclough, 1992). "Temporality refers to the temporal location of a communicative action in relation to other communicative actions and situational features of a social context that influence how agents in that context interpret this action" (Heracleous & Barrett, 2001, pp. 760–761). In order to study and analyze a discourse, we thus need to pay attention to the context into which the relevant text is set (Steinulfsson Skjerdal, 2001). On the one hand, we understand this statement as referring to the immediate context in the studied newspapers, i.e., the category where the text referring to female entrepreneurship is published. We analyze this immediate context by referring to Johannisson et al. (2002). These authors conceptually distinguish between systemic (economic) and substantive (social) embeddedness, drawing attention to the fact that "any business activity reflects a complex socioeconomic phenomenon" (Johannisson et al., 2002, p. 298). The embeddedness of entrepreneurship then refers to the overall institutional regulations and the general environment that influence opportunity fields for entrepreneurship, while values and norms determine the collective and individual perception of entrepreneurial opportunities. This, on the other hand, leads us to analyze the discourse in relation to its broader economic and societal context beyond the newspaper texts.

Empirical studies such as the Global Entrepreneurship Monitor demonstrate that the value placed on entrepreneurship varies across countries: "Among the many factors that contribute to entrepreneurship, perhaps the most critical is a set of social and cultural values along with the appropriate social, economic and political institutions that legitimize and encourage the pursuit of entrepreneurial opportunity" (Reynolds et al., 1999, p. 43). In this respect, discourses on female entrepreneurship in the media could make a difference, as they produce (often gender-specific) categories for structuring the perception and valuation of entrepreneurship. This in turn might influence the nature and extent of female entrepreneurship in two ways. If categories change the values a society attributes to female entrepreneurship positively, women's willingness to create ventures might increase or vice versa. Similarly, where categories are constructed as male-female dichotomies with mutually exclusive meanings of the polar ends (Pietiläinen, 2001) and where female entrepreneurship implicitly is attributed with a lower legitimacy compared to male entrepreneurship, old role models might remain unchallenged and female entrepreneurship be less attractive.

All this implies that in order to analyze the media discourse on female entrepreneurship we also need to look at how gender equality is reflected in German media concepts of female entrepreneurship. What does gender equality refer to? Ahl (2002, p. 16) distinguishes between two main lines of how gender is generally conceived. The first assumes that women and men are essentially the same and therefore need to be treated in the same way. However, she argues that based on existing power relations this would imply applying male standards to women as well, with discriminatory results. The second line assumes that women and men are different from each other, demanding that women's qualities need to be valued higher than they currently are. According to Ahl (2002, p. 16) this approach is criticized for treating women and their qualities uniformly, as well as for valuing some women's experiences higher than others. Thus, Ahl concludes (and criticizes) that the assumptions behind the categories of "women" and "men" are taken for granted.

Discourse analysis in analyzing female entrepreneurship has already been fruitfully employed by a few researchers. Most notably, Ahl (2002) deconstructs the discourse of female entrepreneurship in 81 academic research articles published in high-quality entrepreneurship journals. She finds entrepreneurship to be male gendered, but thought of as neutral. Male and female entrepreneurs are assumed to be essentially different. The articles then, for example, stress small differences in entrepreneurial behavior, present female entrepreneurs as exceptions from "normal" women, or construct an alternative, feminine entrepreneurship model (Ahl, 2002). In a discourse analysis of a Finnish entrepreneurship journal, Pietiläinen (2001) arrives at similar conclusions. She questions the way we tend to decipher gender information with its culturally-bound implications. If equal opportunities really existed, why would it still seem natural to ask female entrepreneurs about combining work and family responsibilities when discussing their entrepreneurial behavior, which would not naturally occur in interviewing male entrepreneurs.

In this study, we are interested in the discourse on female entrepreneurship in German newspapers, because we assume newspapers to have an impact on how people conceive female entrepreneurship. Both studies presented above refer to existing entrepreneurial activities, while we are interested in the valuation attributed to these activities as transmitted to potential entrepreneurs (i.e., readers) by popular newspapers.

THE CONTEXT FOR FEMALE ENTREPRENEURSHIP IN GERMANY

A Statistical Picture of Female Entrepreneurship in Germany from 1991–2001

In Germany, business start-ups, which reached their highest level with a total number of 531,000 in 1991, have been decreasing more or less continuously since 1998, dropping to 455,000 in 2001. This goes hand in hand with increasing rates of market exits until 1999. Only in 2000 and 2001 the trend was reversed, although business closures in 2001 are still considerably higher compared to the early 1990s. In 2001, the net entry rate for all of Germany has dropped to 69,000, which is less than the amount of business start-ups in the West Germany of the late 1980s. With regard to female entrepreneurs, data for all of Germany appears to confirm a "push" hypothesis toward entrepreneurship, although "pull" motives also played an important role. A large share of women who changed or obtained employment in the year 2000 (47%, men 39%), were previously unemployed, another 32% (men 21%) held a non-wage position (i.e., studying, housewife) before setting up their venture (Lauxen-Ulbrich & Leicht, 2002, p. 30). The former goes hand in hand with the latest GEM results for Germany, which indicate a higher share of necessity-based female entrepreneurship, compared to men (women 28%, men 17.4% (cf. Sternberg & Bergmann, 2003, p. 15). Sector-wise, women entrepreneurs (similar to female wage employees) cluster in trade and services, with increasing shares in both sectors since the mid-1990s.

With respect to the overall development of female entrepreneurship, we can observe differences between West and East Germany. Despite an overall increase during the 1990s, in 2001 women still accounted for less than half of the West German work force (Table 4.3). From 1991–2001 the total West German female labor force grew by 10.5%, while female entrepreneurship increased by nearly 24% (+162,000 enterprises), which is considerably higher compared to the 14%-increase in all entrepreneurship. In West Germany, women entrepreneurs now account for 6.4% of the female labor force and 27.5% of all entrepreneurs. Mainly, women are employed as clerks where they represented more than half of all work force in 2001, with this share having grown over the past decade. More and more women also work as civil servants, reflecting the overall trend toward higher education. On the other hand, women still constitute the majority of all family help in small enterprises. Although the share of female family help has been decreasing continuously to less than 2% of the female labor force in 2000, the year 2001 surprisingly saw a considerable increase (+88,000) in this labor category, which might partly be a result of both worsening labor market and overall macroeconomic conditions.

In East Germany total female entrepreneurship increased by a considerable 71.4% (+70,000 enterprises, Table 4.3). However, this could not compensate for the overall loss in female employment, which decreased by nearly 18% (–645,000) in the period 1991–2001. This negative labor market development during the past decade appears to indicate a push toward entrepreneurship, especially as women were the first to be fired and the last to find new employment after transition started. On the other hand, nearly 30% of all East German entrepreneurs are women. Interestingly, this share has been higher in East Germany compared to West Germany from 1991 onward. This might partly be explained by the value the former GDR, like all socialist states, put on qualified female employment, which might have increased women's willingness to become entrepreneurs,

Table 4.3. Development of Female Employment and Female Entrepreneurship in West and East Germany, 1991–2001

	1991	1992	1993	1994	1995	1996	1997	1998	1999	2000	2001
West Germany											
Female employment (in 1,000)											
Total labor force	29,684	30,094	29,782	29,124	29,243	29,277	29,199	29,317	29,729	30,009	30,307
Total female labor force	11,965	12,249	12,161	12,127	12,102	12,275	12,299	12,416	12,738	12,950	13,226
Total entrepreneurs	2,689	2,699	2,746	2,823	2,850	2,921	3,014	3,051	3,049	3,089	3,070
Total women entrepreneurs	682	677	688	725	739	773	806	827	830	845	844
Vertical distribution of female labor force (in %)											
Entrepreneurs	5.7	5.5	5.7	6.0	6.1	6.3	6.6	6.7	6.5	6.5	6.4
Family help	3.6	3.5	3.3	3.2	3.1	2.4	2.2	2.3	1.8	1.8	2.4
Civil servants	4.6	4.7	4.9	5.1	5.1	5.2	5.3	5.3	5.2	5.0	4.9
Clerks	58.8	59.6	61.2	61.5	61.6	62.2	62.1	62.2	62.8	62.6	63.5
Workers	27.2	26.7	24.9	24.2	24.1	23.9	23.8	23.6	23.8	24.0	22.8
Share of women in different labor positions (in %)											
Labor force	40.3	40.7	40.8	41.3	41.4	41.9	42.1	42.4	42.8	43.2	43.6
Entrepreneurs	25.4	25.1	25.1	25.7	25.9	26.5	26.7	27.1	27.2	27.4	27.5
Family help	83.9	83.2	84.1	82.1	82.0	79.8	77.2	77.3	76.0	75.7	78.2
Civil servants	22.9	24.0	25.1	26.8	27.6	28.5	29.7	30.6	31.2	32.1	33.1
Clerks	54.1	54.3	55.0	54.9	54.9	55.9	54.9	54.9	55.2	55.7	54.6
Workers	29.5	29.6	28.3	28.8	28.8	29.1	30.1	30.2	31.0	31.1	31.8

	1991	1992	1993	1994	1995	1996	1997	1998	1999	2000	2001
					East Germany						
				Female employment (in 1,000)							
Total labor force	7,761	6,847	6,599	6,678	6,804	6,705	6,605	6,543	6,673	6,595	6,509
Total female labor force	3,605	3,068	2,923	2,961	3,006	3,003	2,956	2,935	3,006	2,974	2,960
Total entrepreneurs	348	393	428	464	486	488	514	543	546	554	562
Total women entrepreneurs	98	113	129	136	141	143	155	159	161	167	168
				Vertical distribution of female labor force (%)							
Entrepreneurs	2.7	3.7	4.4	4.6	4.7	4.8	5.2	5.4	5.4	5.6	5.7
Family help	0.1	0.3	0.3	0.3	0.5	0.3	0.3	0.4	0.4	0.4	0.7
Civil servants	0.2	0.4	0.5	0.9	1.2	1.8	2.2	2.4	2.7	2.9	2.8
Clerks	66.7	69.7	70.6	70.2	68.8	67.6	66.4	67.7	67.0	66.7	66.8
Workers	30.2	25.9	24.2	23.9	24.8	25.5	25.8	24.0	24.6	24.4	24.0
				Share of women in different labor positions (%)							
Labor force	46.5	44.8	44.3	44.4	44.2	44.8	44.8	44.9	45.0	45.1	45.5
Entrepreneurs	28.2	28.8	30.1	29.3	29.0	29.3	30.2	29.3	29.5	30.1	29.9
Family help	83.3	81.8	80.0	76.9	75.0	71.4	66.7	75.0	73.3	70.6	66.7
Civil servants	6.7	11.1	12.2	16.8	19.7	24.2	26.7	27.5	29.4	30.6	28.9
Clerks	63.4	62.7	63.7	63.5	64.0	65.6	63.9	64.0	63.6	64.5	63.3
Workers	30.9	27.2	25.3	25.6	25.9	26.5	27.6	26.9	27.7	27.2	28.4

Source: own calculations based on micro census.

although growing unemployment also contributed. As in West Germany, most women work as clerks. Additionally, a larger share, compared to the West, are employed as civil servants, reflecting the higher overall level of education in East Germany.

Although the number of East German female entrepreneurs keeps growing, the rapid growth rate that could be observed during the first years of reunification has slowed down. This indicates that the development of female (as well as overall) entrepreneurship in East Germany follows the general pattern which several research studies have outlined for post-Socialist countries (e.g., Piasecki & Rogut, 1993; Tschepurenko, 1998), i.e., after an initial upsurge entrepreneurship development slows down. This "explosion of entrepreneurship" (Piasecki & Rogut, 1993) happened for East German female entrepreneurship from 1991–1995 while growth rates have been decelerating since. Despite the enormous initial growth, the overall level of female entrepreneurship is still lower in East Germany, as compared to West Germany. The share of East German female entrepreneurs in the female labor force amounted to 5.7% in 2001. In comparison to 1991 this indicates considerable progress made since the beginning of the transformation process and reunification. However, the decelerating growth rates since 1996 suggests an ongoing gap in the extent of female entrepreneurship between East and West Germany.

The Institutional Framework for Female Entrepreneurs in Germany: Gendered Institutions?

The institutional and legal contexts play an important role for female entrepreneurship, influencing both its nature and extent as well as its potential economic contribution. Here, the question arises if (and if yes, in which ways) access to entrepreneurship is restricted in Germany. While gender equality is codified in the German Constitution, its implementation throughout the economy and society might still lead to open and subtle discrimination against women. Open discrimination could be observed until the early 1970s concerning legal regulations where women needed their husband's signature on a labor contract to become valid, or regulations with respect to bank accounts where husbands were required to countersign a woman's application. While open discrimination remains a topic, especially concerning wage gaps, hidden constraints, expressing themselves through the institutional environment, might play an even more important role in restricting women entrepreneurship.

Childcare facilities play a role in supporting or constraining female entrepreneurship in practice. While Germany is still characterized by a rather traditional labor distribution, where men contribute incomes and women are mainly responsible for child care, institutional contexts have been much more favorable in Northern European countries, reflecting an egalitarian-individualistic principle in labor market and family policies (Pfau-Effinger, 1995, p. 49f.). In Sweden full-time childcare is the rule, with 60% of Swedish kindergarten children attending an all-day institution. In Germany, only 9% of children of kindergarten age attend all day institutions, while in Great Britain child care is mainly organized on a private basis (Gustafsson & Wetzel, 1997, p. 120).

In addition, social and tax policies could influence women entrepreneurs with respect to the level of social security connected to entrepreneurship. This is an important factor for potential women entrepreneurs who might also consider entrepreneurship for family reasons or in order to improve household income. A consideration of social security regulations in Germany serves to illustrate this issue, indicating that social security problems go hand in hand with entrepreneurship. For example, until 1989 entrepreneurs who employed up to two employees could join the statutory social security health insurance scheme, but since then access has been limited to previous employees now working as self-employed, entrepreneurs, and professional groups, such as artists or journalists (Frick et al., 1998). Moreover, Holst (2001) refers to the gender-restrictive role of the German tax system that mainly favors male participation in the formal labor market and informal, unpaid work of women through discriminating against married women. Gustafsson (1995) demonstrated that if West Germany introduced the Swedish tax system, women's employment would increase by 10%, while the opposite situation in Sweden would decrease women's employment by 20%.

Female entrepreneurship is also influenced to a large extent by the value society attaches to women's employment. An increased labor market participation of women occurred in Western economies only since the 1970s, as Birley (1989) describes: "Until very recently, the major role of women was seen in most Western economies by both men and women to be that of wife and mother. Indeed, even should they take employment, this was almost always in addition to their role as homemaker." Here, evidence for East Germany demonstrates that the decreasing labor market participation of East German women following reunification can only partly be attributed to higher unemployment rates for women, but it also reflects an overall conservative trend in Germany, ascribing a homebound role for women (e.g., Meyer & Schulze, 1995; Rocksloh-Papendieck, 1995) as well as the decrease in childcare facilities.

To sum up, while there has been progress with respect to the legal and institutional environment for female entrepreneurship in Germany, several policy-related factors still (might) restrict women's willingness to become entrepreneurs. (West-) German society still defines women mainly through roles connected to family and household responsibilities. Thus, societal values implicitly understand female entrepreneurship as less desirable, which in turn affects the self-perceptions and individual attitudes of potential female entrepreneurs. In this context, research confirmed that professional choices of women take into account what society deems desirable and "correct" for their sex (Holst, 2001). Consequently, this might (partly) explain lower rates of female entrepreneurs.

A reluctant attitude of women toward entrepreneurship is reinforced through the ambivalent image of entrepreneurs ("*Unternehmer*") and entrepreneurship. In most Western cultures entrepreneurship still is attributed with male characteristics. Research, studying entrepreneurial metaphors for Scandinavian countries where the environment favors female entrepreneurs, demonstrated for the late 1990s, that women assign controversial and negative metaphors to entrepreneurship, while men frequently emphasized idealizing aspects: "It appeared that many females perceived entrepreneurship as perhaps requiring too full a commitment to business, thereby reducing the time and effort required to pursue other important avenues. (...) The traditional view holding that every man has to fend for himself and make due sacrifices in order to succeed surfaced again and again" (Hyrsky, 1999, p. 29). This is even more apparent in the German society, which still puts a higher value on male role stereotypes than on female ones (Holst, 2002). In this context, most women entrepreneurs, especially those having set up a venture in the professions (e.g., as doctors or lawyers), do not see themselves as "Unternehmerin" which they attribute to those women who lead larger industry firms.

Support Policies for Female Entrepreneurs

National policies for female entrepreneurs differ across Europe, reflecting both country traditions and their societies' attitudes toward working women. While support for female entrepreneurs has a long tradition in Northern European countries, the German government only recently started paying attention to the topic of female entrepreneurship as an important means to raise the overall level of entrepreneurship. Currently support for female entrepreneurs is focused on programs taking care of support needs in terms of financial or human capital, but it is neglecting the impact of the overall legal and institutional framework. Most German programs for start-ups concentrate on extending and stabilizing the financial base of the new venture regardless of the entrepreneur's gender. Although consultancy plays a less important role, in recent years there has been a shift toward integrated packages, combining financing, consultancy, and training. Moreover, several new instruments on both the federal and state level stress venture creation by pupils, students, or graduates. Papenheim and Görisch (2001) identified 13 state programs, which exclusively focus on students, although there is only one gender-specific measure, i.e., an online-course for female business founders out of universities (Welter et al., 2003).

Selected support measures, which are exclusively directed at female entrepreneurs, are mainly found on the state level. These include, for example, a program in North Rhine Westphalia, which encourages mentoring for young female ventures (TWIN, i.e., Two Women win), or small credit lines. However, all these programs only support a small number of female entrepreneurs, e.g., in Mecklenburg-Vorpommern 200 female entrepreneurs received loans during the period 1996–2000. State governments also frequently introduce specific regulations into mass loan programs, especially where these programs are jointly financed by federal and state governments. One such example refers to a loan program in North-Rhine Westphalia where the state government allows loan applications of female nascent entrepreneurs without previous industry knowledge. Another such regulation is to be found in Mecklenburg-Vorpommern, where the state investment bank hands out loans directly to female entrepreneurs, provided they previously were rejected by banks (Kehlbeck & Schneider, 1999, p. 29). These regulations aim at leveling out the possibly negative effects of the German "housebank system," where commercial banks take on a gatekeeper function, i.e., all applications for financial support programs are channeled through them.

In this context, the Deutsche Ausgleichsbank (DtA), one of the two public banks involved in financing new ventures, only recently introduced two micro finance programs. These refer to the "Startgeld" program which offers loans amounting up to 50,000 Euro (since 1999), and the new "Mikrokredit" which offers 25,000 Euro loans for starting and new entrepreneurs for up to three years (for an overview on local and/or regional micro-credit programs in Germany; see Evers, 2002; Evers & Habschick, 2001). Both programs allow for applications of full-time *and* (at least initially) part-time start-ups, thus recognizing the diverse paths into entrepreneurship. So far, they appear to be successful in reaching those entrepreneurs (e.g., women, unemployed persons) who perceive themselves (and often are) "neglected" by banks. Between 1999 and 2001, the DtA handed out Startgeld loans to nearly 6,500 women entrepreneurs, and there already have been 600 successful applications (40% women) within the "Mikrokredit" program since its start in October 2002. Both of these programs reflect a shift in support policies. They acknowledge the fact that specific groups of entrepreneurs need smaller amounts of loans and, as in the case of many women entrepreneurs, frequently start as part-time ventures (Piorkowsky, 2001).

Support for female entrepreneurship on the *federal level* shows a thematic focus, taking into account the specific tasks of federal ministries. The Federal Ministry for Women, Senior Citizens, Family and Youth (BMFSFJ) sees its role in fostering societal change, which also implies support for networking initiatives between gender-specific support agencies and "mainstream" business organizations as well as lobbying for gender-specific statistics and financing relevant research studies (e.g., IfM, 2001; Piorkowsky, 2001, 2002). The Federal Ministry for Education and Research (BMBF) support measures that aim to orient women toward "new" employment fields, as well as gender specific research (e.g., Fehrenbach & Leicht, 2002; Lauxen-Ulbrich & Leicht, 2002; Welter et al., 2003). The Federal Ministry of Economics (BMWi) is generally responsible for SME support. Since the elections in September 1998, which ended the 13-year-government of the Christian Democratic Union (CDU) and Chancellor Kohl, the federal government has increased its emphasis on fostering female entrepreneurship. For example, the Federal Action Program on "Innovation and employment in the knowledge society of the 21st century" pursues the goal of increasing the share of female entrepreneurs in entrepreneurship to 40%. Overall, there is an ongoing subtle shift in federal support policies toward an institutionally oriented approach. This is aimed at integrating gender-specific support topics into general entrepreneurship programs and policies, instead of setting up specific measures. This goes hand in hand with a focus on public-private partnerships.

Business Associations, Networking and Public-Private Support Initiatives

In this context, the 1990s saw a considerable increase in gender-specific public-private and wholly private networks for women entrepreneurs (for details, cf. Welter et al., 2003). Women entrepreneurs appear to be more reluctant to address chambers of commerce and industry and crafts, which traditionally play a major role in the German (support) system. The overall dominance of male entrepreneurs in business associations and chambers is reflected in the low shares of women entrepreneurs in boards and committees, although recently more women entrepreneurs showed interest in participating in these business organizations. For example, only one out of 82 chambers of commerce and industry is presided over by a woman, another four have female CEOs, while there are one female president, one female vice-president and six female CEOs across the 55 chambers of craft (Welter et al., 2003).

Women-related organizations fall into different categories: those organizations or networks aiming at working women in general (e.g., the Business and Professional Women Organization, which originally was founded in the 1920s in the United States, and in the 1930s in Germany) and specific associations/networks for female entrepreneurs or female business founders. The latter category includes, for example, the oldest and with 1,700 members also the largest female entrepreneur association in Germany, the "Verband Deutscher Unternehmerinnen" (VdU), which was set up in 1954. It still remains the only women entrepreneur association on federal and regional level, while most of the other organizations either have a mainly sectoral focus (such as "Schöne Aussichten" with 700 members, which is concentrated on female entrepreneurs in professions, or "webgrrls" which focuses on women entrepreneurs in new media) or an explicit regional and local orientation respectively. This overall increase and the focus on regions or sectors reflect a general shift in the organizations' philosophies from general lobbying toward providing direct membership benefits such as acquiring new clients (Frerichs & Wiemer, 2002).

Other public-private or private initiatives to foster female entrepreneurship refer to *awards for female entrepreneurs and female business founders*, which gained importance during the past years. While Sperling and May (2001) could identify only four regional awards, an Internet search in 2002 found eight regional or local and two federal/international initiatives (Table 4.4). Awards are handed out for innovative business ideas, new products or services, or innovative ways of combining work and family. Some of the awards, such as the IDEE-Award, also take into account employment creation through new enterprises. The latter often are considerable, as the example of the Vision-Female Entrepreneur Award demonstrates. The six best female entrepreneurs awarded since its creation had created a total of 85 new employment possibilities (52 of them for women), which amounts to an average 14 new jobs per firm, compared to the overall German average of 4.5 new jobs per new venture within the first five years.

In principle, most awards, especially those on regional and local level, offer only nominal acknowledgments, while mainly federal and international awards are accompanied by considerable prize money. However, especially where large, well-known companies or mass media donate these awards, it is the public recognition of the award-wining entrepreneurs that appears important. Thus, the German environment for female entrepreneurship is characterized by a trend toward increasing the visibility of women entrepreneurs. We now turn to analyzing how this context for female entrepreneurs and its development are reflected in the newspaper discourse.

Table 4.4. Awards for Female Business Founders and Entrepreneurs

Award and year	Initiated by	Requirements	Amount
Regional			
Anna-Westphalen Award (1999, 2000, 2001)	Working party "Female entrepreneurs" in Flensburg	Region Flensburg Female entrepreneur, female business founder	1,500–2,000 DM, golden pin, certificate
Beate-Uhse-Award for Female entrepreneurs (2002)	Company Beate Uhse	Schleswig-Holstein Female business founders and young female-led businesses	10,000 €
Bizzy (2000, 2002)	Fair for female entrepreneurs in Hamburg	Implicitly restricted to Hamburg and Northern Germany	2,002 €
		Female business founder, support for female workers in enterprises, products/services relevant for women	
Existenz-Award for female business founders (since 1997 yearly)	Company for office services in Berlin, Checkpoint Charlie'	Berlin Female entrepreneurs, female business founders	Fully paid office, including postal and fax services for 6 months
Future Award (since 1998 yearly)	Magazine *Super-Illu*	East Germany[a]	5,000 €
Award for female business founders in Saxonia (since 2001 yearly)	State Ministry for Equality of Women and Men	Saxonia Female entrepreneurs Innovative idea for business start	No data
Award for female entrepreneurs in Emscher-Lippe 2001	Go-Emscher-Lippe Region, City Bottrop, City Gelsenkirchen	Region Emscher-Lippe Female entrepreneur	5,000 €
VISION-Female entrepreneur Award (2000, 2002)	Network for female business founders, Aachen	Region Aachen Female entrepreneur, female successor, female professional	1,000, 2,500, and 5,000 DM
Federal level			
IDEE-Award (since 1997 yearly)	Company Albert Darboven	Female business founders or young female-led businesses < 3 years	100,000 DM

Table 4.4. Awards for Female Business Founders and Entrepreneurs

Award and year	Initiated by	Requirements	Amount
Veuve-Cliquot-Award (since 1983 yearly)	Company Veuve Cliquot	Female entrepreneurs, handed out in 11 countries	No data

Welter et al., 2003.

[a] *Super-Illu* offered five prizes in 2002: one each for female and male business founder with a good business idea, one for the best enterprise idea, one for an entrepreneur that started again after bankruptcy, one to a previously unemployed founder. In recent years, the magazine prized 3 concepts, each with 10,000 DM.

THE DISCOURSE ON FEMALE ENTREPRENEURSHIP

When analyzing the newspaper discourse, it becomes obvious that female entrepreneurship is not just an economically important phenomenon. Therefore, we will first discuss the external embeddedness of the discourse on female entrepreneurship, drawing on Johannisson et al.'s (2002) concept of systemic (economic) and substantive (political and cultural) embeddedness of entrepreneurship. Out of a total of 203 articles in the conservative *Welt* in 1995–2001, slightly less than half discuss female entrepreneurship within economic categories, implicitly or explicitly interpreting female entrepreneurship as an economic phenomenon (Table 4.5, Appendix 1, and Appendix 2 give a detailed list of aggregated article categories for both newspapers). This mainly includes portraits of successful female entrepreneurs in different fields, and reports about support programs or the activities of business associations and networks. Several articles take a strong position toward a (desired) link between increasing female entrepreneurship and the creation of new employment. A similar picture is conveyed in the liberal *Süddeutsche Zeitung (SZ)*. The importance attributed to female entrepreneurship as an economic phenomenon is only slightly lower; 46.1 % of all articles fall into this category, as compared to 47.8 % in the conservative *Welt*.

Although nearly 47% of all analyzed articles refer to female entrepreneurship in an economic context, the media discourse is not restricted to the fields of business and economics in general, or entrepreneurship in particular. As Table 4.5 illustrates, the discourse is also grounded in political and cultural discussions, thus reflecting the so-called "substantive embeddedness of entrepreneurship" (Johannisson et al., 2002). Although we expected differences here between the more leftist newspaper *SZ* showing a more pronounced tendency toward a substantive embeddedness compared to the conservative *Welt*, the data collected show a similar picture. Thirty-seven percent of all articles in the *Welt* and 45% in the *SZ* link female entrepreneurship with cultural issues, 15% of the *Welt* articles and 9% of the *SZ* articles see it within political issues.

Table 4.5. External Embeddedness of the Discourse on Female Entrepreneurship in the *Welt* and the *Süddeutsche Zeitung*

Focus of article	Economy		Politics		Culture		Total number
Year	No	%	No	%	No	%	No
Welt							
1995	1	50.0	1	50.0	0	0	2
1996	2	28.6	3	42.9	2	28.6	7
1997	0	0	3	60.0	2	40.0	5
1998	1	11.1	3	33.3	5	55.6	9
1999	14	42.4	5	15.2	14	42.2	33
2000	26	54.2	6	12.5	16	33.3	48
200	53	53.5	10	10.1	36	36.4	99
Total	97	47.8	31	15.3	75	36.9	203
Süddeutsche Zeitung							
1995	16	39.0	2	4.9	23	56.1	41
1996	19	48.7	2	5.1	18	46.2	39
1997	9	34.6	4	15.4	13	50.0	26
1998	23	52.3	6	13.6	15	34.1	44
1999	23	39.7	6	10.3	29	50.0	58
2000	21	42.0	3	6.0	26	52.0	50
2001	44	56.4	7	9.0	27	34.6	78
Total	155	46.1	30	8.9	151	44.9	336

Note: Own calculations.

The category of cultural issues refers, for example, again to articles portraying female entrepreneurs, although with a different emphasis compared to the economic portrays, and describing them in relation to cultural events (i.e., dinner parties, societal meetings or crimes of or against female entrepreneurs). Surprisingly, some articles in the culture sections even report best practices in supporting German female entrepreneurs. Political articles often discuss female entrepreneurs related to an international or, as in the *Welt*, related to an East German context. For the leftist *SZ*, the cultural importance of female entrepreneurship is equally as strong as the economic importance. Interestingly, while the overall importance of female entrepreneurship is increasing, as reflected by an increasing number of articles mentioning the topic in both newspapers, the embeddedness of the discourse is not showing a clear trend of change. Thus, female entrepreneurship is not becoming a predominantly economic phenomenon, as might be expected in view of the public efforts put into increasing its overall level.

How does the discourse on female entrepreneurship in Germany relate to its context? A number of articles discuss the difficulties women experience in combining economic and social roles, referring, for example, to their double burden of work and family or explicitly stating that this particular female entrepreneur chose not to have a family and children *because of* her entrepreneurial role. In this vein, the official (political) discourse argues that female entrepreneurship is important for economic development and also for a modern society with gender equality. This would imply a necessary change in cultural norms toward attributing a higher value to female entrepreneurship. Above, we proposed that the discourse might influence the nature and extent of entrepreneurial activities. Thus, to increase the level of female entrepreneurial activity, the substantive embeddedness (Johannisson et al., 2002) of the discourse (reflected in the number of articles from the political and cultural categories) would have to increase in importance, which is the case in terms of the number of articles mentioning this topic. In addition, the context is characterized by an overall increase in the level of female entrepreneurship as well as an emphasis on support activities. The importance attached to entrepreneurial activity is also reflected in the increasing importance of the economic discourse and the improvement of the entrepreneurship environment. Although there obviously exists a link between the discourse and female entrepreneurial activity, we have to refrain from interpreting this as a linear cause-and-effect relationship, but rather have to draw attention to recursive links.

This leaves the important question of whether the data collected here for a period of seven years (can) show any qualitative changes within this period. In this context, we looked at the *internal embeddedness* of the concept of "female entrepreneur." This is linked to the question of whether female entrepreneurs are a main or side focus of the newspaper discourse (cf. Table 4.6). A "main focus" is associated with a higher internal embeddedness, referring to whole series, company or individual portraits as well as to articles on support measures. The discourse on female entrepreneurs shows a "side focus" or lower internal embeddedness when "female entrepreneur" simply refers to one of the actors in the article, which often goes hand in hand with a totally different article topic. Examples are expressions such as "the female entrepreneur from Milan" in an article about her kidnapping or "the 93-year-old widowed female entrepreneur who was robbed in her apartment."

Table 4.6. Internal Embeddedness of Female Entrepreneurship

	1995		1996		1997		1998		1999		2000		2001	
	No	%	No	%	No	%	No	%	No	%	No	%	No	%
Welt														
Main focus	0	0	4	57.1	0	0	5	55.6	17	51.5	26	54.2	54	54.5
Side focus	2	100.0	3	42.9	5	100.0	4	44.4	16	48.5	22	45.8	45	45.5
Süddeutsche Zeitung														
Main focus	13	31.7	8	20.5	10	38.5	20	45.5	26	44.8	24	48.0	44	56.4
Side focus	28	68.3	31	79.5	16	61.5	24	54.5	32	55.2	26	52.0	34	43.6

Source: Own calculations.

Internal embeddedness has changed over the studied period for both newspapers. From 1995–1998, 60% of all published articles in the *Welt* and 66% in the *SZ* mentioned female entrepreneurs as only a side focus, while in the next three years this share dropped to 46% for the *Welt* and 49% for the *SZ*, respectively. This clearly indicates a growing interest in female entrepreneurship as a main topic of attention, which might have been ignited by the overall political emphasis put on this topic, especially after the German Social-Democratic Party and the Green Party won elections in September 1998.

The discourse on female entrepreneurs in the two German newspapers takes place along a number of broad arguments, which are similar to those found in earlier studies on female entrepreneurship from different perspectives (e.g., Ahl, 2002; Pietiläinen, 2001). For example, the discourse is largely based on the key assumption that (female) entrepreneurship is good for the economic situation and thus for society at large. A number of the articles implicitly state that female entrepreneurship would be better than or complementary to male entrepreneurship. Female entrepreneurship is described as "better" than male in the sense that women are seen as less risk-oriented and using less financial resources. Interestingly, depicting the idea of risk-avoidance as a positive aspect of female entrepreneurship is in contrast to the usual definition of what makes an entrepreneur, which includes the willingness to take risks. Female entrepreneurship is understood as complementary to male entrepreneurship in the sense that it often refers to an emotional dimension, which is believed to be positive but an explicitly female trait.

Another line of discourse states that female entrepreneurship is still too low. Thus, special programs would be needed to facilitate entrepreneurial activity. Here, several articles discuss (the success of) existing programs of fostering female entrepreneurship. The underlying assumption to this line of argument is that female entrepreneurship would be a yet untapped resource. In this context, supporting female entrepreneurship is seen as positive, as running one's own business would allow women to schedule working time and family around one's needs. Thus, the assumption is that the female entrepreneur would still be responsible for the household and family work, and in her spare-time, she could become an entrepreneur. The role patterns as such are not brought into question.

The arising question is: Does the discourse on female entrepreneurship reinforce the men's right to a career, around which women have to organize? Or does it induce necessary societal change in Germany? At a first glance, the newspaper discourse appears to favor societal change, especially looking at the many positive portraits of female entrepreneurs, which in principle establishes them as role models. However, this changes when analyzing the contents and language used in more detail. Although many of those companies portrayed by both newspapers introduced innovative products and services, those are often related to the reality of housewives and mothers. One such example is a woman entrepreneur who set up a company for reusable diapers. In addition, articles frequently portray successful women entrepreneurs in traditional fields, which are typically perceived as female domains, such as fashion or interior design. Where women entrepreneurs appear in non-typical female fields, such as the automobile industry, they often have taken over family businesses.

Moreover, these role models often are created around implicit differences to male behavior and reinforce female stereotypes. For example, the sex appeal of female entrepreneurs is frequently assessed. In addition, female entrepreneurial behavior is described in comparative terms to male behavior, for example, female risk-taking behavior is less frequent and less financing is needed. Female entrepreneurs' businesses are reported to grow slower. Thus, the creation of role models largely builds on a dichotomy it pretends to overcome. Females are depicted in contrast to male entrepreneurs and thus the underlying discourse is one of entrepreneurship being a male phenomenon and female entrepreneurship being the exception to that.

Surprisingly, the implicit definitions ascribed to female entrepreneurs do not appear to differ much across both newspapers. They show a blurred and ambiguous picture of female entrepreneurship. A female entrepreneur is mainly understood as being a hard-working power-woman, showing enthusiasm, energy, firmness, and cleverness, in short: a superwoman standing her "woman" in a male-dominated business world. For example, one female entrepreneur is described as a dazzling personality, a tough power-woman in colorful Chanel costumes with endless energy and enthusiasm. Stereotypical female attributes, such as emotions, fairness, social values, female logic, sympathy and understanding, are also stressed, leading to the implicit assumption that a successful female entrepreneur needs to be more male than any man, but also more female than any woman.

Some portraits of female entrepreneurship (interestingly more often those written by male authors) also reflect a lack of distance (or respect) to the respective person, albeit this appears to be related to the section of the newspaper the article is published in. Traumatic events, interior designs of apartments, age, figure, haircut and clothes as well as family relations are often discussed as part of the portrait, especially when those feature in cultural sections. Women entrepreneurs emerge as "very beautiful" (an ex-model who turned to entrepreneurship), as a "graceful woman with twinkling blue eyes" (a 73-year-old entrepreneur leading a large production company), or as a "45-year-old trained industrial sales representative who turned entrepreneur with three children," although some articles also feel a need to stress their actor's reluctance when asked for their age.

While male entrepreneurship is often associated with the idea of "getting rich quick," this is not a major topic in articles on female entrepreneurship. Rather, the topic of self-fulfilment is stressed. Again, this states a norm for female entrepreneurship which is different from male (and thus "normal") entrepreneurship. All this implies that the creation of female entrepreneur role models is less focused on providing role models in general, but role models for women and for the construction of gender differences in entrepreneurial behavior, which are the basis for the infrastructure support programs. On the other hand, especially portraits implicitly link female entrepreneurship to success, describing successful women entrepreneurs, often those who were awarded one of the prestigious awards for female entrepreneurs (cf. Table 4.4). However, those articles also stress a typical (socially unwanted) behavior of successful women entrepreneurs who had to behave like men, in order to set up successful businesses. And yet again, some articles draw attention to the fact that women entrepreneurs are successful because of their sex. In those cases, the article frequently emphasizes the outer appearance of the entrepreneur as well as her behavior toward the journalist.

OUTLOOK

The presentation of the findings so far has clearly depicted a colorful jigsaw of different complementary and contradictory statements, drawing attention to the different voices and assumptions that are reflected in this discourse. These voices discuss female entrepreneurship seemingly in unison, but this changes when looking at those statements in more detail. The underlying assumptions vary between assuming existing gender equality and acknowledging inequality, but referring to equality as a future goal. A third group of articles, which has increased in importance only in the last few years, renounces reference to gender or gender-biased stereotypes and just presents female entrepreneurs in their own right.

Here, the implications of many articles—that female entrepreneurs would have to subdue "male characteristics" or have to act out "female characteristics" (such as leading emotionally)—are abandoned and instead, female entrepreneurs are presented in their individual strengths and weaknesses. Intuitively, this "new" view seems appealing. However, what does this imply for the public policy of fostering female entrepreneurship with "target-specific" measures? A perspective, which acknowledges the contributions of female entrepreneurship in its own right, is only now emerging in the newspaper discourse. We have stated above that newspaper discourses have an important impact on public opinion, but also that the change of cultural values takes a long time. Thus, this new perspective gives us some hope that in the future gender equality might be accomplished.

However, the analysis of the articles also reveals that too little focus is put on societal changes that would imply a fairer distribution of work in the house and family. Female entrepreneurship is fostered *in addition* to the roles of housewives and mothers. Therefore, even successful role models, as depicted in several articles, can serve to strengthen the traditionally prevailing "housewife"-model in German society instead of inducing societal changes. Therefore, although public policies helping women to develop their entrepreneurial positions seem important, there also has to be a stronger focus on reducing the double burden carried by women not only by facilitating this burden for women, but by redistributing it.

ACKNOWLEDGMENT

Both authors acknowledge support by the Federal Ministry of Education and Research (BMBF).

NOTE

1. The German-speaking countries have recently reformed the spelling of the German language. This changed the spelling of the word from "selbständig" to "selbstständig." As the reform was fiercely debated, the national newspapers only slowly adapted the new spelling, and the old spelling can still be found. Thus, our search had to include both alternatives.

APPENDIX 1

Detailed List of Aggregated Article Categories in the *Welt*

Economy	Politics	Culture
• Wirtschaft *(Economy)*	• Politik *(Politics)*	• Feuilleton *(Feature pages)*
• Berufswelt, Karriere, Management und Karriere *(Job world, Career, Management & Career)*	• Seite Drei *(Page 3)*	• Aus aller Welt *(From all over the world)*
	• Forum *(Forum)*	• Stil *(Style)*
• Menschen und Märkte *(People and markets)*		• Bayern Feuilleton *(Bavaria Feature pages)*
• Webwelt, Webforum *(Web world, Web forum)*		• Bayern Gesellschaft *(Bavaria Society)*
• Medien *(media)*		• Berlin, Potsdam und die Mark *(Berlin, Potsdam and the Mark)*
• Finanzen *(Finances)*		• Berlin Feuilleton *(Berlin Feature pages)*
• Unternehmen *(Companies)*		• Bremen Gesellschaft *(Bremen Society)*
• Bayern Wirtschaft *(Bavaria Economy)*		
• Berlin Wirtschaft *(Berlin Economy)*		• Hansestadt Hamburg *(Hanse City Hamburg)*
• Hamburg Wirtschaft *(Hamburg Economy)*		• Hamburg, Norddeutschland *(Hamburg, Northern Germany)*
• Hamburg Verbandsnachrichten *(Hamburg news from associations)*		• Sport *(Sports)*

Note: Compiled by authors.

APPENDIX 2

Detailed List of Aggregated Article Categories in the *SZ*

Economy	Politics	Culture
• Münchner Wirtschaft *(Munich's economy)*	• Nachrichten* *(News)*	• Vermischtes *(Miscellaneous)*
• Wirtschaft *(Economy)*	• Sonderthemen* st *(Special topics)*	• Meinungsseite* *(Opinion page)*
• Beilage* *(Supplement)*	• Raum München *(Munich region)*	• Themen* *(topics)*
• Seite 3* *(Page 3)*		• Bildung & Beruf* *(Education & Profession)*
• Immobilien *(Real estate)*	• Themen Ausland *(Topics from abroad)*	• Mode* *(Fashion)*
• Medien* *(media)*	• Berliner Seite* *(Berlin page)*	• Briefe an die SZ *(Letters to the SZ)*
• Magazin* *(Magazine)*		• Reise und Erholung *(Travel and Recreation)*

Detailed List of Aggregated Article Categories in the *SZ*

Economy	Politics	Culture
	• Meinungsseite (*Opinion page*)	• Feuilleton (*Feature pages*)
		• Sport (*Sports*)
		• Hochschule (*University*)
		• SZ am Wochenende* (*SZ on the weekend*)
		• Stadtanzeiger* (*City planner*)
		• Kinder- und Jugendliteratur (*Children and youth books*)
		• Literatur (*Literature*)
		• Münchner Kultur (*Culture in Munich*)
		• Theater (*Theatre*)
		• Leserbriefe (*Letters from the readers*)
		• Panorama (*Panorama*)
		• Jugend, Schule, Wirtschaft (*Youth, School, Economy*)
		• Computerseite (*Computer page*)
		• Politisches Buch (*Political book*)

Compiled by authors.
Note: The article categories München (*Munich*), Bayern (*Bavaria*) were relevant in all three categories. Those sections marked with an asterix also appeared in other categories, it is placed here in the most relevant category.

REFERENCES

Ahl, H.J. (2002). *The making of the female entrepreneur: A discourse analysis of research texts on women's entrepreneurship.* Jönköping: Jönköping International Business School Dissertation Series No. 15.

Ainsworth, S. (2001, July 11–13). *Discourse analysis as social construction: Towards greater integration of approaches and methods.* Paper presented at the Second International Conference on Critical Management Studies, Manchester.

Beattie, R. (1999). The creative entrepreneur: A study of the entrepreneur's creative processes. In P.D. Reynolds, W.D. Bygrave, S. Manigart, C.M. Mason, G.D. Meyers, H.J. Sapienza, & K.G. Shaver (Eds.), *Frontiers of entrepreneurship research 1999* (pp. 138–151). Wellesley, MA: Babson College Center for Entrepreneurial Studies.

Berger, P.L., & Luckmann, T. (1969). *Die gesellschaftliche Konstruktion der Wirklichkeit: Eine Theorie der Wissenssoziologie.* Frankfurt: Fischer.

Birley, S. (1989, January). Female entrepreneurs: Are they really any different? *Journal of Small Business Management*, pp. 32–37.
Boje, D.M. (1991). The storytelling organization: A study of story performance in an office-supply firm. *Administrative Science Quarterly, 36*, 106–126.
Burr, V. (1995). *An introduction to social constructionism.* London: Routledge.
Cicourel, A.V. (1981). Three models of discourse analysis: The role of social structure. *Discourse Processes, 3,* 101–131.
Du Gay, P. (1996). *Consumption and identity at work.* London: Sage.
Evers, J. (2002, September 19). *Microlending—Ein neuer Weg zur Finanzierung von Kleinunternehmen. Überblick über Ansätze in Deutschland und Europa.* Presentation to a workshop in Stuttgart.
Evers, J., & Habschick, M. (2000). *Micro finance designed for start ups as an exit out 0f unemployment.* Essen: Schriften und Materialien zu Handwerk und Mittelstand 10, RWI.
Fairclough, N. (1992). *Discourse and social change.* Cambridge, MA: Polity Press.
Fehrenbach, S., & Leicht, R. (2002). *Strukturmerkmale und Potentiale der von Frauen geführten Betriebe in Deutschland.* Mannheim: Veröffentlichungen des Instituts für Mittelstandsforschung der Universität Mannheim, Grüne Reihe Nr. 47. Universität Mannheim.
Foucault, M. (1972). *The archeology of knowledge.* London: Tavistock.
Frerichs, P., & Wiemert, H. (2002). *"Ich gebe, damit Du gibst." Frauennetzwerke—strategisch, reziprok, exklusiv.* Opladen: Soziale Chancen, Schriftenreihe des ISO-Instituts Köln, 2. Leske + Budrich.
Frick, S., Lageman, B., von Rosenbladt, B., Voelzkow, H., & Welter, F. (1998). *Möglichkeiten zur Verbesserung des wirtschafts- und gesellschaftspolitischen Umfeldes für Existenzgründer und kleine und mittlere Unternehmen – Wege zu einer neuen Kultur der Selbständigkeit.* Essen: Untersuchungen des RWI, 25.
Gleich, U. (1998). Politikvermittlung und politische Partizipation durch Medien. In H. Dichanz (Ed.), *Handbuch Medien: Medienforschung, Konzepte, Themen, Ergebnisse* (pp. 54–59). Bonn: Bundeszentrale für politische Bildung.
Gustafsson, S. (1995). Public policies and women's labor force participation: A comparison of Sweden, West Germany, and the Netherlands. In P.P. Schulz (Ed.), *Investments in Women's human capital* (pp. 91–112). Chicago, London.
Gustafsson, S., & Wetzels, C. (1997). Family policies and women's labour force transitions in connection with childbirth. *Vierteljahrshefte zur Wirtschaftsforschung, 1,* 118–124.
Heracleaous, L., & Barrett, M. (2001). Organizational change as discourse: Communicative actions and deep structures in the context of information technology implementation. *Academy of Management Journal, 44*(4), 755–778.
Holst, E. (2001). *Institutionelle Determinanten der Erwerbsarbeit: Zur Notwendigkeit einer Gender-Perspektive in den Wirtschaftswissenschaften.* Berline: DIW Diskussionspapier, 237.
Holst, E. (2002). Institutionelle Determinanten der Erwerbsarbeit. In F. Maier and A. Fiedler (Eds.), *Gender Matters: Feministische Analysen zur Wirtschafts- und Sozialpolitik.* Fhw-Forschung, 42/43, 89–109. Berlin: Edition Sigma.
Hyrsky, K. (1999). Entrepreneurial metaphors and concepts: An exploratory study. *International Small Business Journal, 18*(1), 13–34.

Institut für Mittelstandsforschung (IFM) Bonn. (2001). *Gender-spezifische Aufbereitung der amtlichen Statistik: Möglichkeiten respektive Anforderungen.* Materialien zur Gleichstellungspolitik, 82/2001. Bonn: BMFSFJ.

Johannisson, B., Ramirez-Pasillas, M., & Karlsson, G. (2002). The embeddedness of inter-firm networks, *Entrepreneurship & Regional Development, 14*(4), 297–315.

Kehlbeck, H., & Schneider, U. (1999). *Frauen als Zielgruppe von Existenzgründungen unter besonderer Berücksichtigung der Finanzierungsaspekte.* Hamburg: Eine Untersuchung im Auftrag des Senatsamtes für die Gleichstellung.

Kirzner, I. (1979). *Perception, opportunity and profit: Studies in the theory of entrepreneurship.* Chicago: University of Chicago Press.

Lauxen-Ulbrich, M., & Leicht, R. (2002). *Entwicklung und Tätigkeitsprofil selbständiger Frauen in Deutschland. Eine empirische Untersuchung anhand der Daten des Mikrozensus.* Mannheim: Veröffentlichungen des Instituts für Mittelstandsforschung, 46. Universität Mannheim.

Macdonald, M. (1995). *Representing woman: Myths of femininity in the popular media.* London: Edward Arnold.

Media-Analyse. (2002). (AG.MA) *2002 Tageszeitungen.* http://www.sueddeutsche.de/index.php?url=/ueberuns/mediadaten&datei=index.php, February, 20th, 2002.

Meyer, S., & Schulze, E. (1995). Die Auswirkungen der Wende auf Frauen und Familien in den neuen Bundesländern. In: S. Gensior (ed.), *Vergesellschaftung und Frauenerwerbsarbeit: Ost-West-Vergleiche* (pp. 249–269). Berlin: Edition Sigma.

Papenheim, D., & Görisch, J. (2001). *Landesförderprogramme für Existenzgründungen aus Hochschulen.* Karlsruhe: Fraunhofer-Institut für Systemtechnik und Innovationsforschung.

Pfau-Effinger, B. (1995). Erwerbsbeteiligung von Frauen im europäischen Vergleich. *Informationen zur Raumentwicklung, 1*, 49–60.

Piasecki, B., & Rogut, A. (1993, September). *Self regulation of SME sector development at a more advanced stage of transformation.* Paper presented to the 20th Annual Conference of E.A.R.I.E., Tel Aviv.

Pietiläinen, T. (2001). *Gender and female entrepreneurship in a pro-entrepreneurship magazine.* Stockholm: Swedish School of Economics and Business Administration Working Paper, 458.

Piorkowsky, M.-B. (2001). *Existenzgründungsprozesse im Zu- und Nebenerwerb von Frauen und Männern: Eine empirische Analyse der Bedingungen und Verläufe bei Gründungs- und Entwicklungsprozessen von Unternehmen unter besonderer Berücksichtigung genderspezifischer Aspekte.* Bonn: BMFSFJ.

Piorkowsky, M.-B. with Scholl, S. (2002). *Genderaspekte in der finanziellen Förderung von Unternehmensgründungen. Eine qualitative und quantitative Analyse der Programme auf Bundesebene – unter besonderer Berücksichtigung der Gründung durch Frauen.* Bonn: BMFSFJ.

Rocksloh-Papendieck, B. (1995). Lebensstrategien im Umbruch. In S. Gensior (Ed.), *Vergesellschaftung und Frauenerwerbsarbeit: Ost-West-Vergleich* (pp. 219–248). Berlin: Edition Sigma.

Schmitt-Beck, R. (1994). Politikvermittlung durch Massenkommunikation und interpersonale Kommunikation. Anmerkungen zur Theorieentwicklung und einer empirischer Vergleich. In M. Jäckel & P. Winterhoff-Spurk (Eds.), *Politik* und Medien. Analysen zur Entwicklung der politischen Kommunikation (pp.159–180). Berlin: Vistas.

Soothill, K., & Grover, C. (1997). A note on computer searches of newspapers. *Sociology, 31*(3), 591.

Sperling, C., & May, M. (2001). *Aktivitäten von und für Unternehmerinnen und Existenzgründerinnen im Bereich der Klein- und Mittelbetriebe (KMU) – Bundesweiter Überblick, Band 1, Bundesweites Adressenverzeichnis, Band 2*. Essen/Bonn: BMFSFJ.

Steinulfsson Skjerdal, T. (2001). *Responsible Watchdogs? Normative Theories of the Press in Post-Apartheid South Africa. A Discourse Analysis of 102 newspaper Articles, 1996–99*. Durban, South Africa: Masters dissertation, University of Natal.

Sternberg, R., & Bergmann, H. (2003). *Global Entrepreneurship Monitor: Unternehmensgründungen im weltweiten Vergleich. Länderbericht Deutschland 2002*. Köln: Universität zu Köln.

Stevenson, N. (1995). *Understanding media cultures: Social theory and mass communication*. London/Thousand Oaks, CA: Sage.

Tschepurenko, A. (1998). *Die russischen Kleinunternehmen in der zweiten Hälfte der 90er Jahre. Teil I: Entwicklung, Leistung, Probleme*. Köln: BiOst.

Weick, K.E. (1995). *Sensemaking in organizations*. London/Thousands Oaks, CA: Sage.

Weick, K.E. (1998). *Der Prozeß des Organisierens*. Frankfurt am Main: Suhrkamp.

Welter, F. (2001). *Nascent Entrepreneurship in Germany*. Schriften und Materialien zu Handwerk und Mittelstand, 11. Essen: RWI.

Welter, F., & Lageman, B. with assistance from Stoytcheva, M. (2003). *Gründerinnen in Deutschland: Potenziale und institutionelles Umfeld*. Essen: Untersuchungen des RWI.

CHAPTER 5

WOMEN ENTREPRENEURS

Breaking Through the Glass Barrier

Nan S. Langowitz and Claudia Morgan

ABSTRACT

Women-founded and owned firms represent an increasing percentage of businesses and business revenues in the United States. Yet research has shown that women entrepreneurs may face situational barriers as they develop their businesses. Among the situational barriers women may face is a feminized Horatio Alger stereotype of the woman as entrepreneur. Such a stereotype, and its implications, may serve as a "glass barrier" to the aspirations of potential women entrepreneurs and the expectations of the financial and commercial community with whom she might do business. This chapter examines the coverage of women entrepreneurs by the popular business press and the extent to which media coverage reinforces the glass barrier created by this stereotype. The research identifies the main characteristics and normative messages in a four-year sample of business periodical profiles on women entrepreneurs and contrasts those findings with the experience of sixty-six women entrepreneurs. The research shows that the message provided in the business media about women entrepreneurs and their businesses is substantially but not entirely on target. Where the normative message goes astray, it reinforces the glass barrier for women entrepreneurs.

INTRODUCTION

Women-founded and owned firms represent an increasing percentage of businesses and business revenues in the United States. In 2000, 38% of businesses in the United States were owned by women (Center for Women's Business Research, 2001). These firms contributed $3.6 trillion to the U.S. economy and employed 27.5 million workers (Center for Women's Business Research, 2001). While women entrepreneurs' education, career development, and personal motivations are all known to contribute significantly to the survival and growth of their businesses, situational and cultural influences are also known to affect women and men as they plan, found, and grow new businesses (Birley, 1989; Brush, 1997; Cliff, 1998). Indeed, women entrepreneurs have been called "invisible" because their businesses fail to gain sustained media and academic attention (Baker, Aldrich, & Liou, 1997) and still encounter significant situational and cultural barriers (Brush, 1997).

While U.S. society has largely moved beyond the 1950s era image of a woman earning "pin money" to buy that little something special for herself, there still appears to be a modern stereotype of the woman entrepreneur and her business. Namely, the modern image is that of a woman driven to start her business by dire circumstance, rather than personal drive and desire. One popular view is that a woman starts a business out of economic necessity. The feminized Horatio Alger story invokes a Cinderella theme in which the woman overcomes hardship with the benefit of neither fairy godmother nor handsome prince. The circumstance might vary from welfare mother to divorcee but the frequent underlying message is that something unusual has caused the woman to start her own business. Why else would she do it? Given that circumstance, the goal is personal survival, rather than economic growth, fortune and the desire to lead. The modern stereotype also assumes that the business be in a "woman-related" field, such as food, clothing, service or retailing, allowing her to take advantage of her perceived familiarity with domestic management, caregiving and shopping. Taken as a whole, the modern stereotype implies that a woman entrepreneur is not seriously interested in venture development and will seek a threshold level of financial success rather than significant economic performance. This stereotype and its implications may serve as a "glass barrier" that dampens the aspirations of potential women entrepreneurs and dilutes the expectations of the financial and commercial community with whom she might do business.

In order to study the potential impact of this "glass barrier" we examined popular business press coverage of women entrepreneurs. Our study identifies the main characteristics and normative messages in a four-year sample of business periodical profiles on women entrepreneurs and contrasts those findings with the experience of sixty-six women entrepreneurs. Although the research is exploratory in nature, the findings are systematically derived and represent a study of a relatively large sample of underrepresented subjects, both in terms of business press coverage and academic business research. The findings presented herein are meant to stimulate discussion and further study on women entrepreneurs and their businesses.

The business publications studied all achieve high circulation and thereby shape the perception of reality for hundreds of thousands of readers in the business community, both male and female. The Massachusetts entrepreneurs to whom the media coverage was compared run businesses in one of the most active entrepreneurial state economies in the United States. The research shows that the message provided in the business media about women entrepreneurs and their businesses is substantially but not entirely on target. Where the normative message goes astray, it reinforces the glass barrier for women entrepreneurs. Such reinforcement has the potential to mislead aspiring women entrepreneurs, and the business community with whom they are interdependent, with respect to industries of opportunity, assessment of their personal suitability for entrepreneurship, and aspiration levels for success. This article explains the research and the derivation of our findings.

RESEARCH DESIGN AND METHODS

Popular media is a powerful force in shaping perceptions of reality (Taylor, Hobbs, Nilsson, O'Halloran, & Preisser, 2000; Tuchman, 1978; Turow, 1997). There is substantial theory and some case study research linking media messages and common perceptions of women in different spheres of life (Faludi, 1991; Wolf, 1991). Messages from popular media are known to influence business behavior and response (e.g., Bird, 1989; Renkema & Hoeken, 1998; Swift, 1993). Messages from popular media may therefore have implications for activity by women entrepreneurs in their professional and business development. Certainly, one aspect of media influence is the sheer volume of coverage. In a mid-1990s retrospective study, the coverage of women business owners was found to have declined at precisely the same time period that women were making substantive gains in business ownership (Baker et al., 1997). Another aspect of media influence, however, is how the popular business press, despite the paucity of coverage, portrays women entrepreneurs. This is the issue addressed by our research.

Profile articles of entrepreneurs and their businesses in high circulation magazines perform a number of functions. The articles draw peer attention to subjects of market influence or potential influence; they may draw attention to the subject firm's products or services; and they may affect the perceptions of investors, employees, and current customers or clients by virtue of the broad exposure provided by the magazine (Brody, 1994). Magazine profile articles are a unique opportunity for a business leader to convey a humane image (Bird, 1989). Profiles provide more space than virtually any other approach save for biographical study to document detailed insights into a business leader's vision, beliefs, and life story. A profile article can help consolidate a corporate image into one leading figure, a critical positioning issue in an environment saturated with complex messages about business structure, behavior, and performance (Corning, 1999; D'Alessandro, 1990).

Profiles of women business owners may also serve more subtle but broadly important social functions. Despite enormous gains in social and economic influence in the past several decades, women entrepreneurs work in social settings in which gender stereotypes have been found to persist (Baron, Markman, & Hirza, 2001). The stereotypes, as elements of situational and cultural influence, are thought to bias perceptions and understandings of what women entrepreneurs do. Indeed, the perception that women-owned businesses as less successful, capable, credit-worthy and innovative continues to be experienced as a barrier (Brush, 1997). In this research, we were interested in how the portrayal of women entrepreneurs in popular business press profiles might reinforce the stereotypes, what we are calling the "glass barrier," that previous research has documented. In particular, we examined whether normative[1] themes could be identified across profiles of women entrepreneurs found among the business outlets providing the highest coverage from 1996 to 2000, and the extent to which the norms identified contrasted with the experience of successful women entrepreneurs. We designed the research to explore the following propositions:

1. Business media profiles of women entrepreneurs realistically reflect the motivations and context for venture start-up by women entrepreneurs,

2. Business media profiles of women entrepreneurs and their companies realistically reflect the business characteristics of women founded firms.

We found that the business print media conveys mixed messages about women entrepreneurs, and may reflect the persistence of biases, that is the reinforcement of the glass barrier, to some extent.

RESEARCH METHODOLOGY

The research design included three stages: (a) Identification of articles in the popular business press that profiled women entrepreneurs and their firms; (b) Content analysis of those articles designated as substantive profiles[2] with a minimum 500-word content; and (c) Comparison of the normative themes identified through the content analysis with the experience of a large survey sample of women entrepreneurs.

The entrepreneur profiles were identified from a comprehensive literature search focused on women and entrepreneurship items published or produced and disseminated between July 1, 1996 and June 30, 2000. The approach to the comprehensive search was largely phenomenological. Through a search across 24 of the 46 Online Computer Library Center (OCLC) "FirstSearch" databases for all items in English referencing the keyword term "women entrepreneurs,"[3] we found 514 unique entries. Sources included in the OCLC database included popular journalism, government statistics, business case studies, and other forms of empirical investigation from a variety of sources. Undertaking our search in the summer of 2000, we limited the search to dates between July 1, 1996, and June 30, 2000 in order to bring what was at the time the most recent comprehensive examination of the literature and entrepreneurship up to date (Starr & Yudkin, 1996). In so doing, we determined that the start date should be midyear in order to accommodate sources that may have been produced in 1996 but perhaps not addressed by Starr and Yudkin, as well as to create a full four years of new literature to consider for our study.

One hundred forty-two of the 514 sources in the database were individual or business profiles in the popular press, with seven high-circulation[4] business periodicals accounting for seventy-eight of the profiles, each having a minimum of three articles during the four-year time period (see Table 5.1). Forty-three of these articles were sub-sampled (see Appendix 1 for a list of articles) from the group for a minimum content and 500-word count threshold. In order to focus on sources with the fullest possible coverage of entrepreneurs and their companies, we included articles of 500 or more words that made the entrepreneur and/or her firm the subject of the article. Articles which described niche or performance characteristics of firms that happened to be women-owned or those that gave only brief sidebar information about a woman entrepreneur and her business, for example *Working Woman's* "Top 500 Women- Owned Businesses" annual article, were not included in our content analysis.

Content analysis is among the most frequently used methodologies for communication and media study and is often used to explore the influence of the media upon social understanding (Taylor et al., 2001). We used a basic method of content analysis, focusing on identification of themes

Table 5.1. Annual Count of "Women Entrepreneurs" Profile Articles in Top Seven Business Publications Providing Coverage, July 1 through June 30, 1996–2000

	1996/97	1997/98	1998/99	1999/00	Circulation
Black Enterprise (6)	1	2	1	2	430,464
Forbes (9)	4	2	3	0	907,207
Hispanic (5)	0	1	1	3	260,000
Inc. (3)	0	0	0	3	658,788
Nation's Business (3)	3	0	0	0	850,000
Success (5)	2	1	2	0	475,000
Working Woman (12)	2	3	6	1	636,297
Total Articles (43):	12	9	13	9	

and basic quantitative analysis of their representation (Neuendorf, 2001). We analyzed the forty-three articles in the seven popular business periodicals for the presence of predominant themes with respect to women entrepreneurs.[5] Six domains of content were identified: (1) the origin story of the business, (2) industry context, (3) start-up financing, (4) characteristics and background of the entrepreneur, (5) success indicators for the business and entrepreneur, and (6) future plans for the business. Although the content of these domains was generally exclusive there were some areas of overlap. For example, the entrepreneur's motivation for starting the business is included in both the origin story of the business and as a characteristic of the entrepreneur. Content coding of the articles was conducted by both authors with nearly identical coding of the success indicators domain assuring us of inter-rater reliability. In order to ensure moderate reliability, we shared codes for all sets of themes with one another and independently reviewed their frequency among all forty-three articles (Neuendorf, 2001). Domain content dimensions are provided in Table 5.2.

The thematic analysis of the profile literature was compared to the experiences of a group of women entrepreneurs who participated in a separate research study on woman-led businesses (Langowitz, 2002). The comparison group consists of sixty-six women entrepreneurs who were surveyed regarding facets of the entrepreneurial experience, including firm demographics (revenues, annual rate of growth, geographic location); industries represented, age of firm, and number of employees; and demographics of the subjects themselves (managerial experience, controlling ownership, education, years with current enterprise).

The comparison group is subject to some limitations. First, it is restricted only to the business ventures of women entrepreneurs in Massachusetts.

Table 5.2. Content Domain Dimensions

	Origin Story	Industry Context	Start-Up Financing	Entrepreneur's Characteristics	Success Indicators	Future Plans
Recognition: Life background	✔					
Recognition: Professional background	✔					
Recognition: Serendipity/Research	✔					
Motivation: Change/challenge/dream	✔			✔		
Motivation: Personal achievement:	✔			✔		
Motivation: Personal adversity	✔			✔		
Opportunity in the industry		✔				
Women in the industry		✔				
Women in the socio-economic group		✔				
Personal savings			✔	✔		
Family and friends funding			✔	✔		
Client contracts/advance orders			✔			
VC, corporate investor or private placement			✔			
Bank loan			✔			
Personal credit			✔			
Government supported financing			✔			
Life or career experience qualifications				✔		
Educational qualifications				✔		
Age of entrepreneur				✔		
Childhood family information				✔		
Current family information				✔		
Professional network/mentor				✔		

Table 5.2. Content Domain Dimensions (Cont.)

	Origin Story	Industry Context	Start-Up Financing	Entrepreneur's Characteristics	Success Indicators	Future Plans
Education/training/research				✓		
Hard work				✓		
Uniqueness in field/pioneer				✓	✓	
Risk taker	✓			✓		
Company revenues or assets					✓	
Employees					✓	
Company growth rate					✓	
Business longevity					✓	
Clients					✓	
Personal wealth					✓	
Personal autonomy					✓	
Personal style/status					✓	
Growth/expansion of business						✓
Succession/exit of entrepreneur						✓

Massachusetts, however, is a leading U.S. state economy and as such results for its businesses may be considered reasonably representative of national trends. Second, the respondents are self-selected participants in the study. A potential participant pool of 650 women business leaders was initially contacted by mail with the request that they participate in a study on woman-led businesses. Upon the return of a phase one single-page survey, respondents were asked to participate in an on-line phase two survey. The phase one response rate was 33% (212 chief executives) with a follow-on second stage response rate of 43%. Sixty-six of the ninety-two second-stage women business leader respondents could be characterized as women entrepreneurs (that is, company founders as well as leaders) comparable to those covered by the business press profiles.

The businesses in the comparison group are demographically similar to that of the businesses profiled in the articles in terms of revenues and business longevity. The comparison group's median company revenue is $4.85 million and two thirds of the businesses are older than seven years. In the profiles group, the median revenue range is $1 to $5 million and half of the profiled businesses have been established more than seven years.

MEDIA COVERAGE

The profile articles in our sample represent the journalistic policy of seven different business magazines: *Black Enterprise, Forbes, Hispanic, Inc., Nation's Business, Success,* and *Working Woman.* All of these publications chose to associate the articles with the keyword phrase "women entrepreneurs," with *Working Woman* (14) and *Forbes* (9) publishing the most profile articles during the four-year time period by that keyword definition. Table 5.1 provides the count of articles for each of the four years studied, beginning with June 30, 1996 through July 1, 1997. While article profiles under the keyword phrase "women entrepreneurs" were published by other business periodicals, the seven publications we included in this study are those which provided the highest total coverage across the four-year time-period. Since publications such as *Inc.* and *Nation's Business* were included with only three profiles published, it is clear that many business journals provided essentially no coverage of women entrepreneurs or chose not to identify their coverage with that keyword phrase. The journalistic policy choice of identifying a keyword phrase is not the direct subject of this research. Circulation for these journals ranges from 260,000 at *Hispanic* to more than 900,000 for *Forbes*. Unfortunately, both *Nation's Business*, in 1999, and *Success*, in 2001, ceased publication. In addition, *Working Woman* was listed as "on hiatus" by its publisher in September 2001 and with the sale of its publishing group in mid-2002 is no longer in print.

As a group there are some common characteristics to the profile articles. Most of the articles, 69%, focus on an individual entrepreneur and her company, while the remainder provides data on multiple companies within the article. Most articles provide a description of the business (100%), its origin (91%) and how it was financed (76%) as well as descriptive characteristics of the entrepreneur (96%) and indicators of her entrepreneurial success (89%).

All of the articles provided some descriptive characteristics of the entrepreneurial businesses profiled. The leading industries in which companies were profiled were professional services (21%), followed by consumer products (12%), apparel and accessories (11%), and technology (10%). Less than half of the profiles provided any background information on the industry and only 22% provided context information about women in the industry. As a result, profiles tended to reinforce the stereotype that women entrepreneurs found businesses in "woman-related" industries and yet they do little to educate the reader about those industries or the role of women within them.

Revenues were provided for 74% of the firms described within the sample articles. Of those firms, the median size firm reported upon had revenues between $1 and $5 million, with the largest firm at $200 million. With respect to company age, the profiles placed an emphasis on newer companies, with 50% of the companies profiled in business for less than seven years and only one third of companies profiled in business more than fourteen years. There was no obvious tendency by any one publication to favor firms of particular size, age or industry among the companies profiled. The focus on newer companies may simply be a reflection of reporting on what's new or hot, yet by focusing on newer companies and particularly those with low revenue size, little coverage is given to women entrepreneurs with sustainable high revenue businesses. The nature of this coverage leaves open the possibility of reinforcing the notion that women are not really serious about long run, high growth ventures.

Ninety-one percent of the articles provided information about the origin of the business. Opportunity recognition was most often attributed to recognizing a business idea through serendipitously finding or researching an unmet need (51%), as well as developing an idea based upon prior business experience (42%). Essentially the "eureka" approach to business venturing. The desire for a change or challenge was also a significant aspect of business origin, identified in nearly half (47%) of the profiles. These business origin themes overlapped within profiles so that often the business origin story was that of a desire for a change or challenge combined with a spark of a new idea.

The majority of the profiles (76%) also pointed to personal achievement as the source of the entrepreneur's motivation to found her firm, as follows:

- Desire for a change or a challenge (47%).
- Determination to achieve personal control (47%).
- Determination to overcome personal tragedy or circumstances (40%).
- Determination to achieve personal financial success (29%).
- Determination to overcome discrimination (20%).{\BL}

A feminized Horatio Alger story was a sub-text in many of these profiles.

In addition to mentioning the motivation to start the firms, most profiles, 76%, give an indication of the form of financing used at start-up. Personal savings is the leading source of financing mentioned (42%), followed by funding through family and friends (36%). Only 13% of the profiles mentioned venture capital or private placement start-up financing and 11% mentioned an advance client contract as an initial financing arrangement. Focusing on those businesses started with personal savings rather than bank or outside financing, may serve to reinforce the glass barrier that women entrepreneurs are not building significant businesses oriented toward growth. For the businesses profiled, scraping together financing from personal contacts was all that seemed to be required.

Finally, many of the articles gave the reader a sense that the business was ongoing but often did not specifically say so. Future plans were explicitly mentioned in 56% of the articles, with most of those citing growth or expansion as a deliberate plan. Nonetheless almost half of the articles gave no indication of future direction for the business. By leaving out the future so frequently, the business profiles potentially leave would be entrepreneurs or their business collaborators with the impression that women's ventures have no significant forward outlook.

Descriptions of the women entrepreneurs were present in nearly all of the profiles (91%); however, the descriptors used varied. The most frequently mentioned descriptors were as follows:

- Source of business or industry experience (89%).
- Prior career or life experience relevant to the business (64%).
- Circumstance of personal adversity (64%).
- Current family information (58%).
- Age of the entrepreneur (56%).
- Indication of risk-taking posture (53%).
- Indication of hard work and resourcefulness (47%).

Most profiles intermingled discussion of the entrepreneur with discussion of her business. As a result, indications of the firm's success could be easily construed as indications of the entrepreneur's success. Eighty-four percent of the profiles provided some indication of success. Not surprisingly, given the business focus of the publications, the profiles predominantly emphasized indicators of business success as a measure of personal success. The primary entrepreneurial success indicators mentioned were the traditional business measures of revenues (73%), firm growth rate (44%), and number of employees (38%). Other success indicators were longevity of the business (31%) and clients (31%). Indicators that gave a sense of the entrepreneur's personal success, beyond the immediate success of the business, were the uniqueness of the entrepreneur in her field (24%) and personal wealth (20%). Again, it is interesting to note that growth rate and longevity were far less frequently noted as measures of success than revenue size, particularly since the typical company profiled was of relatively small size ($1 to $5 million on average).

COMPARATIVE ANALYSIS

Taken as a whole, the media profiles provide significant messages about social norms regarding women entrepreneurs and their businesses. To evaluate the extent to which these articles reflect levels of reality and stereotype, we compared the findings of our content analysis with the experience of a larger group of women entrepreneurs and their businesses with respect to both the characteristics of the ventures and the motivations of the founders.

Through the choice of industries covered, media outlets promote specific (although not necessarily realistic) norms about opportunities for women entrepreneurs within certain industries. The frequent stereotype is that women entrepreneurs will establish businesses in "woman-related" areas. The industries highlighted in the forty-three profile articles suggest that professional services (21%), apparel and accessories (12%), consumer products (11%), and technology (10%) are, respectively, the most favorable industries for women to start businesses. The first three of these industries fit the stereotype of industries about which women are traditionally expected to be knowledgeable. Yet, this choice of industries is only a partial reflection of the reality of opportunity for women entrepreneurs. While professional services was the leading industry in the comparison group (28%), the second and third leading industries were travel and leisure (16%) and construction services (16%), whereas apparel and accessories and consumer products each represented less than 5% of the comparison group.[6] Eleven percent of the comparison group firms were technology companies, similar to the 10% representation in the profile articles. Aspiring women entrepreneurs may be misdirected about the true level of opportunity within industries if they follow the examples of those companies profiled in the media. Indeed, the highest growth industries for women-owned businesses nationwide included construction, but neither apparel nor consumer products (Center for Women's Business Research, 2001).

The profile articles also provide norms concerning business start-up by women. Personal achievement is mentioned in more than three-quarters of the profile articles as the leading motivation to start the business. Further, the profiles emphasized equally (47%) the desire for a change or challenge and the desire for personal control as aspects of start-up motivation. The implication therein is that it is normative for women to pursue entrepreneurship due to personal drivers. This norm is confirmed by the comparison group, in which the most frequently reported motivation for entrepreneurship was personal achievement (72%) and personal autonomy (65%). Both the profiles and the comparison group confirm prior research about entrepreneurial motivations for women and for men (Moore & Buttner, 1997). However the media downplays personal achievement and autonomy in its coverage of entrepreneurial motivation, crowding it out in its level of mention with the old stereotypes of business start-up as a means to overcome personal adversity or achieve economic stability.

Our content analysis showed overcoming adversity as a distinct theme in the profiles of women's entrepreneurial experience. Nearly two-thirds of the profiles highlighted the entrepreneur's personal adverse circumstance such as family tragedy, illness, divorce, economic impoverishment, or discrimination. This was augmented by the focus on self-sacrifice through long hours and hard work in nearly half of the articles. The normative message of the profiles is that a woman's business venture is formed primarily as a result of difficult life experience, with the implication that adversity is a requisite catalyst for women entrepreneurs. Why else would a woman work that hard? This implied norm stands in sharp contrast to the experience of the comparison group of entrepreneurs. Only a third of the comparison group entrepreneurs cited economic need as an important motivator for founding their firms. The journalistic emphasis on adversity as a motivation for entrepreneurship bears the risk of reinforcing the stereotype of women as victims. In this regard, the "human interest story" angle may dilute positive messages of women as active agents of enterprise, adding to the glass barrier to women's entrepreneurship.

The media message also drifts a field with respect to coverage of the origins of the businesses described. The profiles most frequently cited serendipitous opportunity (51%) or need recognition as the catalyst for start-up of the business. Yet, in the comparison group, only 34% of respondents said that "having a great idea" was the source of their initiation of the business venture. It would be a shame if aspiring entrepreneurs interpreted the message in the profiles to mean that unless they have a "Eureka!" moment they should not set out to establish their own firms.

Start-up financing is also the subject of more than three-quarters of the profiles, with a tendency to profile companies in which personal savings (42%) or funding from family and friends (36%) was the financing source. The comparison group provided no comparable data on start-up financing. However, this pattern of financing has been found to be commonplace among women-owned firms (Coleman & Carsky, 1996; Haynes & Haynes, 1999). Even in high-growth firms, women-owned firms have been shown to make less use of external financing (National Foundation for Women Business Owners, 2001). Unfortunately, the business profiles do little to positively influence women entrepreneurs in this regard.

Finally, the profile articles favor company revenues as the most frequent indicator of entrepreneurial success. Yet, the companies profiled have median revenues in the $1 to $5 million range. This promotes an unnecessarily low revenue success target to an aspiring woman entrepreneur. In the larger research pool from which the comparison group was drawn, the average company size of the top one hundred woman-led firms in Massachusetts was $46.1 million (Langowitz, 2002), suggesting a much higher success target might be more appropriate for business media coverage. In addition to unnecessarily lowering aspirations of women entrepreneurs, profiles of lower revenue companies may contribute to the persistence of stereotyping in the general business community that women-owned businesses are not as successful, credit-worthy or legitimate.

CONCLUSION

Overall, popular business media coverage establishes clear norms regarding women entrepreneurs and their companies. Because only some of these norms can be confirmed against the reality of the broader base experience of women entrepreneurs, this media coverage tends to reinforce old stereotypes, thereby supporting the glass barrier women entrepreneurs often face. Business periodical coverage of women entrepreneurs and their ventures accurately reflect two of the four leading industries in which women entrepreneurs have most recently found success. With respect to business origins, personal achievement is the most frequently cited motivator for start-up by women entrepreneurs. However, business periodicals tend to emphasize the theme of personal adversity and hardship as a precondition for business start-up, supporting the misconception that women would not otherwise run their own businesses. Further, serendipitous recognition of a business idea is the primary source of business origin mentioned, whereas having a great idea is only mentioned by one-third of the comparison group entrepreneurs. Most women entrepreneurs start their business through a deliberate process, driven by the goal of personal achievement. Yet, media coverage persists in covering stories of women entrepreneurs who were struck by an idea and burdened by adverse circumstances. Finally, although there are ample examples of higher revenue companies funded with external financing that might be profiled, the typical company reported upon by the popular business press was a company of only $1 to $5 million in size funded through personal savings from friends and family. Such coverage sets a low target threshold for women's entrepreneurial success and aspirations, thereby reinforcing the attitude that women entrepreneurs "aren't really serious." In the areas in which the business press profiles stray from a realistic reflection of women entrepreneurs and their businesses, the media risks reinforcing those situational barriers that stereotype women in business and society. Because of the influence the business media has on all members of the business community, media coverage contributes to the glass barrier that women entrepreneurs currently encounter and influences its persistence as an obstacle for those who may follow in the future.

ACKNOWLEDGMENT

The authors gratefully acknowledge the support of the Babson College Board of Research for partial funding of this research. In addition, Babson College librarians Frances Nilsson and Rachel Zyirek provided invaluable assistance with the details of our literature search. We are solely responsible for any errors or omissions.

NOTES

1. For this study, we use the term "normative" to describe (theoretically) common or even imitable characteristics of the entrepreneur that are positioned in the profile as significant contributors to the success of the subject's venture (per Maruso &Weinzimmer, 1999). For example, the sheer frequency of appearance of experiences that are conventionally understood to be barriers to personal success in the profiles might lead consumers of the literature to interpret that the overcoming of personal obstacles is normative and even motivating for women engaged in entrepreneurship.
2. In the strictest sense, a profile is a "concise biographical sketch" (Merriam-Webster, 2002). For this study, we defined a profile to be a substantive article with features of both business case studies and personal biographies, such as the entrepreneur's inspiration for participation in a market or industry, characteristics of the firm or industry, references to the subject entrepreneur's motivation for start-up and related personality characteristics, among others. More than two-thirds of the articles studied focused on an individual entrepreneurial profile, with 31% of the articles including profiles of multiple ventures and entrepreneurs.
3. Use of the keyword phrase "women business owners" was also examined however one of the major databases, ABI/INFORM, did not begin using this keyword phrase as a category until 1998. Furthermore, some of the subjects of interest for this study do not own their businesses, although they may have founded the business and continue to lead them. Therefore, we determined that "women entrepreneurs" was the more powerful search phrase.
4. Circulation numbers for *Black Enterprise, Forbes, Inc., and Working Woman* were taken from eCirc, accessed on 1/15/02 indicating analyzed paid circulation averages for six months ended 6/30/01. See http://abcas1.access-abc.com/ecirc. Circulation numbers for *Nation's Business* (p. 1193) and *Success* (p. 5516) are taken from Ulrich's International Periodical Directory, 1998. Circulation for *Hispanic* is a guaranteed BPA-audited circulation from http://www.hispanicmagazine.com/advertising/hispanicrates02-nat.html accessed on 1/16/02.
5. Phenomenologically, we recognize that women entrepreneurs are active agents in, and authorities about, their business achievements (per Lindlof, 1996) but reasoned that their agency and authority may be tempered by other content in individual articles. (In other words, we reasoned that there were many other variables that influenced the profile subject's control over, and understanding of, her business and personal circumstances, whether

she articulated those influences or not. The interviewing and editing processes may have also modified the importance that the profile subject may have attributed to particular issues.)
6. A larger study of 212 woman-led firms in Massachusetts also showed a concentration among professional services, construction services, travel & leisure, and technology as the leading four industries (Langowitz, 2002).

REFERENCES

Baker, T., Aldrich, H. E., & Liou, N. (1997). Invisible entrepreneurs: The neglect of women business owners by mass media and scholarly journals in the USA. *Entrepreneurship and Regional Development, 9*(3), 221–233.

Baron, R., Markman, G., & Hirza, A. (2001). Perceptions of women and men as entrepreneurs: Evidence for differential effects of attributional augmenting. *Journal of Applied Psychology, 86*(5), 923–929.

Bird, D. (1989). Corporate ad savvy (Part 1). *Direct Marketing, 52*(4), 62–66.

Birley, S. (1989). Female entrepreneurs: Are they really any different? *Journal of Small Business Management, 27*(1), 32–37.

Brody, E.W. (1994). PR is to experience shat marketing is to expectations. *Public Relations Quarterly, 39*(2), 20–22.

Brush, C. (1997). Women-owned businesses: Obstacles and opportunities. *Journal of Developmental Entrepreneurship, 2*(1), 1–24.

Center for Women's Business Research (CWBR). (2001). *Women-owned businesses in 2002: Trends in the U.S. and 50 States.* Washington, DC: CWBR in conjunction with the U.S. Bureau of the Census.

Cliff, J. (1998). Does one size fit all? Exploring the relationship between attitudes towards growth, gender, and business size. *Journal of Business Venturing, 13*(6), 523–542.

Coleman, S., & Carsky, M. (1996). Understanding the market of women-owned businesses. *Journal of Retail Banking, 18*(2), 479.

Corning, B. (1999). Great reputations. *Accountancy, 123*(1267), 38–39.

D'Alessandro, D. (1990). Image building—Why is it so difficult? *Executive Speeches, 5*(4), 7–13.

eCirc. (2001). http://abcas1.accessabc.com/ecirc Retrieved March 2002.

Faludi, S. (1991). *Backlash: The undeclared war against American women.* New York: Anchor Books.

Galen, M. (1999). Realizing benefits from a merger. *Executive Excellence, 16*(10), 14.

Gartner, W.B. (1990). What are we talking about when we talk about entrepreneurship? *Journal of Business Venturing, 5*, 15–28.

Gundry, L., & Ben-Joseph, M. (2001). *Women entrepreneurs in the new millennium: Recent progress and future directions for research, entrepreneurship development and teaching.* Coleman Council for Entrepreneurship Education White Paper, CEAE Coleman Foundation.

Gunning, J. (2000). *The idea of the entrepreneur role as distinctly human action: A history of progress.* Oman: College of Commerce and Economics. Sultan Qaboos University.

http://www.gunning.cafeprogressive.com/subjecti/workpape/role_ent.htm (Retrieved October 2001).

Haynes, G.W., & Haynes, D.C. (1999). The debt structure of small businesses owned by women in 1987 and 1993. *Journal of Small Business Management, 37*(2), 1–19.

Hispanic Magazine circulation. (2002). http://www.hispanicmagazine.com/advertising/hispanicrates02-nat.html (Retrieved March 2002).

Knight, F. (1921). *Risk, uncertainty, and profit.* New York: Houghton-Mifflin.

Langowitz, N. (2002). *The top woman-led businesses in Massachusetts.* Wellesley, MA: The Center for Women's Leadership at Babson College.

Lindlof, T. (1996). Seeking a path of greatest resistance: The self becoming method. In D. Grodin & T. Lindlof (Eds.), *Constructing the self in a mediated world* (pp. 179–205). Thousand Oaks, CA: Sage.

Maruso, L., & Weinzimmer, L (1999). *A normative framework to assess small-firm entry strategies: A resource-based view.* Paper presented at the Annual Meeting of the Small Business Institute Directors' Association, San Francisco, CA.

Merriam-Webster Company. (2002). *Merriam Webster-Online Language Center: The Dictionary.* http://www.m-w.com/netdict.htm (Retrieved January 2002).

Moore, D.P., & Buttner, H. (1997). *Women entrepreneurs: Moving beyond the glass ceiling.* Thousand Oaks, CA: Sage.

National Foundation for Women Business Owners (NFWBO). (2001). *Entrepreneurial vision in action: Exploring the growth among women- and men-owned firms.* Washington, DC: National Foundation for Women Business Owners [name changed after publication to the Center for Women's Business Research].

Neuendorf, K.A. (2001). *The content analysis guidebook.* Thousand Oaks, CA: Sage.

Renkema, J., & Hoeken, H. (1998). The influence of negative newspaper publicity on corporate image in the Netherlands. *Journal of Business Communication, 35*(4), 521–535.

Shelby, A. (1988). A macro theory of management communication. *Journal of Business Communication, 25*(2), 13–27.

Starr, J., & Yudkin, M. (1996). *Women entrepreneurs: A review of current research.* Wellesley, MA: Wellesley College Centers for Women.

Swift, P. (1992–93). The conscience of a mercenary. *Public Relations Quarterly, 37*(4), 3–32.

Taylor, N., Hobbs, R., Nilsson, F., O'Halloran, K., & Preisser, C. (2000). *The rise of the term social entrepreneurship in print publications.* Paper presented at Babson-Kauffman Entrepreneurial Research Conference, Boston, MA.

Tuchman, G. (1978). *Making news.* New York: Free Press.

Turow, J. (1997). *Media systems in society: Understanding industries, strategies and power.* White Plains, NY: Longman.

Ulrich's International Periodical Directory. (1998). New York: R.R. Bowker.

Von Mises, L. (1966). *Human action: A treatise on economics.* Chicago: Henry Regnery Company.

Wolf, N. (1991). *The beauty myth.* New York: William Morrow.

APPENDIX 1

Profile Articles Used in Content Analysis

Alexander, J. (1998). Tough as nails. *Working Woman, 23*(10), 58–62.
Asirvatham, S. (1997). Fast learner. *Success, 44*(8), 68–71.
Boram, J. (1996). Looking for Ms. Goodwrench. *Nation's Business, 84*(10), 14.
Borrego, A.M. (1999). Motherhood gives birth to companies, too. *Inc., 21*(16), 17–18.
Brown, A. (1997). A new lease on life. *Black Enterprise, 27*(12), 28–30.
Chapa, J. (1998). Conquering the recruitment challenge. *Hispanic, 11*(6), 62.
Clarke, R., & Wright, M. (2000). Running with the big dogs. *Black Enterprise, 30*(7), 250–252.
Clarke, R. (1998). A tough act to copy. *Black Enterprise, 28*(7), 195.
Conlin, M. (1996). Massages while you wait. *Forbes, 158*(15), 132–133.
Crowley, L. (1996). Fueling your own success. *Working Woman, 21*(10), 40–43.
Cubbage, J. (1999). In pursuit of artistic endeavors. *Black Enterprise, 30*(1), 28–30.
Dentzer, S. (1997–1998). Q & A: Merle Aiko Okawara. *Working Woman, 23*(1), 30–31.
Dillon, K. (2000). Three women and a kiosk. *Inc., 22*(1), 60–62.
Donovan, D. (1998). Where are they now? *Forbes, 161*(10), 88–90.
Gite, L., & Baskerville, D. (1996). Black women entrepreneurs on the rise. *Black Enterprise, 27*, 72–74.
Godfrey, N. (1998). Just B. *Working Woman, 23*(10), 30–32.
Godfrey, N. (1998–1999). Talent scout. *Working Woman, 24*(1), 28–31.
Gorr, Y. (1998). The art of creating Christmas cards. *Hispanic, 11*(12), 64.
Granados, C. (1999). Corporate exodus. *Hispanic, 12*(7/8), 49.
Grover, M.B. (1998). Starting a company is like going to war. *Forbes, 162*(10), 184–193.
Hayes, C. (1998). Business dynamos. *Black Enterprise 29*(1), 58–60.
Hurt, H. (1997). Anatomy of an IPO. *Working Woman, 22*(6), 28–33.
Maynard, R. (1996). If the shoe fits.... *Nation's Business, 84*(10), 16.
McMenamin, B. (1998). Pistols and perfume. *Forbes, 161*(12), 45–46.
Morais, R. (1999). An artisan discovers cash flow. *Forbes, 164*(10), 150–152.
Moran, T. (1996). A business maximized at home. *Success, 43*(10), 52–56.
Munk, N., & Oliver, S. (1996). Women of the valley. *Forbes, 158*(15), 102–108.
Nelton, S. (1997). A scrappy entrepreneur. *Nation's Business, 85*(6), 12–14.
Oliver, S. (1996). How Katherine Hammer reinvented herself. *Forbes, 158*(4), 98–103.
Parch, L. (1998). Beyond Alice's restaurant. *Working Woman, 23*(5), 15.
Pofeldt, E, (1997). The self-made woman. *Success, 44*(5), 36–40.
Post, T. (1999). The convergence gamble. *Forbes, 163*(4), 112–117.
Riley, J. (1999). Latinas: Natural-born entrepreneurs? *Hispanic, 12*(10), 86.
Rubin, H. (1999). The loneliness of the long-distance soloist. *Inc., 21*(18), 128–30.
Terry-Azios, D.A. (2000). Carmen Bermudez. *Hispanic, 13*(6), 28.
Visser, M. (1999). Breaking the mold. *Success, 46*(5), 38–39.

Wallach, J. (1997–1998). Q & A : Linda E Harnevo. *Working Woman, 23*(1), 42–43.
Walmac, A. (1998). Paper chase. *Working Woman, 23*(9), 36–38.
Walmac, A. (1999a). Full of beans. *Working Woman, 24*(2), 38–40.
Walmac, A. (1999b). Tools for recovery. *Working Woman, 24*(3), 32–34.
Walmac, A. (1999c). Baking for dollars. *Working Woman, 24*(7), 36–37.
Young, J. (1996). Object lesson. *Forbes, 158*(5), 80–81.
Zimmerman, E. (1998). Shelving prejudice. *Success, 45*(12), 36–37.

CHAPTER 6

WOMEN MICRO ENTREPRENEURS IN HONG KONG

Balancing the Personal with the Business

Evelyn G. H. Ng and Catherine W. Ng

ABSTRACT

Recent census and statistical data show that the number of female self-employed persons and female employers in Hong Kong is rising. Also, female sole proprietors and joint owners, compared to male, are younger, less likely to be married, more likely to be living alone and increasingly more educated. Information about female micro entrepreneurs in Hong Kong and elsewhere suggest that applying conventional conceptions of business success in terms of company size, sales volume and net profit to this group is problematic. Instead, intangibles such as independence, self-esteem and family well-being are equally important considerations. Interviews conducted with women micro-business owners reveal that they are extremely independent, resilient and hardworking, and that they are alert to business opportunities and set high standards of customer service quality for themselves and their staff. They are also found to be hampered by familial obligations which often fall mainly on them. To better facilitate the development of entrepreneurial spirit, there is a need for the government and business associations to adopt a more gendered perspective of entrepreneurship and to recognize female entrepreneurs' struggle with personal and business matters.

INTRODUCTION

There has been a vast array of academic interest in the many aspects of economic development in Hong Kong as one of the "Asian Dragons," and its miraculous rise within a capitalist framework. Entrepreneurship has been seen as an important facet of Hong Kong's industrial development, and has garnered a fair share of research interest (e.g., Cheah & Hu, 1996; Enright, Scott, & Dodwell, 1997; Lau & Snell, 1996; Siu & Martin, 1992). However, much of the research focus has mostly been on small and medium size manufacturing enterprises (e.g., Lau, Chan, & Man, 1999; Sit, 1985; Sit & Wong, 1989) and in the main, does not deal separately with female or male business ownership. Comparatively, women business owners or entrepreneurs are an invisible group.[1] A start however, has been made by some researchers (Ho, 1997; Siu & Chu, 1994) to open up some space for gendered perspectives in the study of entrepreneurship in Hong Kong, although their focus continues to be in the manufacturing sector.

Stevenson (1986) finds that while research interest in women entrepreneurs began in the 1970s in North America, some of the research methods were questionable, often using a structured survey questionnaire to impose male-centered notions on female respondents. There was little attempt to find out the "world of the female business owner." In our present exploratory study, we have chosen to delve into issues that are relevant to women micro entrepreneurs by conducting in-depth interviews with a number of Hong Kong respondents to understand a little of this world. We define micro entrepreneurs as business owners who are self-employed or who employ fewer than 10 employees. Based on the data from two female micro entrepreneurs, three women business owners' associations, and government census and statistics figures, this paper is an initial attempt to see if Hong Kong women business owners share some of the information that we know about their counterparts in North America and in developing economies which have different cultural and economic systems. Our study also aims to examine the possible reasons for the invisibility of this unique group of Hong Kong women, and to shed light on what, if any, can be done to enhance their satisfaction level as micro entrepreneurs.

In an influential report by Reynolds et al. (2000), *Global Entrepreneurship Monitor: 2000 Executive Report*, which surveyed 21 countries worldwide,[2] it is found that entrepreneurship is strongly associated with national economic growth. The report finds that increased participation of women entrepreneurs is critical to long term economic prosperity. It is strongly suggested that women's participation in entrepreneurship is a potential economic resource of real significance to most nations. While recognizing that it would prove to be a cultural challenge, the report calls for policies that would release the capacity of women to engage in entrepreneurship. We hope our paper contributes to that policy direction.

WOMEN BUSINESS OWNERS IN NORTH AMERICA

Stevenson (1986), researching within the North American context, contends that historically women have been confined to the domestic realm and so were denied access to the resources that enable entrepreneurship, namely capital, business and technical education, and prior management experience.

More recently, Nelton (1998) traces a more positive outlook for women business owners in the United States indicating that since the 1970s, women have gained in management experience to move on and start their own companies and to take over family firms. She identifies a 1997 study by the National Foundation for Women Business Owners (NFWBO) which reportedly finds that American women today own about a third of all U.S. companies, and in addition, appear to be moving rapidly into areas largely dominated by men, namely, construction, wholesale trade, transportation, communications, agribusiness and manufacturing. It is claimed that this rising presence of successful women entrepreneurs has changed the business climate. It is now more acceptable for women to take over companies run by their fathers or husbands, and for local chambers of commerce to accept gradually the idea of women as business leaders and business owners. What this means is that the presence of good female business owners as role models has created a cyclical effect of encouraging more acceptance of women business owners, thus generating a positive climate for their increase. She notes further that venture capitalists are now beginning to invest in companies run by such women.

WOMEN BUSINESS OWNERS IN DEVELOPING COUNTRIES

The amount of data regarding women entrepreneurs in developed economies is steadily increasing, but as noted by Singh, Ruthie, and Muhammed (2001), there is a paucity of research on women enterprises in developing economies where the milieu is very different. The lack of attention has been acknowledged by Tinker (1990), who, working within the "women in development" paradigm, explains that if size of enterprise is an important criterion, then women are not seen as significant economic actors, and this was largely the case in the early 1970s when they were invisible in the informal sector studies. Since then, though, enterprises run by women have slowly begun to be recognized as a major source of employment, especially for a developing economy.

In addition, Tinker (1990) finds that enterprises run by women tend to cluster around "micro enterprises," which loosely refers to those enterprises involving individual women and their family members. Their business (e.g., operating as street vendors or market sellers in urban areas) however, is perceived as an extension of their domestic activity. Because they do not offer employment to others in any significant way, they are not popular subjects in economic research projects. Such enterprises have been considered lacking in business acumen because the profits are not reinvested back into the enterprises in order to expand, but instead are used to improve children's education or family nutritional needs. Furthermore, such self-employed women operate enterprises that have weak market integration and strong face-to-face customer relations instead. Enterprises by women who work from home (such as knitting with hand machines, rolling cigarettes, or assembling toys) are vertically integrated into a larger economic activity, but again these do not generate large profits or employ many workers. Tinker (1990) argues that women micro entrepreneurs may have a different set of priorities and values, and that programs designed to help them should accept their values, and not undermine their effort by requirements of growth. Their resistance to business growth may be traced to fears that men may take over when the enterprise gets big or that an increase in size brings higher risks which they are not prepared to take.

While Hong Kong is considered as a developed economy belonging to a group known as "Newly Industrialized Countries" (NICs), women micro entrepreneurs in Hong Kong similar to those in developing economies, have also been rather "invisible." It might therefore be worthwhile to examine relevant studies conducted in developing economies to see if the findings are instructive for our understanding of Hong Kong's case.

Singh et al. (2001) conducted a gender-based performance analysis of 200 micro and small enterprises in four villages in Java, Indonesia. The majority (94%) of the respondents are sole proprietors within the informal sector. Women own or operate 56% of these enterprises. Their analysis is primarily about the factors influencing the performance of these female enterprises. Their findings suggest a number of broad themes common in many women entrepreneurship studies, such as:

1. Male enterprises dominate in the production/manufacturing sector while women enterprises dominate in food processing and trade subsectors.
2. The average annual growth rate is higher for enterprises by male entrepreneurs, and the growth rate for male and female owned enterprises varies significantly between them in the same sector.
3. Male entrepreneurs are younger and have more training.
4. Enterprises with a higher number of workers perform better than those with a lower number.
5. Family members constitute a major share of the total workforce for both male and female enterprises.

In summation, Singh et al. (2001) conclude that in developed countries, significant variables influencing performance are level of education, previous experience, environment, occupational experience, and skills. In contrast, in developing economies, important variables are total number of family workers and industry sector. Compared to male enterprises, female enterprises are usually found in traditional and less dynamic markets where prospects for growth are relatively limited. In addition, age of enterprise and age of entrepreneurs are significant variables. More important, similar to Tinker's (1990) conclusions, Singh et al. (2001) also suggest that female entrepreneurs have different objectives from their male counterparts. This gender difference might be because women are more likely than men to be in sectors which are less oriented to growth.

WOMEN BUSINESS OWNERS IN HONG KONG

Demographic Profile

Our examination of the latest census data suggests that there are two categories of business owners: (1) Self-employed—A person who works for profit or fees in his/her own business/profession, neither employed by someone nor employing others, and (2) Employer—A person who works for profit or fees in his/her own business/profession and employs one or more persons to work for him/her.

Table 6.1 shows the proportion of self-employed and employer persons by sex for the years 1986, 1991, 1996, and 2001. Over the years, the proportion of female self-employed persons has increased from 12.4% in 1986 to 13.4% in 1991, 15.3% in 1996 and 17.9% in 2001; so has the proportion of female employers, correspondingly, from 7.1% to 10.3%, 12.6% and 16.4%.

Table 6.1. Number of Self-Employed Persons and Employers by Sex (1986, 1991, 1996 & 2001)[a,b]

	Self-employed persons				Employers			
	Male		Female		Male		Female	
	'000	(%)	'000	(%)	'000	(%)	'000	(%)
1986	131.9	(87.6%)	18.7	(12.4%)	109.4	(92.9%)	8.4	(7.1%)
1991	124.6	(86.6%)	19.3	(13.4%)	137.0	(89.7%)	15.7	(10.3%)
1996	121.5	(84.7%)	22.0	(15.3%)	148.2	(87.4%)	21.4	(12.6%)
2001	166.4	(82.1%)	36.3	(17.9%)	137.5	(83.6%)	26.9	(16.4%)

[a] Source: Census and Statistics Department, Hong Kong Government.
[b] Figures are rounded to the nearest hundred, and the percentages therefore may not add up to 100.0%.

Male self-employed persons have become older (highest percentage group was 28.8% in the age range 30–39 in 1986 and 38.0% in 40–49 in 2001). In contrast, female self-employed persons have become younger. In 1986, close to half (48.7%) of them were at 50 or over. In 2001, the number dropped to 19.3%, and 32.8% were in the age range 40–49. In 2001, 47.9% of female self-employed persons were under 40 years of age; the corresponding number for male self-employed persons was 31.1% (see Table 6.2a).

With reference to female and male employers, their age profiles share a similar pattern over the years, with female employers slightly younger than male employers. In 2001, for both sexes, about 40% of employers fell in the age range of 40–49 (see Table 6.2b).

Table 6.2a. Number of Self-Employed Persons by Age by Sex (1986, 1991, 1996 & 2001)[a,b]

	1986		1991		1996		2001	
Age	Male	Female	Male	Female	Male	Female	Male	Female
15–19	*	*	0.4%	2.1%	0.4%	2.7%	0.3%	2.5%
20–29	11.3%	11.2%	10.0%	14.0%	8.0%	18.6%	7.5%	17.9%
30–39	28.8%	17.6%	29.8%	24.4%	28.8%	28.2%	23.3%	27.5%
40–49	23.1%	21.4%	27.9%	23.3%	34.8%	29.1%	38.0%	32.8%
50–59	23.2%	25.7%	19.8%	15.5%	18.3%	12.3%	22.4%	13.2%
60 and over	13.4%	23.0%	12.0%	20.7%	9.7%	9.5%	8.4%	6.1%

[a] Source: Census and Statistics Department, Hong Kong Government.
[b] Figures are rounded to the nearest hundred, and the percentages therefore may not add up to 100.0%.
* Figures collected in the census exercise that are too small for estimation purpose are suppressed.

Table 6.2b. Number of Employers by Age by Sex (1986, 1991, 1996 & 2001)[a,b]

	1986		1991		1996		2001	
Age	Male	Female	Male	Female	Male	Female	Male	Female
15–19	*	—	*	—	*	—	*	—
20–29	9.0%	10.7%	7.8%	12.1%	5.1%	9.4%	3.6%	5.6%
30–39	30.8%	39.3%	33.6%	43.9%	31.4%	42.5%	24.4%	29.4%
40–49	27.1%	28.6%	32.3%	27.4%	36.8%	33.6%	39.7%	39.8%
50–59	21.7%	11.9%	17.2%	12.7%	17.5%	11.2%	22.5%	19.3%
60 and over	11.3%	9.5%	9.1%	4.5%	9.1%	3.7%	9.8%	5.9%

[a] Source: Census and Statistics Department, Hong Kong Government.
[b] Figures are rounded to the nearest hundred, and the percentages therefore may not add up to 100.0%.
— Insignificant figures.
* Figures collected in the census exercise that are too small for estimation purpose are suppressed.

Tables 6.3a and 6.3b show the proportion of self-employed persons and employers by marital status by sex for the years 1986, 1991, 1996 and 2001. The proportion of married male self-employed persons remained stable between 81.7% in 1986 to 79.8% in 2001. In comparison, the proportion of married female self-employed persons dropped from 61.0% in 1986 to 56.5% in 2001. This might partially be due to the age factor as discussed above. There was also a huge increase in the proportion of never married female self-employed persons from 12.3% in 1986 to 31.4% in 2001. Ng and Ng (2002) have found that not only has the number of never-married

Table 6.3a. Number of Self-Employed Persons by Marital Status by Sex (1986, 1991, 1996 & 2001)[a,b]

	1986		1991		1996		2001	
Marital Status	Male	Female	Male	Female	Male	Female	Male	Female
Never married	15.0%	12.3%	16.5%	17.6%	16.1%	29.1%	16.8%	31.4%
Now married	81.7%	61.0%	80.4%	64.2%	80.9%	58.2%	79.8%	56.5%
Widowed	2.0%	24.1%	1.6%	14.0%	1.1%	7.3%	0.7%	3.6%
Divorced/Separated	1.2%	3.2%	1.4%	4.1%	1.9%	5.5%	2.6%	8.5%

[a] Source: Census and Statistics Department, Hong Kong Government.
[b] Figures are rounded to the nearest hundred, and the percentages therefore may not add up to 100.0%.

Table 6.3b. Number of Employers by Marital Status by Sex (1986, 1991, 1996 & 2001)[a,b]

	1986		1991		1996		2001	
Marital Status	Male	Female	Male	Female	Male	Female	Male	Female
Never married	8.7%	16.7%	10.0%	17.2%	8.0%	15.0%	8.3%	14.1%
Now married	89.4%	64.3%	88.2%	68.8%	90.1%	76.6%	89.6%	74.3%
Widowed	1.3%	14.3%	0.7%	8.3%	0.7%	2.8%	0.7%	4.8%
Divorced/Separated	0.6%	4.8%	1.1%	5.7%	1.1%	6.1%	1.4%	6.7%

[a] Source: Census and Statistics Department, Hong Kong Government.
[b] Figures are rounded to the nearest hundred, and the percentages therefore may not add up to 100.0%

women in Hong Kong been rising, Hong Kong's single working women are driven, achievement-oriented, focused, responsible, disciplined, inquisitive, worldly and proud of themselves. More of them are feeling more affirmative and assertive about their singleness. This might have boosted their confidence in self-employment.

As for the employers group, married men remained at the 90% level over the years, while married women increased slightly from 64.3% in 1986 to 74.3% in 2001. In other words, about half of female self-employed persons are not married while the majority of female employers are married.

Table 6.4 reveals that a higher proportion of female than male self-employed persons and employers live by themselves. This is true throughout the years. In 2001, for example, 5.7% of male self-employed persons (and

Table 6.4. Number of Self-Employed Persons and Employers by Sex and Whether Living Alone (1986, 1991, 1996 & 2001)[a,b]

	Self-employed persons				Employers			
	Male		Female		Male		Female	
	Yes	No	Yes	No	Yes	No	Yes	No
1986	8.7%	91.3%	11.7%	88.3%	3.8%	96.2%	6.0%	94.1%
1991	7.6%	92.4%	7.8%	92.2%	4.3%	95.7%	7.0%	93.0%
1996	6.3%	93.7%	10.0%	90.0%	4.5%	95.5%	6.6%	93.5%
2001	5.7%	94.3%	7.2%	92.8%	4.2%	95.9%	4.8%	95.2%

[a] Source: Census and Statistics Department, Hong Kong Government.
[b] Figures are rounded to the nearest hundred, and the percentages therefore may not add up to 100.0%.

4.2% of male employers) live by themselves, while the corresponding number for female self-employed persons (and female employers) is 7.2% (4.8%).

As regards the education level of self-employed persons, the pattern has changed significantly over the years for both sexes (see Table 6.5a). In 1986, about two-fifths of male self-employed persons were at or above secondary school education level. The proportion rose to about three-quarters in 2001. The corresponding figures for female self-employed persons were about one quarter in 1986 and about four-fifths in 2001. The jump in education level is of course higher among women than among men. What is also interesting is that in 1986, three quarters of female self-employed persons were at primary or lower educational levels. This reflects that education level has not been a major obstacle for women becoming sole proprietors and joint owners. In fact, throughout the years, the proportion of female self-employed persons in the category of "no schooling/kindergarten" is higher than that for male self-employed persons (40.6% vs. 7.1% in 1986, 24.9% vs. 6.3% in 1991, 10.5% vs. 2.8% in 1996 and 4.4% vs. 1.4% in 2001). This might be because the labor market is less accessible to women with poorer educational background, pushing them into considering self-employment as the alternative option. By 2001, female self-employed persons are on the whole slightly more educated than male self-employed persons. Many of these educated female self-employed persons have started companies providing professional and business services (see Tables 6.6a and 6.6b).

As for the education level of employers, females and males share the same pattern (see Table 6.5b). Over the years, the highest percentage is at the secondary/matriculation group (about 50%), and there is a decrease in the lower-end (no schooling/kindergarten) and an increase in the higher-end (tertiary: degree).

Table 6.5a. Number of Self-Employed Persons by Education Attainment by Sex (1986, 1991, 1996 & 2001)[a,b]

Education Attainment	1986		1991		1996		2001	
	Male	Female	Male	Female	Male	Female	Male	Female
No Schooling/ Kindergarten	7.1%	40.6%	6.3%	24.9%	2.8%	10.5%	1.4%	4.4%
Primary	50.7%	35.8%	43.7%	32.1%	33.5%	22.3%	25.7%	16.3%
Secondary/ Matriculation	38.7%	19.3%	44.9%	32.1%	54.6%	44.1%	62.0%	54.8%
Tertiary: non-degree	1.4%	2.1%	1.7%	3.6%	3.2%	7.3%	3.7%	8.0%
Tertiary: degree	2.0%	2.7%	3.4%	7.3%	5.9%	16.4%	7.1%	16.8%

[a] Source: Census and Statistics Department, Hong Kong Government.
[b] Figures are rounded to the nearest hundred, and the percentages therefore may not add up to 100.0%.

Table 6.5b. Number of Employers by Education Attainment by Sex (1986, 1991, 1996 & 2001)[a,b]

Education Attainment	1986		1991		1996		2001	
	Male	Female	Male	Female	Male	Female	Male	Female
No Schooling/ Kindergarten	2.6%	7.1%	2.0%	2.5%	1.3%	*	0.8%	1.5%
Primary	28.3%	20.2%	21.5%	15.3%	17.1%	12.1%	15.2%	11.2%
Secondary/ Matriculation	52.8%	54.8%	57.3%	55.4%	57.7%	60.3%	57.1%	58.4%
Tertiary: non-degree	4.5%	4.8%	5.5%	4.5%	6.8%	8.4%	7.0%	7.4%
Tertiary: degree	11.9%	13.1%	13.6%	22.3%	17.2%	18.2%	19.9%	21.6%

[a] Source: Census and Statistics Department, Hong Kong Government.
[b] Figures are rounded to the nearest hundred, and the percentages therefore may not add up to 100.0%.
* Figures collected in the census exercise that are too small for estimation purpose are suppressed.

So, what we are seeing is that female self-employed persons, in comparison to male self-employed persons, are younger, less likely to be married, more likely to be living alone, and increasingly more educated. In contrast, the demographic gender differences are not so marked in the employers group. It appears that female sole proprietors and joint owners constitute a very unique group among business owners in Hong Kong.

As expected, gender segregation by industry is obvious among self-employed persons (see Table 6.6a). Females congregate in the categories of "Wholesale, retail and import/export trades, restaurants and hotels" (41.9% of female self-employed persons fell in that category in 2001) and "Community, social and personal services" (31.7%). Males, in contrast, congregate in the categories of "Transport, storage and communications" (35.6% of male self-employed persons fell in that category in 2001) and "Construction" (14.1%). In the employer group, both females and males congregate in the industry "Wholesale, retail and import/export trades, restaurants and hotels" (45.5% for men and 54.3% for women in 2001) (see Table 6.6b).

Not only are women and men closer in their demographics in the small- and medium-size business sector (i.e., the employers group), they are also more similar in their choice of industry type. In contrast, in the micro-business sector (i.e., the self-employed group of sole proprietors and joint owners), women and men pursue different industries.

Table 6.6a. Number of Self-Employed Persons by Industry by Sex (1986, 1991, 1996 & 2001)[a,b]

Industry	1986 Male	1986 Female	1991 Male	1991 Female	1996 Male	1996 Female	2001 Male	2001 Female
Manufacturing	10.3%	2.7%	7.1%	3.6%	6.3%	2.3%	5.6%	1.4%
Construction	1.4%	*	3.1%	—	3.5%	*	14.1%	1.7%
Wholesale, retail and import/export trades, restaurants and hotels	35.3%	66.8%	32.3%	59.6%	32.7%	50.0%	26.9%	41.9%
Transport, storage and communications	31.9%	3.7%	41.7%	5.7%	41.4%	2.7%	35.6%	2.8%
Financing, insurance, real estate and business services	0.8%	1.6%	1.6%	2.1%	3.8%	9.1%	6.7%	19.6%
Community, social and personal services	9.3%	10.2%	8.9%	22.3%	9.2%	33.2%	10.2%	31.7%
Others	11.0%	15.0%	5.3%	6.2%	3.0%	3.2%	1.0%	1.1%

Table 6.6b. Number of Employers by Industry by Sex (1986, 1991, 1996 & 2001)[a,b]

Industry	1986 Male	1986 Female	1991 Male	1991 Female	1996 Male	1996 Female	2001 Male	2001 Female
Manufacturing	33.6%	29.8%	30.4%	20.4%	23.5%	15.9%	18.5%	13.8%
Construction	7.6%	*	8.9%	1.9%	9.6%	1.4%	12.0%	2.2%
Wholesale, retail and import/export trades, restaurants and hotels	40.8%	51.2%	42.4%	52.9%	45.1%	56.5%	45.5%	54.3%
Transport, storage and communications	4.4%	*	4.5%	3.8%	5.9%	2.8%	5.7%	4.1%
Financing, insurance, real estate and business services	4.5%	6.0%	6.1%	7.0%	7.5%	11.2%	8.9%	13.0%
Community, social and personal services	7.3%	8.3%	6.4%	12.7%	7.2%	11.7%	8.5%	12.3%
Others	1.9%	*	1.3%	*	1.3%	*	0.9%	*

[a] Source: Census and Statistics Department, Hong Kong Government.
[b] Figures are rounded to the nearest hundred, and the percentages therefore may not add up to 100.0%.
— Insignificant figures. * Figures collected in the census exercise that are too small for estimation purpose are suppressed.

Lastly, as expected, on the whole, there is an earnings gap between the sexes in both the self-employed persons and employers sectors (see Tables 6.7a and 6.7b). However, the gap has narrowed over the years. In 1986, 78.1% of female self-employed persons earned less than HK$3,000, compared to 36.2% of male self-employed persons earning the same. Although in 2001, the percentage was still higher for women (18.7%) than for men (5.2%), it had narrowed quite substantially. More important, in 2001, a higher proportion of female self-employed persons (5.2%) earned HK$30,000 and over than male self-employed persons (3.7%). While the earnings gap between women male employers had also narrowed over the years, by 2001, the proportion of female employers earning HK$20,000 and above (49.8%) was lower than that of male employers (59.9%).

Table 6.7a. Number of Self-Employed Persons by Monthly Employment Earnings by Sex (1986, 1991, 1996 & 2001)[a,b]

Monthly employment earnings	1986		1991		1996		2001	
HK$	Male	Female	Male	Female	Male	Female	Male	Female
<3,000	36.2%	78.1%	7.1%	28.0%	2.9%	19.1%	5.2%	18.7%
3,000–3,999	33.7%	13.9%	7.1%	18.7%	2.1%	7.3%	3.2%	6.3%
4,000–4,999	18.1%	3.2%	10.4%	19.7%	3.0%	7.3%	3.0%	6.1%
5,000–5,999	6.6%	*	15.2%	9.3%	5.0%	8.6%	5.2%	6.3%
6,000–6,999	2.5%	1.6%	19.7%	8.8%	6.0%	8.6%	6.3%	6.9%
7,000–7,999	1.2%	*	13.9%	3.1%	7.2%	6.8%	7.2%	5.2%
8,000–8,999	0.5%	*	10.9%	3.1%	12.8%	7.3%	12.1%	7.2%
9,000–9,999	*	*	2.9%	*	9.1%	3.2%	7.5%	3.3%
10,000–14,999	0.8%	*	8.7%	6.2%	31.5%	15.0%	27.7%	19.8%
15,000–19,999	*	*	2.2%	1.6%	10.2%	7.7%	10.8%	6.9%
20,000–29,999	*	—	0.9%	*	6.8%	6.4%	8.2%	8.3%
30,000 and over	*	*	0.9%	*	3.1%	2.7%	3.7%	5.2%

[a] Source: Census and Statistics Department, Hong Kong Government.
[b] Figures are rounded to the nearest hundred, and the percentages therefore may not add up to 100.0%.
— Insignificant figures.
* Figures collected in the census exercise that are too small for estimation purpose are suppressed.

Table 6.7b. Number of Employers by Monthly Employment Earnings by Sex (1986, 1991, 1996 & 2001)[a,b]

Monthly employment earnings	1986		1991		1996		2001	
HK$	Male	Female	Male	Female	Male	Female	Male	Female
<3,000	8.7%	26.2%	1.6%	4.5%	*	*	2.4%	3.3%
3,000–3,999	13.6%	15.5%	0.9%	4.5%	0.2%	*	0.4%	*
4,000–4,999	16.1%	14.3%	2.2%	6.4%	*	1.4%	0.3%	*
5,000–5,999	16.2%	15.5%	5.0%	8.9%	0.6%	2.8%	0.9%	1.9%
6,000–6,999	11.5%	9.5%	6.8%	7.6%	1.0%	2.8%	0.9%	1.5%
7,000–7,999	5.7%	*	6.4%	4.5%	1.1%	2.8%	1.2%	2.2%
8,000–8,999	6.3%	*	9.6%	8.9%	2.5%	5.1%	2.3%	3.3%
9,000–9,999	0.9%	*	4.0%	2.5%	1.6%	1.9%	1.7%	2.2%
10,000–14,999	10.8%	9.5%	29.6%	22.9%	19.4%	22.4%	15.7%	19.0%
15,000–19,999	3.4%	*	11.6%	9.6%	18.7%	17.3%	14.3%	15.2%
20,000–29,999	3.7%	*	11.7%	9.6%	25.2%	21.5%	27.3%	24.9%
30,000 and over	3.1%	*	10.7%	10.2%	29.5%	21.5%	32.6%	24.9%

[a] Source: Census and Statistics Department, Hong Kong Government.
[b] Figures are rounded to the nearest hundred, and the percentages therefore may not add up to 100.0%.
* Figures collected in the census exercise that are too small for estimation purpose are suppressed.

The earnings gap between female and male self-employed persons and employers could be due to the size of their businesses as measured by number of personnel inclusive of the owner(s) as well as salaried and unpaid employees. We were unable to obtain female and male self-employed persons' and employers' firm sizes. The best estimate we could get is the Census and Statistics Department's category of "unpaid workers," which includes "working proprietors, active business partners and unpaid family workers." Table 6.8 shows that the proportion of female unpaid workers working in establishments of size 1–9 was 95.7% while the corresponding figure for male unpaid workers was 93.6%. In all other categories of larger size of establishment, the percentage for female unpaid workers was lower than the percentage for male unpaid workers. Presuming that female and male unpaid family workers follow the same distribution pattern across establishments of different sizes, it is reasonable to deduce that the statistics above indicate that female business owners (working proprietors and business partners) are more likely to be owners of smaller establishments than male business owners. It is worth noting that Hong Kong thrives on small firms. In 2001, 87.5% of establishments in Hong Kong have fewer than 10 personnel, and 94.6% fewer than 20 (see Table 6.8).

Table 6.8. Number of Establishments and Unpaid Workers Analyzed by Size of Establishment and Gender, First Quarter 2001[a,b]

			Number of Unpaid Workers [d]			
			Male		Female	
Size of establishment (in terms of number of persons engaged) [c]	No. of establishments	(%)	'000	(%)	'000	(%)
1–9	262,461	(87.5%)	122,619	(93.6%)	62,206	(95.7%)
10–19	21,380	(7.1%)	5,612	(4.3%)	1,969	(3.0%)
20–49	10,725	(3.6%)	1,897	(1.4%)	598	(0.9%)
50–99	3,386	(1.1%)	390	(0.3%)	101	(0.2%)
100–199	1,191	(0.4%)	188	(0.1%)	54	(0.1%)
200–499	487	(0.2%)	57	(0.0%)	18	(0.0%)
500–999	138	(0.0%)	101	(0.1%)	21	(0.0%)
≥ 1,000	79	(0.0%)	107	(0.1%)	15	(0.0%)

[a] Source: Census and Statistics Department, Hong Kong Government.
[b] Figures may not add up exactly to the total due to rounding.
[c] Persons engaged: Exclusive of civil servants and comprise (a) individual proprietors and partners, (b) unpaid family workers, and (c) full-time and part-time salaried personnel.
[d] Unpaid workers: Exclusive of civil servants and comprise (a) individual proprietors and partners, and (b) unpaid family workers.

In sum, women business owners in Hong Kong own smaller firms than male business owners. Female self-employed persons' earnings levels are fast catching up with male self-employed persons', while the earnings gap between female and male employers is closing far more slowly. Many women micro-business owners have entered the "Community, social and personal services" and "Financing, insurance, real estate and business services" sectors. A higher proportion of them are highly educated, living alone, not married, and younger. As regards the employers group, women still lag behind men in terms of earnings. They seem to be competing hard against men in the "Wholesale, retail and import/export trades, restaurants and hotels" sector. Women and men employers have similar age profiles and educational backgrounds, although the females are more likely to be unmarried and living alone.

Invisibility of Women Micro-Business Owners

While 17.2% of self-employed persons and employers are female in 2001 (see Table 6.1), literature about women business owners, particularly female mirco entrepreneurs, is few and far between. Siu and Chu's (1994) study is about 18 female entrepreneurs who own manufacturing firms. No data is provided about the size of their enterprises. Their findings point to female entrepreneurs' strained personal relationships with family members and in terms of business-related problems, to operational difficulties and marketing. The researchers call for a specially tailored training program and a consultation center for female entrepreneurs. Ho's (1997) study of factory owners expands the size of the sample of interviewees to 22 female and 22 male "established entrepreneurs." However, it too is confined to the manufacturing industry (clothing). Her findings suggest that among female respondents, their role as an entrepreneur has a greater effect on their domestic role than their male counterparts. Married female entrepreneurs have difficulties maintaining a marriage and single female entrepreneurs have problems finding a partner. Her female respondents reported that unlike other entrepreneurs elsewhere who spoke in terms of personal achievements or job satisfactions, they became entrepreneurs because of "family obligations" or what she terms "entrepreneurial familism" (Ho, 1997, p. 343). In her study, entreprencurial behavior comprises innovation, financial risk-taking and reinvestment. Risk-taking is relatively low for both female and male respondents; innovation for both groups consists of a search for new markets and new product development, and reinvestment is higher among female entrepreneurs.

Sit and Wong's (1989) study on small and medium enterprises focuses also on manufacturing, as well as on export-oriented industries. Apart from a short section under "Sex" in which comparisons are made between female and male entrepreneurs, respondents in their survey are often treated as a whole, with some references to the differences between "petty" (0–9 workers) and "small" (10–49 workers) enterprises, where appropriate. There are about 20 female respondents (8.2% of total respondents), but only 11 replied to the question about their spouses' activities. Six have husbands in trade, three husbands are industrialists, and two husbands are manual workers. The researchers postulate that these women's entry to the manufacturing industry is facilitated by their husband's occupational background, and while they are curious about the lack of women entrepreneurs in manufacturing, are unable to give any solid explanation for their small number.

One slightly different exposition of micro-entrepreneurship in Hong Kong is Smart's (1989) study of the activities of illegal street hawkers in Hong Kong. She attempts to explain the smaller number of women hawkers compared to men as a consequence of the prevailing social perception of street hawking as an "unsuitable vocation for women" (Smart, 1989, p. 25). It is maintained that culturally, the Chinese are averse to letting their women into situations which involve frequent interaction with strangers. She gives detailed anthropological information of the tough conditions under which the illegal hawkers operate, for example dealing with people who may have triad connections, suffering the stress of harassment from law enforcement personnel, and fighting for working space. One would therefore expect that there are few female hawkers. On the contrary, the female to male ratio among hawkers is higher than that reported for self-employed persons. In 1986, government statistics show 7.1 self-employed men to one self-employed woman (i.e., only 12.4% of the self-employed persons group is female; see Table 6.1). Yet, according to the 1981 census data, there are 2.4 male hawkers to every female hawker (Smart, 1989). This implies that female micro entrepreneurs in Hong Kong can be competitive in small dynamic enterprises that demand constant attention to consumer wants.

The interest for us in her study is our broad understanding of (micro) entrepreneurship as the capacity for business owners to take advantage of opportunities to start a new enterprise. Smart (1989) portrays street hawkers in Hong Kong as "independent entrepreneurs" and claim that they occupy a wide range of niches in the existing retailing structures, and are deeply embedded in commodity distribution in the world market. She also finds that street hawking can generate very attractive incomes vis-à-vis wage employment in industrial and commercial sectors. Echoing Tinker's (1990) argument that self-sufficiency is an important component in the trajectory toward economic development, Smart (1989) rightly sites micro entrepreneurship, of which street hawking is but one manifestation, as a positive contribution to the economy. Her findings about street hawking in an urbanized, industrialized society like Hong Kong leads her to conclude that further enquiry about other forms of micro entrepreneurship in developed economies should be encouraged.

Tinker's (1990) and Smart's (1989) work about the importance of micro entrepreneurs suggest to us that entrepreneurship is not only about successful male entrepreneurs and prominent business personalities.[3] In addition, the "petty" (0–9 workers) entrepreneurs in manufacturing (Sit & Wong, 1989) and street hawkers (Smart, 1989) are in a labor intensive sector that often involves paid and unpaid family members. Furthermore, both sectors attract people who lack formal education or social or cultural capital, and provide aspirations for the upwardly mobile. Micro enterprises can be regarded as viable economic activities for people who are disadvantaged because of their position as recent migrants, or for people who are socially dislocated, with limited formal education, limited access to social and economic resources, and who are relatively vulnerable to exploitation and low wages. We see that while women in Hong Kong may not own readily identifiable enterprises like factories in significant numbers, they do participate in independent enterprises. Both the Hong Kong female factory owners and the female hawkers in the studies cited so far show an appreciation for economic initiatives and sheer hard work, and possess the "entrepreneurial element" (Anderson, 1986, p. 157), which is not only about a capacity to maximize given market data but also the alertness to new possibilities.

Life Stories of Two Hong Kong Women Micro-Business Owners

We have seen above that while some information is emerging about female entrepreneurship in Hong Kong, they have tended in the main, toward larger businesses and the manufacturing sector. There is still a general lack of perspective and little insight into women micro-business owners' unique circumstances and experiences, especially in the service sector. Given the large number of women in the wholesale and retail sector and the personal services sector (see Tables 6.6a and 6.6b), specifically in the garment industry, we examine the experiences of two female micro entrepreneurs in these sectors to enable us to obtain a sense of what we earlier referred to as "the world of the female business owner."

Maureen (early 40s): Sole proprietor offering garment alteration services. When she was fifteen, Maureen gave birth to a son, but after 18 years of marriage is now divorced from her former husband who was in business. She now lives with her son, who is a graduate of a local university. She has operated her garment alteration shop in the same shopping mall in a retail and commercial district in Hong Kong for about nine years. She started working since she was 12 in the garment industry, and was an assistant in the sample department of an international sportswear company before it laid off staff in Asia. She was in her 30s when made redundant, and by chance came across the present vacant shop space.

> I thought it might be fun to start my own business. My friends encouraged me and I made the decision in three days ... I had no idea what the economic environment was like. I had no idea if I was in a competitive industry or not. In fact, there were about five to six alteration shops in the mall. I wasn't planning to stay in the business long; in fact I just wasn't planning at all. (Maureen)

Maureen stayed on for nine years but at the time of the interview, confessed that she is at the end of her tether. During the last three years (1999–2002, a period still reeling from the 1997 Asian economic crisis) her business volume has shrunk so much that her average take-home pay (after deducting rent for shop) is only HK$3,000 per month. She would prefer to change her status to become an employee ("a security guard or a salesperson"), but given her age and low educational level, realizes that it would be difficult for her to be hired. What appears to keep her going with the business is her need to earn a living as her son has not contributed to the household expenses ("He asked me to give him a few more years to enjoy himself"), and the support of loyal clients that she has retained, some of whom have become personal friends.

Maureen hires no help and prefers to run the business by herself. A brief stint employing a part-time worker was not satisfactory as she found that the hired help was not hard-working. Maureen's deliberate strategy is to keep her business small so that she can work on her own, and to avoid the stress of managing an employee. Maureen's emphasis on the quality of her work is evident and she hints that a helper would probably not be able to meet her high standard of work. The advantage gained in not depending on an employee, however, has not helped her when she is ill and unable to meet her workload.

Mary (mid 40s): Sole proprietor of a clothes and accessories boutique. Mary had been a full-time homemaker until her son was in his teens. She then ventured into designing and producing small quantities of handbags, or buying them from overseas and selling them to boutique owners that she had befriended when she was their customer. Although she picked up some information from these contacts, she learnt to build up her own network slowly from scratch. She then expanded to clothes and accessories.

She has spent so far about HK$1 million of her savings starting this enterprise and buying stock. She has not been earning a salary for the three years since she began, but explains this lack of returns as equivalent to the fees that she has to pay if she enrolled at a formal business course. The outlay is perceived as buying business knowledge that she would not have obtained at any other business course. Her current foray into retail and as a small-scale wholesaler, is seen as part of a skills training process to hone her personal interest in fashion and a future role as clothes consultant to a loyal clientele.

When she travels to buy new stock, a trusted salesperson is needed to look after the boutique located on the first floor of a building block in a busy shopping area. The availability of such help has proved unstable and the shop would sometimes be closed temporarily. Her clients would ring before they visit although there would be drop-in customers some of the time. She depends on the help of two women to distribute flyers on the pavement right in front of the entrance of the building twice a week, and they would verbally encourage potential customers to visit the shop upstairs. This direct marketing aimed at pedestrians has been helpful, but the small number who eventually visited her shop has not been sufficient as a stable source of customers. Besides selling from her shop, Mary advertises in the "Yellow Pages" (of the telephone directory) and on an ad-hoc basis, takes part in hotel fairs to sell her stock.

DEFINITIONS OF SUCCESS

Drawing from the life stories of the two female micro entrepreneurs interviewed, we find two possible reasons why women become self-employed in Hong Kong. Maureen has to make a living for herself and her son instead of relying on welfare when her husband could not contribute to the family after the dissolution of the marriage. Mary, after many years as a homemaker and primary child care provider, has decided to retrain herself for self-employment in a second career by learning a new trade. She had previously worked in an administrative position in a large company. Both recognize that their age works against them if they had to compete for jobs with younger applicants. In Mary's case, stereotypes about homemakers are another unfavorable factor, and in Maureen's case, low education level and poor English language ability pose additional barriers for her in seeking paid employment.

The two micro entrepreneurs above show some interesting characteristics. They started their own businesses without borrowing money from any agency. Both, as business owners, have not given profit and business growth particular emphases. In fact, Maureen resisted growth, a facet also noted by Tinker's (1990) study of women micro-business owners in developing economies. Their attitude toward their business reflects an emphasis toward self-sufficiency and a decent wage level for themselves after deducting the costs of doing business.

Feminist researchers like Marlow and Strange (1994) contend that the trend in small business research is to treat all women as "honorary men." This is problematic because some presumed business goals may not be achievable for a group where social and economic barriers exist. They note that attention has to be paid to the issue of domestic and waged labor conflicts that many women have to face. It is argued that since women continue to bear the major part of family and home responsibilities, women who undertake business ownership are likely to have different expectations of their experiences of entrepreneurship and hence different conceptions of success. Since business "success" is an important line of enquiry for policymakers and funding organizations, women business owners are disadvantaged when they have different aspirations from the normative (male) model. Most women may accept that profit, growth and employment are important indicators of performance, but social and family constraints can retard their realization for higher accounting figures. Hence, some women already see themselves as having "succeeded" when they can balance their books. This appears to be what Maureen and Mary are aiming for.

A survey of female business owners in Singapore and elsewhere (Mayasami & Goby, 1999) has identified some major motivating factors for female business owners. The factors can be re-configured as: (1) job satisfaction, desire to be one's own boss, freedom and flexibility, independence, (2) presence of opportunities, to put knowledge to use, (3) achievement, personal challenge, desire to realize an ambition, and (4) the need to make more money. Teo (1996), whose findings about women in Singapore are extensively quoted in the above review, finds that successful business women are driven to provide financially for their family and to have control over their lives.

Our two interviewees have reflected some very similar sentiments. Their satisfaction from being self-employed is not solely in relation to financial gains, but also to a large extent to a heightened sense of self-esteem. While devoting much of themselves to their businesses, they remain solely responsible for the domestic duties in their household, and continue to feel a strong sense of obligation toward their family. Our data suggest that women without much prompting, would bring in issues of domestic and family responsibilities when they relate their career development, and so the topic of entrepreneurship and self-employment reflects a complex mix of highly personal and cultural factors at play. The "reconciliation of the competing demands of waged and domestic labor" (Marlow & Strange, 1994, p. 182) is an important variable in small business studies because in the final analysis, this would affect the way these female business owners perceive their success.

WOMEN BUSINESS OWNERS ASSOCIATIONS IN HONG KONG

From our conversations with Hong Kong women micro-business owners, we understand that many of them know little about women business owners associations. Some have heard of a few professional, business and trade associations, but do not feel the need to join. Given that women micro-business owners are often not considered as significant business people, to what extent can they benefit from organized support networks, socially and economically?

Sit and Wong (1989) found that nearly 90% of small and medium business owners have not joined any voluntary associations. They note that while there are a variety of potential associations in Hong Kong (e.g., occupationally-related ones like the Chinese Manufacturers' Association; social and welfare ones like the *kai fong*, literal translation of which is "street workshop," and mutual aid committees or surname or clan organizations), only about 5.1% of the small and medium enterprise respondents in their survey joined industrial associations, and 4.4%, the Chinese Manufacturers' Association. The researchers observe that the respondents operate as "independent entities without any clear sense of sectorial interest or a perceived need to organize among themselves" (Sit & Wong, 1989, p. 125). Smart (1989) also finds that other than informal rotating credit associations[4] and the Hawkers' Association, street hawkers do not appear to be members of religious or other types of associations, although many hawkers are triad members or users of their services in order to advance their interests in a competitive marketplace.

We examine three women business owners organizations that purport to gather together women in business. They are the Ladies' Subcommittee of the Chinese General Chamber of Commerce (LS of the CGCC), the Women Business Owners Club (WBOC), and the Hong Kong Women Professionals and Entrepreneurs Association (HKWPEA) (see Table 6.9). The longest one in existence is the LS of the CGCC. It was established in 1958, 58 years after the founding of the CGCC. The WBOC came about in 1990 as a breakaway group from the Hong Kong Business and Professional Women Association (HKBPW). In 1996, the HKWPEA was established as a sister organization of the Chinese mainland's Women Entrepreneurs of All China Federation of Industry and Commerce.

Of the three associations, the WBOC has the largest membership base (about 200). The majority of the members in WBOC are Westerners, with the remainder of the membership consisting mostly of overseas-educated English-speaking Chinese. In contrast, it is stipulated in CGCC's membership application form that applicants must be Chinese nationals. The LS of the CGCC has a membership of about 100, half of which are called "associates" who belong to an older generation from the present membership. Almost all of the 88 members of HKWPEA are ethnic Chinese. The language adopted in these three groups naturally follows the membership pattern: English for the WBOC, Chinese for the CGCC, and a mixture of English (dominant) and Chinese (minor) for the HKWPEA.

The WBOC consists mostly of women who are business owners or interested in starting businesses. The Chairperson we interviewed is single and 38 years old. She is an English-speaking ethnic Chinese born and educated overseas, and owns a small CPA firm of six staff members set up in 1995. The majority of HKWPEA's members are managers or professionals and we spoke to the incumbent vice-president (incoming President in her early 50s) who was born and raised in Hong Kong. She has two grown-up sons, and has been working for an MNC for 25 years, and now holds several senior positions (Executive Vice President, Regional CEO and Chairman).

Table 6.9. Hong Kong's Women Business Owners Associations

	Ladies' Sub-committee of the Chinese General Chamber of Commerce (LS of CGCC)	Women Business Owners Club (WBOC)	Hong Kong Women Professionals and Entrepreneurs Association (HKWPEA)
Year of establishment	1958 (1900)	1990	1996
Aims	To network among women members of the Chamber by organizing activities for them.	To promote the interests of women in business in general and to promote the specific interests of women business entrepreneurs and owners or women who desire to own their own business.	To enhance professional standard, training and business opportunities and consolidate mutual support for the members.
	To raise women members' involvement in the Chamber's affairs.	To promote women as entrepreneurs and to increase skills in business.	To develop networking opportunities for women executives in business and professions in Hong Kong, mainland China and overseas.
	To assist various committees' works as entrusted by the Chamber's Committee or the General Affairs Sub-Committee.		To respond to the HKSAR Government on various policy consultations.
	To liaise with local and overseas business and professional women associations.		
	To recruit Hong Kong business and professional women into the Chamber's membership.		
Organizational structure	One of the sub-committees under the Committee of CGCC	Run as a business	Non-profit organization
	Chairman, 3 Vice-Chairmen, 2 Honorary Chairmen and about 40 members	Board of directors elected from among the membership (President, Treasurer, Secretary, plus eight directors)	Patron: Anson Chan, former Chief Secretary for Administration
		Administrator	Honorary Advisor: Elsie Leung, Secretary for Justice
			Honorary President: Annie Wu
			Executive Committee: President, two Vice-Presidents, Secretary, Treasurer and Directors
			Eight sub-committees

Table 6.9. Hong Kong's Women Business Owners Associations (Cont.)

	Ladies' Sub-committee of the Chinese General Chamber of Commerce (LS of CGCC)	Women Business Owners Club (WBOC)	Hong Kong Women Professionals and Entrepreneurs Association (HKWPEA)
Membership size	108	About 200	88
Membership profile	All Chinese nationals	70% Westerners	45 business executives
		30% overseas-educated Chinese	20 business owners or entrepreneurs
			17 professionals (inclusive of academics)
			6 retired or non-categorized
			Almost all Chinese
Membership fee			
Joining fee	HK$2,000	HK$350	HK$5,000
Yearly subscription	HK$1,000	HK$500	HK$3,500
Activities/events organized			
Formal	Luncheon seminars	Luncheon/dinner talks	Trips to mainland China
	Local, mainland China and overseas trips and exchanges	Seminars and workshops	Seminars
	Visits to various types of organizations and associations		Government policy consultations
	Interest and hobby courses		Meeting with overseas visitors
			Representatives attending overseas conferences/seminars
			Outstanding Women Professional and Entrepreneurs Award
			"Helping Women to Start a Business" Social Service Project

Table 6.9. Hong Kong's Women Business Owners Associations (Cont.)

	Ladies' Sub-committee of the Chinese General Chamber of Commerce (LS of CGCC)	Women Business Owners Club (WBOC)	Hong Kong Women Professionals and Entrepreneurs Association (HKWPEA)
Informal	Luncheon meetings Various social activities	Christmas celebration	Social gatherings
Newsletter	Nil	Monthly newsletter with advertisements	Quarterly newsletter
Average cost of activities	Whole-day visit to China costs from HK$1,000 to HK$2,000 Lunches and dinners compliment of Chairman and Vice-Chairmen	e.g. Half-day seminar costs HK$300 member HK$400 guest	e.g. Open forum is free
Average number of functions/events per year	Biggest two events are March 8th International Women's Day and October 1st National Day celebrations (over 100 tables) Several mainland and overseas trips a year Several training courses a year	14 meetings—dinners and luncheons—per annum (no meetings in July and August)	About 4 social meetings a year About 4 business meetings a year
Primary language adopted			
Written	Chinese	English	Chinese (dominant) and English (minor)
Oral	Cantonese and Putonghua	English	Cantonese

The earlier members of the LS of the CGCC are wives of the male members, and their activities had focused on charity work in the community and taking part in the performing arts. We spoke to the Vice-Chairperson (60 years old) who had previously worked in the Chinese Foreign Affairs Office in the 1970s and 1980s. She started a small consultancy firm on China Trade five years ago, but the greater part of her commitments are mostly taken up by voluntary social and political services as a member of a number of agencies in the Chinese mainland and Hong Kong.

The membership of the LS of the CGCC and the HKWPEA appears to be based on a closed network of recommendations and contacts, while the WBOC recruits more members openly through promoting their organization in the media, newsletters of other organizations and in the events it organizes. The WBOC has more training seminars for small business start-ups and is very focused on business networking, while the other two groups organize more social functions for its members. The HKWPEA, however, claims that it is concerned about public policies affecting the business community as a whole, rather than those only affecting women. The leadership in the LS of the CGCC is now beginning to see that its brief should extend beyond socializing, and activities now include more networking with the business community in China, Europe, Taiwan and South East Asia.

It is worth noting that while there are 53,200 female self-employed persons and employers in Hong Kong in 2001 (see Table 6.1), the combined membership of the three associations is less than 400. This may be due to the restricted membership goal of the LS of the CGCC and the HKWPEA. The former considers only ethnic Chinese professional and business women who are of high social status and socially recognized high achievers. The latter is satisfied that its membership consists of an exclusive list of prominent women or women in senior positions. In contrast, the WBOC appears to be the most active in expanding its membership to include anyone who owns a business. However, the organization may exclude many micro entrepreneurs like Maureen. Its joining fee (HK$350), yearly subscription fee (HK$500), and the cost of its monthly event (about HK$300), are probably beyond the reach of Maureen, whose monthly income is only about HK$3,000. Even if membership and the cost of event participation is within her means, there still remains the issue of differences in educational background and language barrier. Maureen has a primary level education and speaks little English. Although Mary, with an overseas university education, would fit into WBOC's membership profile, the long hours that she puts in into her business would not appear to fit the times that the events are held. However, she made an attempt to attend a seminar, and while she views the gatherings as useful for networking, would not consider joining the group as a member because she feels her business knowledge can only come about through practical experience.

Women Micro Entrepreneurs and Women Business Owners Associations

As micro entrepreneurs, Maureen and Mary put great store on improving their skills through doing, and principally, they need to rely on themselves to build up a good network. There is a gap between this group of women micro-business owners and the membership in the HKWPEA and the LS of the CGCC. In these two organizations, there is a tendency to welcome members who are recognized as "industrialists" or who are socially recognized as important business owners with relatively high business turnover. There is no motivation for these two organizations to recruit micro entrepreneurs although the HKWPEA may see this happening if there had been such members in the first place (its vice-president explained the greater membership number of professionals as "like attract like"). The LS of the CGCC coming from a more traditional male-dominated business chamber see their immediate objective as redefining their goals, and any substantial impact they may have regarding the increase of female entrepreneurs in the community would entail much more work and negotiation within CGCC's organizational hierarchy.

While it is not apparent that the HKWPEA, nor the LS of the CGCC, are actively recruiting micro entrepreneurs into their memberships, they claim they advocate policies that would support women entrepreneurs. For instance, partially in response to the government's broad economic policies toward stimulating employment of which self-employment is one strategy, the HKWPEA (despite the predominance of business executives and professionals over business owners within its ranks) recently launched its current initiative—"Helping Women to Start a Business" Social Service Project—to help aspiring women entrepreneurs start a small business project by acting as a guarantor for a small loan (maximum HK$100,000) from a local bank, and providing a mentor. Out of a total of about forty odd applications, only about three have been successful and another two are borderline cases. The HKWPEA's evaluation is that the rest of the proposals lack innovative ideas.

CONCLUSIONS

The predominance of a gender blind approach to entrepreneurship in past studies presumes that women behave the same way as their male counterparts. Siu and Chu's (1994) and Ho's (1997) studies argue otherwise and propose that female entrepreneurs need special attention because of their gender. Our paper contends that women micro-business owners face additional barriers such as age discrimination, low educational level and lack of work experience due to long periods of absence from employment in order to perform their homemaker role. Ironically, these barriers are also reasons for their choosing self employment over paid employment and for staying self-employed even when profit margins are extremely thin. On the one hand, it would seem that some women micro-business owners wish for financial security and independence for themselves as well as for the family they need to support, on the one hand, and yet on the other, they are hampered by familial obligations which often fall mainly on them. Recent census statistics reveal that the young women micro-business owners, particularly female self-employed persons, are becoming more educated than men, and are increasingly earning as much as men. Family, though, could be sacrificed along the way as statistics also show that these young female entrepreneurs are more likely than their male counterparts to be unmarried and living alone.

Despite the steady increase in the number of women business owners in Hong Kong, the proportion (17%) is nowhere near that in some developed countries, such as in North America (30%). Female enterprises in Hong Kong tend to be smaller than male enterprises, and sex segregation across industry sectors is marked. Hong Kong female entrepreneurs are similar to female entrepreneurs in some developing economies in that they tend not to put business expansion as the first priority. Furthermore, women micro-business owners in Hong Kong are similarly "invisible," as are their counterparts in developing economies (Singh et al., 2001; Tinker, 1990), even though Hong Kong is considered to be an economically developed territory.

Since the Asian economic crisis in 1997, the Hong Kong government has been encouraging citizens to be more self-reliant and more resourceful, and to recapture the entrepreneurial spirit that Hong Kong has been so renowned for in the past. Some women business owners associations that are close to the government have been trying to promulgate this policy direction. The HKWPEA's "Helping Women to Start a Business" Social Service Project is one example of such initiatives. On the whole, however, these women business associations are too remote in its orientation and outlook for women micro-business owners. They appear to be locked within a conventional framework of valuing "successful business" in terms of company size and sales volume and are not explicitly supportive of other values that may be equally important. There is a need to better understand women entrepreneurs, in particular, female micro entrepreneurs, in order to facilitate their attempts to achieve goals that they have set themselves, however modest in accounting terms. Reynolds et al.'s (2000) global report singles out the importance of according due recognition to an entrepreneur whether the person is successful or not. A community that does not resent successful entrepreneurs or stigmatize failed ones provides the crucial social context for promoting economic growth. It would be Hong Kong's social and economic loss if female entrepreneurs especially those in micro enterprises are neglected.

The existence of an independent enterprise culture in Hong Kong and a history of the government's *laissez faire* policy have given the impression that people are free agents, and that business opportunities abound equally for men and women. Our study shows otherwise. There is a unique group of women micro-business owners in Hong Kong who, while alert to business opportunities, need a wider support network to help them balance their familial responsibilities and business aspirations. They are extremely independent, resilient, and hardworking, but could benefit from a wide variety of mentorship programs set up by government, and professional, business or trade associations.

In the process of our research, we find that we are not able to obtain from the Hong Kong Government's Census and Statistics Department any statistics regarding the sizes of companies owned by women or men.[5] Until and unless the government and associations adopt a more gendered perspective of business operations and a wider definition of business success, and start to recognize female entrepreneurs' struggle with personal and business matters, women business owners' energies will remain untapped to the detriment of Hong Kong's long term economic development.

NOTES

1. A distinction has been made between "entrepreneurial ventures" and "small businesses" in some entrepreneurship literature (e.g., Coulter, 2003, pp. 9–11). The distinction is not germane to the discussions in this paper, however, because we are interested in micro-business owners who feature little in entrepreneurship studies and how they might be different from the entrepreneurship norm.
2. The countries surveyed are: Canada, France, Germany, Italy, Japan, the United Kingdom, the United States, Denmark, Finland, Israel, Argentina, Australia, Belgium, Brazil, India, Ireland, Korea, Norway, Singapore, Spain, and Sweden.
3. Contrast, for example, Wang and Wong's (1997) focus on prominent male business personalities in their collection.
4. Informal rotating credit associations are formed by pooling cash among a small group of participants who may take turns to borrow the accumulated total. Interest is paid by the borrower to the rest of the lenders.
5. "Size of establishment" is not equivalent to "size of company." Each branch/shop of a company is called an establishment.

REFERENCES

Anderson, B.L. (1986). Entrepreneurship, market process and the industrial revolution in England. In B.L. Anderson & A.J.H. Latham (Eds.), *The market in history* (pp. 157–175). NH: Croom Helm.

Cheah, H.B., & Hu, T.F.L. (1996). Adaptive response: Entrepreneurship and competitiveness in the economic development of Hong Kong. *Journal of Enterprising Culture, 4*(3), 241–266.

Coulter, M. (2003). *Entrepreneurship in action* (2nd ed.). Upper Saddle River, NJ: Prentice-Hall.

Enright, M.J., Scott, E.E., & Dodwell, D. (1997). *The Hong Kong advantage.* Hong Kong: Oxford University Press.

Ho, P. (1997). *The making of female entrepreneurs in Hong Kong.* Hong Kong: University of Hong Kong. Unpublished Ph.D. dissertation.

Lau, A., & Snell, R. (1996). Structure and growth in small Hong Kong enterprises. *International Journal of Entrepreneurial Behavior and Research, 2*(3), 29–47.

Lau, T., Chan, K.F., & Man, T.W.Y. (1999). Entrepreneurial and managerial competencies: Small business owner/managers in Hong Kong. In P. Fosh, A.W. Chan, W.W.S. Chow, E. Snape, & R. Westwood (Eds.), *Hong Kong management and labor: Change and continuity* (pp. 220–236). London: Routledge.

Marlow, S., & Strange, A. (1994). Female entrepreneurs: Success by whose standards? In M. Tanton (Ed.), *Women in management: A developing presence* (pp. 172–184). London: Routledge.

Mayasami, R.C., & Goby, V.P. (1999). Female business owners in Singapore and elsewhere: A review of studies. *Journal of Small Business Management, 37*(2), 96–105.

Nelton, S. (1998). The rise of women in family firms: A call for research now. *Family Business Review, XI*(3), 215–218.

Ng, E.G.H., & Ng, C.W. (2002, July 7–13). *Single working women in Hong Kong: Thoughts on family and work.* Paper presented at the XV World Congress of Sociology, Brisbane.

Reynolds, P.D., Hay, M., Bygrave, W.D., Camp, S.M., & Autio, E. (2000). *Global entrepreneurship monitor: 2000 executive report.* London: Babson College/London Business School and Kauffman Centre for Entrepreneurial Leadership at the Ewing Marion Kauffman Foundation.

Singh, S.P., Ruthie, G., & Muhammed, S. (2001). A gender-based performance analysis of micro and small enterprises in Java, Indonesia. *Journal of Small Business Management, 39*(2), 174–182.

Sit, V.F.S. (Ed.). (1985). *Strategies for small-scale industries promotion in Asia.* Hong Kong: Longman.

Sit, V., & Wong S.L. (1989). *Small and medium industries in an export-oriented economy: The case of Hong Kong.* Hong Kong: Centre of Asian Studies, University of Hong Kong.

Siu, W.S., & Chu, P. (1994). Female entrepreneurs in Hong Kong: Problems and solutions. *International Journal of Management, 2*(2), 728–736.

Siu, W.S., & Martin, R.G. (1992). Successful entrepreneurship in Hong Kong. *Long Range Planning, 25*(6), 87–93.

Smart, J. (1989). *The political economy of street hawkers in Hong Kong*. Hong Kong: Centre of Asian Studies, University of Hong Kong.

Stevenson, L.A. (1986). Against all odds: The entrepreneurship of women. *Journal of Small Business management, 24*(4), 30–36.

Teo, S.K. (1996). Women entrepreneurs of Singapore. In A.M. Low & W.L. Tan (Eds.), *Singapore business development series: Entrepreneurs, entrepreneurship and enterprising culture* (pp. 254–289). Singapore: Addison-Wesley.

Tinker, I. (1990). The making of a field. In I. Tinker (Ed.), *Persistent inequalities: Women and world development* (pp. 27–53). Oxford: Oxford University Press.

Wang, G., & Wong, S. (1997). *Dynamic Hong Kong: Business and culture*. Hong Kong: Centre of Asian Studies, University of Hong Kong.

CHAPTER 7

ARE THE BARRIERS TO BUSINESS START-UP GREATER FOR FEMALE RECENT GRADUATE ENTREPRENEURS (FRGES) THAN MALE RECENT GRADUATE ENTREPRENEURS (MRGES)?

Richael Connolly, Bill O'Gorman, and Joe Bogue

ABSTRACT

This article explores the phenomenon by which the recent graduate without post-graduation work experience becomes self-employed shortly after graduation. The objective of this research is to compare and contrast female recent graduate entrepreneurs (FRGEs) with their male counterparts, testing the need for "practical experience from employment."

A phenomenological methodology was used, which allows for a deep understanding of the Recent Graduate Entrepreneur (RGE) giving an insight into their start-up processes and experiences. It is important to gain this insight into the RGE, as they are a latent source of wealth for a country's economy. From this research it was found that a supportive environment, which fosters entrepreneurial characteristics and clearly provides advice on starting a business, is imperative for an increase in the number of RGEs and specifically FRGEs becoming self-employed shortly after graduation.

INTRODUCTION

Creating an "enterprise culture" within a country is highly correlated with its economic growth (Reynolds et al., 2001). The Irish Government, as noted by Imnick and O'Kane (2001), deem that *"Aspiring entrepreneurs represent an untapped resource with great potential for future development in Ireland."* Although Recent Graduate Entrepreneurs (RGEs) represent a source of latent socioeconomic potential, there is little research conducted in this area (Tackey & Perryman, 1999). The investigation into the RGE for this paper has implications for public policy, the education system and future graduates who aspire to self-employment.

Different countries have developed enterprise programs to encourage graduate self-employment. As part of Ireland's National Development Plan 2000 to 2006, the *Graduate Enterprise Programme* was introduced to support graduates to make the leap from employment to full-time self-employment. This paper points to the need for a similar support program for graduates making the leap from attending university into full-time self-employment. Parsons and Walsh's (1999) research in the UK found that only 1% of graduates move into self-employment soon after graduation, with even fewer recent graduates with no post graduation work experience (RGEs). Five reports conducted in the UK by the Department for Education and Employment found that women represent less than half of the recent graduate entrepreneur population (Parsons & Walsh, 1999; Tackey & Perryman, 1999; Woodhull, 1999).

Previous research conducted on female entrepreneurs found that females tend to have less pre start-up experience compared to their male counterparts and that this seriously infringed on their ability to acquire start-up resources (Carter et al., 2001, Centre for Enterprise and Economic Development Research, 2000; Cheskin Research et al., 2000). The research for this paper however examines whether the lack of practical experience has a greater impact on female recent graduate entrepreneurs (FRGE) than male recent graduate entrepreneurs (MRGE). The approach chosen was a phenomenological methodology, whereby the essence of the phenomenon of starting a business for the FRGE and MRGE was sought through five in-depth interviews with the selected recent graduates. In order to understand the context of the RGE and to gain an insight into the difficulties that they faced, interviews and surveys were also conducted with Deans and lecturers from relevant faculties within the university studied and enterprise support agencies in the region.

LITERATURE REVIEW

The Importance of Pre-start-up Experience

Although many researchers such as McLarty (2000), Parsons and Walsh (1999), Tackey and Perryman (1999), Woodhull (1999) and Brown (1990) examined RGE's lack of practical experience, Reuber and Fischer (1994, 1999) and Jo and Lee (1996) found that there was no direct relationship between the founder's experience and the success of the venture. As Reuber and Fischer (1999) observed, there was no exact measure of experience and the studies were fragmented and inconclusive. However, knowledgeable practitioners, such as venture capitalists (Reuber & Fischer, 1999) and people engaged in business (Jo & Lee, 1996) believed that founders' experience was important to the success of a new venture.

Experience was categorized into education and work experience by Jo and Lee (1996). Graduates possess education experience and have learned certain skills through this (Garavan et al., 1997; McLarty, 2000; Parsons & Walsh, 1999; Tackey & Perryman, 1999; Woodhull, 1999). Work experience is subdivided into management and industrial experience also termed practical experience. The lack of management experience is not unique to graduates and the importance of this experience is questioned (Jo & Lee, 1996). However, it is the lack of industrial, or practical experience, that is most common for RGEs (Parsons & Walsh, 1999) and female entrepreneurs (Carter et al., 2001). Yet this lack of practical experience has not been comprehensively examined in the literature (Reuber & Fischer, 1999).

According to Carter et al. (2001) female business owners generally lack prior experience and are attracted to self-employment to try and avoid the "glass ceiling" effect found in the work place. Watkins and Watkins (1986) found that the background and experiences of females differed substantially from their male counterparts; females were found to have a lot less relevant experience to enable them to enter into self-employment.

Comparing and Contrasting Age and Female Entrepreneurs in the Literature

The decision to become self-employed is in essence a very personal decision. However, through empirical studies, patterns of motivation for graduates to enter self-employment have emerged, such as the need for independence and autonomy (Brown, 1990; Flemming, 1996, 1993; McLarty, 2000; Parsons & Walsh, 1999; Scott & Twomey, 1998; Tackey & Perryman, 1999; Woodhull, 1999).

The broad profile of female business owners in the UK and USA is that they are relatively young, their businesses are relatively new, concentrated in retail and service industries, and are of modest size with regard to receipts and revenues (Carter et al., 2001). This profile of female business owners is similar for Ireland (Fitzsimmons et al., 2000). Even though there are similarities between male and female entrepreneurs across individual characteristics there are differences in background work and practical experience (Alsos & Ljunggren, 1998). Comparing the literature on female entrepreneurs and RGEs there are many similarities between the two groups with regard to characteristics and pre-start-up experience, both groups represent a significant potential for increased employment (Centre for Enterprise Education Development Research, 2000).

Research has found the RGE's main motive for starting a business was freedom and self-determination. The second most important factor was securing independence (Parsons & Walsh, 1999). These motivations were similar for female entrepreneurs, who were also driven by independence (Carter et al., 2001; Danish Agency for Trade and Employment, 2000; Watkins & Watkins, 1986). Family background has an important influence on RGEs both for financial and emotional support (Tackey & Perryman, 1999), for business knowledge, and as a way of networking (Parsons & Walsh, 1999; Scott & Twomey, 1988).

Empirical research has shown that there are many barriers to graduate start-ups such as: lack of experience; the lack of finance; the lack of confidence; and lack of targeted advice from support agencies (Brown, 1990; Flemming, 1993; Garavan et al., 1997; McLarty, 2000; Parsons & Walsh, 1999; Tackey & Perryman, 1999). These barriers were also similar for female entrepreneurs (Centre for Enterprise and Economic Research, 2000; Cheskin Research et al., 2000). Parson and Walsh (1999) when examining barriers to graduate start-ups found that graduates were disproportionately disadvantaged, as they needed great amounts of persistence to overcome their lack of practical experience. This persistence was especially important when they sought external advice and support as experience and age were selection criteria for start-up support (Garavan et al., 1997; McLarty, 2000; Tackey & Perryman, 1999). Scott and Twomey (1988) noted that the RGE needed to display a high internal locus of control, high need for achievement and risk seeking, and that they should have a strong self-perception of themselves as an entrepreneur. Parsons and Walsh (1999) found the RGE had to have the confidence to go through the start-up process and McLarty (2000) and Watkins and Watkins (1986) established the RGE had to be highly motivated.

Characteristics of the Environment and Its Impact on the RGE

The decision to become self-employed can depend on pull factors or predisposing factors, and push factors also termed triggering factors. Pull factors can be a result of family background or work and hobbies the graduate has experienced (Scott & Twomey, 1988). Push factors generally result from an external environment change, such as an unstable labor market, where graduates will look to self-employment as an alternative to underemployment or unemployment (Parson &Walsh, 1999). Scott and Twomey (1988) used a framework to identify the main variables that influence student aspirations toward self-employment—(1) predisposing factors, (2) triggering factors and (3) possessing a business idea (see Figure 7.1), all three factors act both in concert and independently in shaping graduate career aspirations. Their study suggested that programs can be developed that can enhance students' entrepreneurial competence through increasing their ability to generate new ideas, take risks and recognize new opportunities (Scott & Twomey, 1988).

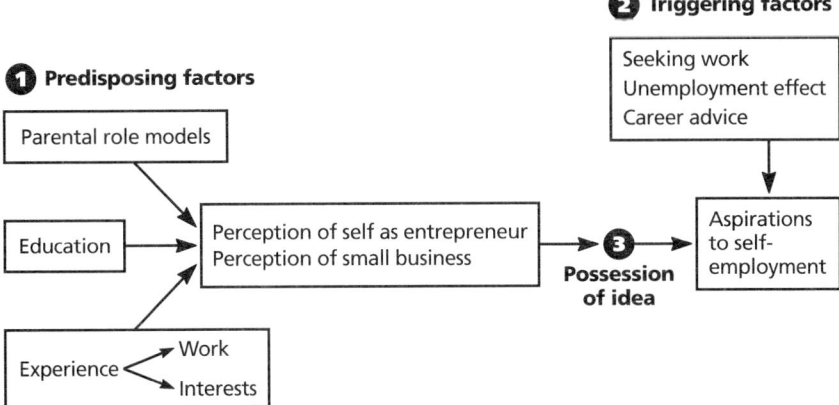

Figure 7.1. Main factors affecting career aspirations (adapted from Scott & Twomey, 1988, p. 7)

Various studies have shown that there is a greater willingness among female graduates to consider self-employment compared to their male counterparts (Brown, 1990; Flemming, 1993, 1996; Parson & Walsh, 1999; Tackey & Perryman, 1999). One reason for this could be that, as pointed out by the Danish Agency for Trade and Employment (2000), in Europe female graduates are more likely to consider self-employment; this is due to the lack of career opportunities, and female entrepreneurs are generally pushed into self-employment.

Education as a Characteristic of the RGE's Environment

Education is a central element of the RGE's environment. The Global Entrepreneurship Monitor 2001 concluded there is a strong relationship between educational participation in a country and its observed level of entrepreneurial activity (Reynolds et al., 2001). Ireland is ranked 5th among the 21 countries surveyed with regard to third level education participation as a percentage of the population. Ireland has a high proportion of graduates from the general population and according to Fitzsimmons et al. (2000) would benefit from greater in-depth graduate entrepreneurship research.

Many studies have observed that educational institutions may not be conducive to inspiring self-employment among graduates, as there is a discrepancy between entrepreneurial aspirations and graduates actually starting a business, (Brenner et al., 1991; Brown, 1990; Flemming, 1993; McLarty, 2000; Parsons & Walsh, 1999; Scott & Twomey, 1988; Tackey & Perryman, 1999; Woodhull, 1999). To encourage more entrepreneurial graduates, students need to learn how to deal with ambiguity and complexity, and to develop all the skills necessary to develop a business (Flemming, 1993). Education should also reinforce innovation, creativity, flexibility, autonomy, and self-expression (Flemming, 1993).

In Boden and Nucci's (2000) study the impact of prior work experience and education on the survival prospects of female and male business ventures was examined. They found that, where other factors were equal, businesses whose owners had four or more years of college and ten or more years of prior work experience, were more likely to survive the first few years in business. In general, the greater the amount of education the more likely women were to succeed in business ownership (Dolinsky et al., 1993).

The Start-Up Process

Reynolds (1997) noted that the process of start-up is a complex interaction among personal, life course, and contextual factors that do not fit into a linear model. Much research has been conducted on understanding this start-up process. This research includes: the key factors in start-up events (Gibb & Ritchie, 1982); the sequence of start-up events (Vesper, 1980); the impact of start-up events on new venture success (Timmons, 1977); the external factors that influence new venture formation (Harrison & Hart, 1983); and the concept of the incubation organisation (Cooper, 1981). These researchers examined different aspects of the start-up process. However, few researchers have approached start-up behaviors in a holistic way (Shabir & Gregorio, 1996).

The greatest barriers to business formation and success are access to capital and mobilizing start-up capital for both males and females (Carter et al., 2001). Cheskin Research et al. (2000) established that male entrepreneurs put more emphasis on networking to further business goals compared to female entrepreneurs. This lack of networking was found to hinder females' business success. The Cheskin Research also found that those who fund new ventures look for specific types of experience that female entrepreneurs were less likely to have. In addition, Parsons and Walsh (1999) noted that securing finance and support in the early stages, realistic mentoring, personal determination, a good business proposal and realistic ambitions were also deemed success factors for RGEs.

OBJECTIVES AND RESEARCH QUESTIONS

Objectives of Research

The main objective of this research was to explore the start-up experiences of RGEs, without prior practical work experience, and in particular to ascertain if there were greater barriers to start-up for FRGEs than MRGEs. A qualitative methodology was chosen to understand the RGEs' start-up experience.

Questions Posed

Based on the literature review it is evident that there is a significant gap in the literature as regards RGEs with no post graduation work experience. This research study asked whether the reason for the low percentage of recent graduate entrepreneurs entering self-employment soon after graduation was directly related to the obstacle of having to overcome the lack of practical experience. In particular this research examined whether the start-up experience of FRGEs was different than that for MRGEs and had FRGEs greater barriers to start-up than their male counterparts. In addition, patterns of motivation to start a business have been uncovered by past empirical research on the graduate entrepreneur but how these patterns of motivation differ between MRGE and FRGE have not been comprehensively examined.

METHODOLOGY

Even though it is universally understood that there is no single entrepreneurial experience for either males or females, many of the factors associated with the start-up process can only be identified through an in-depth investigation at the micro-level of the new business and its founders (Shabir & Gregorio, 1996). According to Bjerke (2000) entrepreneurship is a very human activity and by examining it at the individual level, phenomenology aims to understand the construction of the entrepreneurial social reality.

Phenomenology is an interpretative methodology, which takes the perspective that people's behavior is a product of how they interpret the world (Bogdan & Taylor, 1975). Moustakas (1994) identifies that scientific investigation is made valid when the knowledge sought is arrived at through descriptions that make possible an understanding of the meanings and essences of the experience; and that it is important to take into account the experiencing person and the connection between human consciousness and the objects that exist in the material world. The essence of the phenomenological method is to describe the meaning of an experience from the world view of those who have that experience and as a result attach meaning to it (Kvale, 1996). This is achieved through long-interviews with participants, termed co-researchers, as the purpose of a phenomenological study is to establish a supportive context in which people can build on each other's insights (Li, 2000).

Parameters of Research

The data collected for this study was generated from semi-structured in-depth interviews with 5 co-researchers: 2 females and 3 males. This information was further enhanced through data collected from key informants within the environment in which co-researchers operated. Miles and Huberman (1994) note that the number of co-researchers varies depending on the study with numbers between one and ten being acceptable. Phenomenological research aims to understand human experience rather than statistically generalize and it is therefore based on a small sample size. The co-researchers were purposively sampled by fulfilling all of the criteria necessary to be a recent graduate entrepreneur (Kvale, 1996).

Criteria for RGE

For this research the co-researcher must have received his, or her, primary degree from University College Cork (UCC), Ireland within the period 1990–2002. The definition of RGE, based on the 5 reports from the Department for Education and Employment, UK, (Parsons & Walsh, 1999) and involves:

- Graduate entrepreneurs in the narrower sense, i.e., people who have started a business, even if they are now technically employees of that business;
- Those graduates who consider themselves to be self-employed, i.e., those with more than one customer or client such as freelances; and
- Excluding graduates who are self-employed because it suits their employers' tax arrangements and "entrepreneurs."

In addition for this research the RGE must have had no post-graduation work experience. Work experience was defined as a full-time professional job, where the graduate had worked at a regular activity performed in exchange for payment in a career or occupation and this was their primary source of income. Full-time work was defined by the Organisation for Economic Co-operation and Development (OECD) as 30 or more hours per week. For a graduate to have had no post-graduation work experience means that they have not worked at a full time professional job from the time they received their primary degree to when they became self-employed. The definition of post-graduation work experience is narrow because many graduates obtain part-time work experience. However, this is not considered under the heading of managerial experience and industrial experience as outlined in the literature review.

Data Collection

A list of potential co-researchers was formed through a survey conducted in the UCC alumnus' magazine, circulation of 40,000 graduates. Parallel to this, a survey was sent through email to all 600 academic personnel within UCC, requesting information on recent graduate entrepreneurs. In addition, explorative telephone interviews were conducted with enterprise support agencies in the Cork area. This resulted in a list of 39 graduate entrepreneurs. A letter, which introduced the researcher and stated the purpose of the research was sent to potential participants. This was followed up by a phone call where a screening questionnaire was administered in order to assess if the respondent fitted the RGE criteria, a total of five graduate entrepreneurs fulfilled the criteria and all were willing to participate in the research.

As is consistent with other phenomenological research (Li, 2000) contact was also made with the co-researchers through a pre-interview survey. The points of contact before the interview allowed the researcher to establish rapport, develop participant interest, gain consent for the interview, collect demographic information and to minimize constrained answers during the interview.

The in-depth interviews were semi-structured and consisted of three phases each lasting approximately twenty minutes. Kvale (1996) recommended a three-phase interview format for this process. The three phases for this research consisted of: co-researcher background experiences and what led them to the self-employment decision; their start-up behaviors; and finally what the start-up experience meant to them. Each phase began with a broad introductory question followed by probing and specifying questions where necessary. Direct questions were also asked on different dimensions of the topic. The interviews were audio taped and transcribed later for analysis. The researcher then summarized the interview for the co-researcher to ensure the information was valid and to assess if anything else needed to be added (Kvale, 1996).

Before each interview the researcher bracketed the topic to be examined through the "Epoche" process (Moustakas, 1994). This process, as explained by Moustakas (1994), entails concentrating on the specific person, as prejudgements and preconceptions enter consciousness, they are examined until they no longer have a hold on consciousness, then the researcher is ready to encounter the person freshly and naively.

Data Analysis

The transcript from each interview was read in full, giving each statement equal value, in order to get a sense of the perspectives of the co-researcher, and insight into their life world. Categories (words in bold in Tables 7.2, 7.3, 7.4, and 7.5) specific to the research questions were formulated and specific statements that referred to these categories were selected. An example of a category is "*P1—mot*," which means motivation (mot) to become self-employed in phase 1 (P1) of the interview. The theme that dominated each significant statement was expressed as simply as possible. This is called a "natural meaning unit" (Moustakas, 1994). Each "natural meaning unit" (indented words in Tables 2, 3, 4, and 5) was examined and coded, for example "*P1—mot—con*" meant the motivation to become self-employed was control (con). The elimination of superfluous material and irrelevant themes that did not serve to find answers to the research questions reduced the data further. The essential non-redundant themes were tied together into a descriptive statement. Further analysis was conducted on these statements, which examined the underlying dynamics of the experience, the themes and qualities that accounted for "how" self-employment was experienced by the co-researcher.

Understanding the Context of the RGE

An integral part of this research was to understand the environment that the co-researchers had come from and the impact this environment had on them becoming self-employed. A survey was sent to all academic personnel in UCC. The Deans of relevant faculties and the director of career guidance in UCC and the CEOs of local enterprise support agencies were also interviewed. These surveys and interviews added validity to the data by giving another perspective to the phenomenon of self-employment through triangulation and allowed for the examination of whether there was a need for targeted support for the RGE within the higher education institute and/or the enterprise support agencies.

RESULTS

The results for this research paper were analyzed under the four headings of: the characteristics of the individual (Table 7.2); the characteristics of the RGE's environment (Table 7.3); the start-up behaviors of the RGE (Table 7.4); and what the experience of becoming self-employed has meant for the RGE (Table 7.5). In the tables a "tick" represents the co-researchers that experienced a particular factor, for example, in Table 7.2 three co-researchers experienced the "natural meaning unit" money as a factor in the category motivation.

Profile of Co-researchers

The profile of the five co-researchers was varied: four of the businesses were involved in the Services sector and one was involved in the Manufacturing sector; primary degrees were spread across five different faculties and four co-researchers had post-graduate degrees. The length of time in business ranged from 1 to 9 years (Table 7.1). All of the co-researchers were engaged in part-time work during their time in college and three started their business in a discipline similar to that of their part-time work. All of the co-researchers came from middle class backgrounds.

Table 7.1. Profiles of the Co-researchers

CASE CODE	FRGE1	FRGE2	MRGE1	MRGE2	MRGE3
Gender	Female	Female	Male	Male	Male
Age	28–33	28–33	28–33	28–33	22–27
Business	French school	Manufacturer of fishing flies	Food consultancy	Multimedia	Web design & software development
Degree	Law & French	Commerce	Food Business	Arts	Computer Science
Number years from primary degree to business opening	3 years	3 years	1 year	4 years	0 years (started business during degree)
Post-graduate degree	MBS in Entrepreneurship	MSc in Competition & Strategy	MBS in Agribusiness	Diploma in Film production	NONE
Part-time work	French grinds	Family business	Family business	Theatre	Computer technician

Characteristics of the Individual RGE (Table 7.2)

For both FRGEs control was a significant motivation for self-employment. They expressed a need to be in control of their time. Having control over the development of their careers was very important to them:

> I am able to control my own time and everything I do myself now—that has always been important to me. (FRGE2)

Control was not mentioned by any of the MRGEs. However, across all interviews with the male co-researchers, perseverance came out strongly, but did not emerge in the female co-researchers interviews, however each MRGE spoke about their drive and determination to succeed:

> I had the drive and the determination to make it work whereas other people may not have had it in them. (MRGE2)

Both FRGEs experienced their youth as an advantage when they were starting their business. FRGE2 found she came across as less of a threat to store owners, as she was a lot younger than the typical business representative selling products. This worked to her advantage when selling her prod-

Table 7.2. Characteristics of the individual RGE

	Female		Male		
	FRGE1	FRGE2	MRGE1	MRGE2	MRGE3
Motivation:					
Money	✔		✔	✔	
Control	✔	✔			
Freedom	✔	✔		✔	✔
Different Lifestyle		✔		✔	
Risk taking propensity low	✔	✔	✔	✔	✔
Perseverance			✔	✔	✔
Impact of age:					
Positive getting support	✔	✔	✔		
Negative getting support					✔
Positive impact on business	✔	✔			
Negative impact on business			✔	✔	✔

uct. FRGE1 found it easier to get support as she was seen as the enterprise board's prodigy. This gave her an edge on other applicants for grants:

> I was brought to every function ... I was their [County Enterprise Board's] prodigy being under 25, female and setting up a business. (FRGE1)

In contrast, MRGEs found their youth a hindrance in building up credibility in their business:

> We had a meeting with the County Enterprise Board and basically they told us that they couldn't help us because we were too young and we had not yet graduated. So that wasn't very helpful and as far as I could see there wasn't really any support out there for us. (MRGE3)

From all the interviews there was a low propensity to risk among the co-researchers. The circumstances that surround a recent graduate translated into the feeling that each RGE felt they had little to lose:

> There is no point being nervous about it [becoming self-employed] ... what is a year out of your life? (FRGE2)

This perception of low risk that each RGE held may also be a factor of their entrepreneurial characteristics:

> Whether I was ready or not in I went [became self-employed] ... whereas other people might shy away and say "oh no I'm not ready." (FRGE1)

Characteristics of RGEs' Environment (Table 7.3)

All RGEs displayed entrepreneurial characteristics. These included: an internal locus of control where they felt in control of their own destiny; a strong self-perception; and an aspiration to self-employment. MRGE1 was the only co-researcher who formed his aspiration for self-employment during his time at university.

Family support was very important to all of the co-researchers. All were influenced in some way by their parents. It was found across all interviews that in their childhood certain entrepreneurial characteristics were fostered such as an internal locus of control. MRGE3 explained:

> If there is a negative attitude at home toward self-employment such as your parents saying that you will never succeed—I mean you look up to your parents to a certain extent, so if they weren't behind me I would say it would have been very difficult to have started a business. (MRGE3)

Under the category education (Table 7.3), there are few gender differences evident. All co-researchers mentioned that their self-employment endeavor benefitted from their participation in university life in certain ways, such as provided an environment to find business partners, contacts with industry and facilitated finding initial clients for the business. MRGE3 found university to be the least helpful, even though he started his business while doing his primary degree. The four co-researchers that did post-graduate degrees, found their courses helpful in starting their business, either through technical education or through acquiring the vocabulary to help them communicate in the business world:

> UCC gave me a lot of knowledge to help me negotiate my way through starting up a business. (FRGE1)

The University did not directly impact on the majority of RGEs' businesses. However, it transpired that UCC helped foster their confidence and self-belief in what they did in business. This was consistent with 36% of respondents from the UCC academic survey, who believed UCC should foster confidence. One respondent from the survey stated that:

> By fostering self-confidence with the right connections and support system, graduates should be able to overcome the impact of lack of work experience.

Table 7.3. Characteristics of RGEs' Environment

	Female		Male		
	FRGE1	FRGE2	MRGE1	MRGE2	MRGE3
Perception of Self as Entrepreneur:					
Internal locus of control	✔	✔	✔	✔	✔
Long-term aspiration to self-employment s/e	✔	✔		✔	✔
Strong self-perception	✔	✔	✔	✔	✔
Parental Influence:					
Awareness of self-employment (S/E)		✔	✔	✔	
Advice for S/E		✔	✔	✔	✔
Parental influence negative	✔	✔	✔		
Entrepreneurial Siblings			✔	✔	
Positive Family Support		✔	✔	✔	✔
Part-Time Work	✔	✔	✔	✔	✔
Education:					
Extra courses for starting business	✔	✔			
Post-grad benefited S/E	✔	✔	✔	✔	
Self-taught			✔		✔
Education system needs to educate for S/E	✔	✔	✔	✔	✔
Benefits of UCC degree for SE	✔	✔	✔	✔	
UCC building confidence in individual	✔	✔	✔	✔	
UCC Influence in S/E:					
Broadened skill base				✔	
Provided an environment to find partners		✔	✔		✔
Provided industry contacts (networking)		✔	✔		
UCC Support in S/E:					
Advice			✔		
Too cautious			✔		
Facilitated in finding clients		✔	✔		
No support				✔	✔

Table 7.3. Characteristics of RGEs' Environment (Cont.)

	Female		Male		
	FRGE1	FRGE2	MRGE1	MRGE2	MRGE3
Entered Enterprise Competitions			✔		
Expertise:					
Area of interest used in business	✔	✔	✔	✔	✔
Skill base used in area				✔	✔
Expertise acquired used in business	✔	✔	✔		
Triggering Factors:					
No jobs			✔	✔	✔
The need to bring something to the industry			✔		✔
Opinion of Conventional Career—Negative	✔		✔		
Expectation of S/E—Positive	✔	✔			
Idea Generation:					
Encouragement from another person	✔	✔			
Development of idea from original plan			✔	✔	✔
Further idea generation for future business		✔	✔	✔	✔
Strong vision of business			✔	✔	✔

Fifty-three percent of respondent's from the academic survey felt that graduates would need an interim period of experience before going into self-employment *"I think work experience is vital for people."* MRGE1 received advice and support from UCC but he found the advice too cautious. This was supported by the Deans themselves, who agreed that they only have academic experience, and would not be able to give the best, start-up advice. However, they would be able to use their connections with industry to provide the potential entrepreneur with contacts and guide them to where they should go for advice.

However all co-researchers were adamant that an aspect of education needed to be directly geared toward self-employment, such as signposting what support was needed to start a business and what support was available. A quote from one co-researcher was typical of others:

> What you should learn in the classroom is where to get help, what kind of help you need, help in finding a niche for the business. Advice like that would

certainly have been beneficial. I mean that could have changed my whole life. Basically my business could be a lot more successful now. (MRGE3)

As regards the idea generation category, the decision to become self-employed for both FRGEs was triggered by someone else. For example FRGE1 started to see her talent in teaching as a business venture when someone suggested it to her:

> When I was 19, after my first year in college, a student's father came to me and said that I had been teaching his daughter for years ... and that I should start up on my own, I should really start teaching because the way I teach is really good ... So that started it, I thought to myself very interesting, I could start a business. (FRGE1)

Similarly, FRGE2 decided to become self-employed when her present business partner approached her with an idea that needed to be developed.

In contrast, all MRGEs held a very strong vision for their businesses, in terms of what they wanted to do and where their businesses were going in the future. MRGE1 and MRGE2 were early to market with their business ideas and MRGE3 found his service was in an overcrowded market doing web design but planned to move into the virtual reality field as soon as he acquired the capital to do so. This was in contrast to what the FRGEs spoke about with regard exploring their interests and talents. The strong vision, held by the three MRGEs, gave them an added push into self-employment.

Conversely the FRGEs expressed that they were pulled into, or attracted to, self-employment by a positive expectation of it:

> I suppose a lot to do with the flexible hours and my father's way of life would have influenced me. (FRGE2)

> I could be married with kids because this is an ideal job to have with kids. (FRGE1)

The importance of the family environment was evident for all RGEs. However both FRGEs, when speaking about their parents, spoke about being taught to be independent and not to have to rely on anyone else for an income.

> My father would have been very aware of marriages that had split up and he always instilled in me to be self-sufficient, independent, and not to rely on anyone else. So maybe part of the working for myself came from that. (FRGE2)

Both FRGEs did postgraduate degrees in UCC and managed their degrees to allow them to set up their business while still attending university. Both FRGEs took on extra courses in order to help them set up their business, whereas the MRGEs went straight into self-employment.

Start-up Behaviors (Table 7.4)

The start-up behaviors varied across co-researchers, but there were little differences across gender. However certain issues did emerge and greater insight can be gained from these patterns through linkages with the contextual variables in Tables 7.2 and 7.3 above.

Four out of the five co-researchers formed business partnerships. The three MRGEs formed these partnerships for both emotional (MRGE1 and MRGE3) and financial (MRGE2) support:

> There were three of us in the business. I suppose it was easier for three of us to do it together. We could just look at each other and say well the three of us can't be all wrong. (MRGE1)

FRGE2's business partner had the original business proposal. She formed this partnership to further develop and build on her partner's ideas. She has since started a new business on her own. FRGE1 did not form a partnership. An important gender difference was evident from the first action or initial step, to become self-employed having made the decision. For all MRGEs the initial step was to network in the industry they operated in and find customers:

> The first step was to get a client. We did that by literally pounding the streets and roads of the country, you don't have a business if you don't have clients. (MRGE1)

However, the FRGEs placed greater importance on perfecting the business proposal before going to market. FRGE2 developed a prototype and FRGE1 did a start your own business course.

Three of the RGEs received enterprise support from the County Enterprise Boards. MRGE2 and MRGE3 did not receive any support. MRGE2 felt his business did not need any support and MRGE3 was unable to get support. This was because he had not yet graduated at the time he was setting up his business. The RGEs that did receive support found it invaluable to compensate for their lack of "practical experience" and also to provide financial support. FRGE1, FRGE2 and MRGE1 were involved in PLATO, a business network and mentoring scheme for new ventures in Southern Ireland:

> I could go in and say, one of my teachers isn't performing as well as she can ... I have never disciplined someone in my life. How do I do it? I didn't have a clue what I was doing. You just have to rely on something like that [PLATO]. (FRGE1)

Table 7.4. Start-Up Behaviors

	Female		Male		
	FRGE1	FRGE2	MRGE1	MRGE2	MRGE3
Formed Partnership		✔	✔	✔	✔
Initial Step after Self-Employment:					
Invest own money		✔			
To network			✔	✔	✔
Work from home					✔
Start your own business course (FAS)	✔				
Created a Business Plan	✔			✔	✔
Enterprise Support:					
Enterprise boards very supportive	✔	✔	✔		
No support received					✔
PLATO (business network and mentoring scheme)	✔	✔	✔		
Cork BIC (Business Incubation Centre)			✔		
No support needed				✔	
Business Networks:					
Compensate for lack of experience	✔	✔	✔		
Formed contacts through part-time work					✔
Finance:					
Invest own money		✔		✔	
Cash flow problems			✔		✔
Little overheads	✔	✔	✔		✔
Grants:					
Full funding for business	✔				
Employment grants	✔	✔	✔		
Relationship with Employees:					
Problems getting motivated staff			✔	✔	✔
Staff for admin. Work			✔		✔

Table 7.4. **Start-Up Behaviors (Cont.)**

	Female		Male		
	FRGE1	FRGE2	MRGE1	MRGE2	MRGE3
Relationship with Customers:					
Loyalty to customers		✓	✓	✓	
Difficulty acquiring customers					✓
Work Details:					
Multi-tasking		✓	✓	✓	✓
Importance of publicity	✓	✓	✓		
Firm Growth			✓	✓	✓
Problems:					
Production problems		✓	✓	✓	
Supply problems		✓			
Partnership problems				✓	✓
Labour problems			✓	✓	✓
Acquiring resources					✓

Both FRGEs were flexible with their business proposals in order to maximize the availability of support to them. FRGE2 emphasized the export side of her business and FRGE1 also focused her business in order to avail of grants:

> The Enterprise Board will only give you grants if it is a new niche product. So I had to give French grinds to guesthouse owners and to airport staff ... whereas I just wanted to teach French to primary and secondary school kids. (FRGE1)

Personnel from the enterprise agencies recommended that the graduate should first get practical experience before becoming self-employed, regardless of gender. Those RGEs that did get support had to persevere until they received the support, and in the end they found it invaluable.

All of the co-researchers had little overheads and ensured they kept them low when starting their business, as large amounts of finance were not available to them. FRGE2, MRGE1 and MRGE3 worked from home at business start-up. MRGE2 had greater overheads but formed a partnership in order to get financial backing.

Under the "problems" category all of the MRGEs discussed labor problems, in employing motivated staff. MRGE2 found that he did not have the finance to recruit the best and MRGE1 and MRGE2 employed people their own age (e.g., their classmates):

> Employees just drift, take the wages and they do not contribute anything to the level you would expect from an older employee. The problem with that is that you spend your time unproductively managing those people, when they should be able to manage themselves. (MRGE1)

MRGEs proclaimed, when asked about their start-up problems, having to rely on others who were less motivated was the problem:

> It's tough when you have to take on consultants. It's hard when you have to rely on other people. That is the hardest part because it is impossible to get people as motivated as you are about your business. (MRGE2)

Labor problems were not reported by the FRGEs. This might be due to the fact that they did not employ as many people as their male counterparts. FRGE2 for example did not employ anyone, as she preferred to do everything herself. FRGE1 employed a number of staff but her main problem with this staff was reprimanding them. Communicating with people is a very important aspect of business and all of the MRGEs expressed the importance of interacting with their customers:

> You are not dealing with machines, you are dealing with people and building relationships is very, very important. (MRGE1)

Building the right image in business was also important for the MRGE. However, although this experience was felt by all of the males it was not reported by the females.

The Meaning of the Experience for the RGE (Table 7.5)

The third phase of the interview was for the co-researchers to explain the essence of their experience in their own words. The meanings of the experience of becoming self-employed varied greatly across RGEs. Certain "natural meaning units" had a strong gender bias. The differences on how self-employment was experienced have greater implications for the development of the business.

Both FRGEs put greater emphasis on personal success rather than business success. FRGE1 described her success as:

> Well it [setting up a business] is life changing. It is different if you set up on your own, it is fulfilling. I would never take back one minute of it. I would never work for anybody. (FRGE1)

Table 7.5. The Meaning of the Experiences for the RGE

	Female		Male		
	FRGE1	FRGE2	MRGE1	MRGE2	MRGE3
Success:					
Starting new business		✔	✔	✔	
Increased sales and customer satisfaction		✔	✔		
Personal success	✔	✔			
Success not achieved					✔
Success Factors:					
Constantly learning	✔			✔	
Building up experience	✔	✔			
Focus on vision			✔	✔	✔
Personal selling			✔		✔
Market niche			✔		
Barriers:					
Finance		✔		✔	
Lack of experience					✔
Business climate in Ireland					✔
Lessons:					
Learning from experience		✔	✔		✔
The importance of support					✔
Advice:					
Get enterprise support		✔			✔
Recruit motivated staff			✔	✔	✔
Be 100% focused			✔	✔	

FRGE2 echoed similar experiences:

> Every time I finish a market research project that to me is a success. Every time I get rewarded a contract that to me is the happiest day. People have that much trust in you to do the job. (FRGE2)

The MRGEs equated success with increasing their market share. The FRGEs cited building up experience as a success factor. They placed great emphasis on making use of what they had learnt in the past in their business, and the extra courses they had done before becoming self-employed. The MRGEs, on the other hand, all believed in being focused on a vision for the business, to constantly make sure that the vision was being executed and not get distracted from the goal of the business.

Across all interviews with RGEs a strong factor that came across was the importance of a support network. This support network took various forms such as enterprise support agencies, family support, and support from business partners.

DISCUSSION AND CONCLUSIONS

The shared experiences of the five co-researchers are presented in Figure 7.2. By adapting the framework from the research study by Scott and Twomey (1988) the gender differences in the factors that influenced the self-employment decision for the RGE are displayed. The effect of these gender differences on start-up behaviors and the subsequent success of the business are also presented in Figure 7.2. The impact of lack of practical experience on starting a business for the RGE can be observed. A pertinent part of past empirical research on both female entrepreneurs (Carter et al., 2001; Centre for Enterprise and Economic Development Research, 2000; Cheskin Research et al., 2000) and recent graduate entrepreneurs (Garavan et al., 1997; McLarty, 2000; Parsons & Walsh, 1999; Tackey & Perryman, 1999) is that there are more barriers to self-employment for these two categories of entrepreneurs compared to entrepreneurs in general. These researchers found that the two groups of entrepreneurs have to be highly motivated in order to overcome barriers to start-up.

Initial Motivation to Self-Employment

The results show that all RGEs were highly motivated, displayed an internal locus of control and had a strong self-perception. This is consistent with the literature examining motivation for both the RGE (Brown, 1990; Flemming, 1993; Garavan et al., 1997; McLarty, 2000; Parsons & Walsh, 1999; Tackey & Perryman, 1999) and the female entrepreneur (Carter et al., 2001; Danish Agency for Trade and Employment, 2000; Watkins & Watkins, 1986).

It was evident from this research that motivation powered the decision to start a business. This results in motivation having far reaching implica-

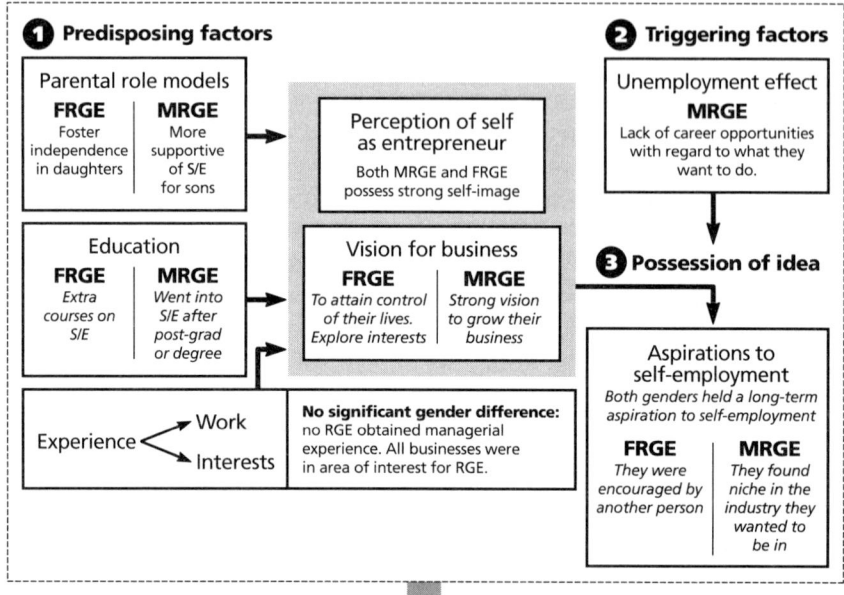
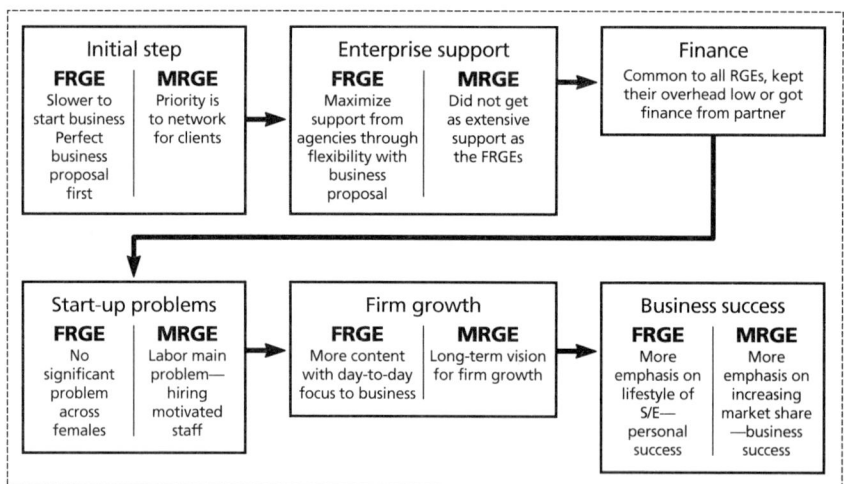

Figure 7.2. MRGE and FRGE gender differences in factors affecting career aspirations and the effects of these in start-up behaviors, adapted Scott and Twomey, 1998

tions for the future of the business. For the FRGEs control was the main motivation to self-employment. As can be seen from Figure 7.2, the vision for the business held by both FRGEs was to achieve control of their lives and to be in control of their time. This can be connected to the Firm Growth box in Figure 7.2, as both FRGEs were content with where their business was. Conversely, the MRGEs held an intense focus on their business, a long-term vision, and ambitious plans for the future of their business. The FRGEs had satisfied their initial motivation and they were in control of what they did, therefore they did not have a need to grow their business. The profile of women business owners in previous literature (Carter et al., 2001; Fitzsimmons et al., 2000) was that they were generally not positioned in high growth industries. A factor for low growth among the FRGEs' businesses in this research was linked to their initial motivation to become self-employed.

Control motivation can also be further linked to Predisposing Factors in Figure 7.2, i.e., parental role models and their family background. Independence was fostered in a way that they were both encouraged not to become reliant on anyone for financial support.

Interestingly both FRGEs' mothers desired their daughters to work in a routine 9 to 5 job, and this made the decision to become self-employed more difficult compared to their male counterparts. All three MRGEs received full family support for their self-employment decision.

Vision for Business

This research concurs with previous research by Carter et al. (2001) and Centre for Enterprise and Economic Development Research (2000) that perseverance and strong vision is evident in male entrepreneurs. This earlier research suggested that this vision resulted in male entrepreneurs receiving greater support than female entrepreneurs. Females were found to be less growth oriented. Contrary to this previous research, this current research found (Enterprise Support, Figure 7.2), that the FRGE received greater support compared to the MRGE. This was due to the FRGEs' willingness to comply with enterprise support requirements, whereas the MRGEs were too focused on their vision for the business, to adapt fully to these requirements.

Predisposing and Triggering Factors

The strong vision held by the MRGEs can be linked to a triggering factor that propelled them into self-employment, (Unemployment Effect, Figure 7.2). It is not that there were no jobs for them, but rather no jobs that fitted their vision of what they wanted to do. Previous research (Cheskin, 2000; Centre for Enterprise and Economic Development Research, 2000) found that female entrepreneurs tended to be pushed into self-employment due to a lack of career opportunities. In this research the reasons surrounding the FRGEs decision to become self-employed were less to do with lack of career opportunities, a factor important for their male counterparts, and more to do with following their interests.

Both FRGEs set up their business while still studying for their Masters degrees, availing of the comfortable environment of a university rather than fully taking the plunge into self-employment. This may be linked back to parental role models, as they were initially coming from a less supportive family environment compared to their male counterparts.

Initial Step into Self-employment

The gender differences in the individual's background culminated in the differences in start-up behavior across gender. The main priority for the MRGE was to network with people and attain clients. This is consistent with the outcome of Cheskin's (2000) research, which compared male and female entrepreneurs. The emphasis on networking and building up a business persona can be connected back to the strong vision of the business held by the MRGEs. In contrast the FRGEs were slower to start their businesses. This was due to a need to perfect the business proposal by attending additional business courses, and due to the lack of initial family support. The MRGEs started their businesses straight away, but they were more likely to run into difficulties during the start-up process.

Start-Up Problems and Business Success

The MRGEs experienced great problems with having to depend on other people when starting their business. This can be linked again to their strong vision and business persona. The FRGEs did emphasize the importance of hiring in the expertise they did not have. The FRGEs were also less likely to hire administrative staff as they felt they were giving up control of their business.

The difference in growth orientation of the FRGE and MRGE was also found to be related to their perception of business success (Business Success in Figure 7.2). Success for the FRGEs translated into the lifestyle they achieved through self-employment, the achievement of control over their lives and their time. Success for the MRGEs translated into market share, and hence their growth orientation as they aimed to increase their market share in the future, and their strong vision for the business had not yet been satisfied.

The start-up behaviors for the RGEs were complex and fragile, which resulted in the need for encouragement and support. The general attitude of support providers was to recommend that the graduate acquire experience first, before becoming self-employed, regardless of gender. Yet this support, achieved through the RGEs' perseverance was invaluable to them in order to compensate for their lack of experience.

RGEs Propensity to Risk Taking

Interestingly, this research found that the jump from attending university into self-employment is perceived as less risky compared to the jump from full-time employment into self-employment. This explains why the RGE displays a low propensity to risk, which is contrary to previous research on entrepreneurs in general (Chell et al., 1991).

Fostering More RGEs

The sample of co-researchers for this research was obtained through a survey of 40,000 of the graduate population in UCC, from which only five respondents complied with the criteria. The small amount of RGEs is consistent with previous research undertaken in the UK (Parsons & Walsh, 1999; Tackey & Perryman, 1999; Woodhull, 1999).

With the appropriate support available to potential RGEs, the transition from university to self-employment would be further facilitated, and result in an increase in RGEs. This research found that the FRGEs did not have any greater barriers to self-employment compared to the MRGEs.

Creating an Enterprise Culture in the Education System

As expressed by the RGEs in this research there should be changes made to education in order to promote the drive to succeed, to increase the focus on business proposals and to foster entrepreneurial spirit within students. There is also a need for signposting of support that is available to the RGE, which would require that the university form closer linkages with local enterprise agencies.

Enterprise Support

There is a need for targeted enterprise support for the RGE, and to differentiate support for the FRGE and MRGE. The FRGEs would benefit best from support networks particularly at the initial stages of starting a business. In this research, the FRGEs' tentative exploration into starting a business, needed to be supported fully by encouragement and nurturing through mentoring and business networks. The MRGEs would have benefitted best from support and assistance for the ongoing development of the business, especially in acquiring assistance to overcome their lack of experience in certain areas. Financial support and accounting procedures needed to be more available to all RGEs.

FUTURE RESEARCH

This was a qualitative phenomenological study. Further understanding into the need for targeted support for the FRGE and MRGE will be gained through a large-scale comparison study on recent graduate entrepreneurs with no post graduation experience, graduate entrepreneurs with post graduation experience and non-graduate entrepreneurs. This will statistically test gender differences identified in this research and give further insight into the importance of education and experience on the entrepreneurial process. Results from this future research may be of great importance to policymakers and educators who are concerned with the enhancement of a country's enterprise culture and economic growth.

REFERENCES

Alsos, G., & Ljunggren, E. (1998). Does the business start-up process differ by gender? A longitudinal study of nascent entrepreneurs. In *Frontiers of entrepreneurship research*. Wellesley, MA: Babson College.

Bjerke, B. (2000, June). *Understanding entrepreneurship—A new direction in research?* Paper presented at the International Council for Small Business, Australia.

Boden, R.J., & Nucci, A.R. (2000). On the survival prospects of men's and women's new business ventures. *Journal of Business Venturing, 15*(4). 347–326.

Bogdan, R., & Taylor, S.J. (1975). *Introduction to qualitative research methods: A phenomelogical approach to the social sciences*. New York: Wiley and Sons.

Brenner, O.C., Pringle, C.D., & Greenhaus, J.H. (1991). Perceived fulfilment of organizational employment versus entrepreneurship: Work values and career intentions of business college graduates. *Journal of Small Business Management, 29*(3), 62–74.

Brown, R. (1990). Encouraging enterprise: Britain's graduate enterprise program. *Journal of Small Business Management, 28*(4), 71–77.

Carter, S., Anderson, S., & Shaw, E. (2001). *Women's business ownership: A review of the academic, popular and Internet literature.* Glasgow: Report to the Small Business Service.

CEEDR. (2000). *Young entrepreneurs, women entrepreneurs, ethnic minority entrepreneurs and co-entrepreneurs in the European Union and Central and Eastern Europe.* Middlesex: Centre for Enterprise and Economic Development Research, Middlesex University Business School.

Chell, E., Haworth, J., & Brealey, S. (1991). *The entrepreneurial personality, concepts, cases and categories.* London: Routledge.

Cheskin Research, CIE., & The Center for New Futures. (2000). *Women entrepreneurs study.* NJ: Cheskin Research.

Cooper, A.C. (1981). Strategic management: New ventures and small business. *Long Range Planning, 14*(5), 39–45.

Danish Agency for Trade and Employment. (2000). *The circumstances of women entrepreneurs.* Copenhagen: Author.

Dolinsky, A.L., Caputo, R.K., Pasumarty, K., & Quazi, H. (1993). The effects of education on business ownership: A longitudinal study of women. *Entrepreneurship Theory and Practice, 18*(1), 32–53.

Fitzsimmons, P., O'Gorman, C., & Roche, F. (2000). *The global entrepreneurship monitor 2000, the Irish report.* Dublin: Department of Administration, University College Dublin, Cahill Printers Ltd.

Flemming, P. (1993, July 5–7). *The role of a structured intervention in shaping graduate entrepreneurship.* Paper presented at the Conference Internationalizing Entrepreneurship Education and Training, Vienna, Austria.

Flemming, P. (1996). Entrepreneurship education in Ireland: A longitudinal study. *Academy of Entrepreneurship Journal European Edition, 2*(1), 94–118.

Garavan, T., O Cinneide, B., & Flemming, P. (1997). The graduate entrepreneur in Ireland. In T. Garavan (Ed.), *Entrepreneurship and business start-ups in Ireland* (pp. 133–167). Dublin: Oak Tree Press.

Gibb, A., & Ritchie, J. (1982). Understanding the process of starting small business. *European Small Business Journal, 1*(1), 26–45.

Harrison, R.T., & Hart, M. (1983). Factors influencing new-business formation: A case study of Northern Ireland. *Environment and Planning, A.15,* 1395–1412.

Imnik, R., & O'Kane, B. (2001). *Starting your own business* (2nd ed.). Department of Enterprise, Trade and Employment, Dublin: Oak Tree Press.

Jo, H., & Lee, J. (1996). The relationship between an entrepreneur's background and performance in a new venture. *Technovation, 16*(4), 161–171.

Kvale, S. (1996). *Interviews: An introduction to qualitative research interviewing.* Thousand Oaks, CA: Sage.

Li, Y. (2000). Geography consciousness and tourism experience. *Annals of Tourism Research, 27*(4), 863–883.

McLarty, R. (2000). *Graduate entrepreneurs and their enterprises.* Norwich: University of East Anglia.

Miles, M.B., & Huberman, A.M. (1994). *Qualitative data analysis.* Thousand Oaks, CA: Sage.

Moustakas, C. (1994). *Phenomenological research methods.* Thousand Oaks, CA: Sage.

Parsons, D., & Walsh, K. (1999). *TEC role in supporting graduate enterprise.* West Sussex: HOST Consultancy & Labour Market Intelligence Unit.

Reuber, A., & Fischer, E. (1994). Entrepreneurs experience, expertise, and the performance of technology—based firms. *IEEE Transactions an Engineering Management, 14*(4), 365–373.

Reuber, A., & Fischer, E. (1999). Understanding the consequences of founder's experience. *Journal of Small Business Management, 35*(2), 30–45.

Reynolds, P. (1997). Who starts new firms?—Preliminary analysis of firms in gestation. *Small Business Economics, 9,* 449–462.

Reynolds, P.D., Camp, S.M., Bygrave, W.D., Autio, E., & Hay, M. (2001). *Global entrepreneurship monitor: 2001 Executive summary.* United Nations Association of the United States of America and the Business Council for the United Nations. Babson College, Ewing Marion Kauffman Foundation, London Business School.

Scott, M., & Twomey, D. (1988). The long-term supply of entrepreneurs: Students career aspirations in relation to entrepreneurs. *Journal of Small Business Management, 26*(4), 5–13.

Shabir, A., & Gregorio, S. (1996). An examination of the relationship between women's personal goals and structural factors influencing their decision to start a business: The case of Pakistan. *Journal of Business Venturing, 11*(6), 507–529.

Tackey, N.D., & Perryman, S. (1999). *Graduates mean business.* Brighton: IES Report 357.

Timmons, J.A. (1977). *New venture creation: A guide to small business development.* Homewood, IL: Irwin.

Vesper, K.M. (1980). *New venture strategies.* Englewood Cliffs, NJ: Prentice-Hall.

Watkins, J.M., & Watkins, D.S. (1986). The female entrepreneur: her background and determinants of business chaos—British data. *International Small Business, 2*(4), 21–31.

Woodhull, R. (1999). *Gradient project.* London: University of East London.

CHAPTER 8

ACCOUNTING FOR CHANGE

Professionalism as a Challenge to Gender Disadvantage in Entrepreneurship

Sara Carter and Sue Marlow

ABSTRACT

Research investigating female entrepreneurship has often highlighted gender-based differences in the performance of women-owned firms. Some studies have linked the underperformance of women-owned firms to the lower levels of capitalization used at business inception. Research studies have generally treated women entrepreneurs as an undifferentiated group, failing to distinguish the growing number of women entering self-employment from professional careers and with the potential to mobilize substantial business capital. This chapter explores the influence of gender in the work and career experiences of women and investigates whether professional status and experience compensate for gender disadvantage within self-employment. Results of an exploratory study of male-owned and female-owned accountants in independent practice suggest that gender disadvantage persists, even within the context of professional practice.

INTRODUCTION

A consistent finding of research investigating female entrepreneurship has been that the performance and growth of women-owned firms in terms of turnover, profit realization and job creation is weaker than that found in male-owned enterprises (Fasci & Valdez, 1998; Rosa et al., 1996). Collectively, these studies suggest a bimodal profile of male-owned and women-owned businesses, with women-owned firms being younger, smaller and achieving a lower level of performance across a range of direct, indirect and proxy measures. Underperformance has been both conceptually and empirically linked to the initial undercapitalization of women-owned firms (Boden & Nucci, 2000; Brush, 1992; Moore & Buttner, 1997; Rosa et al., 1996). The capitalization of a new enterprise is not only dependent on access to finance, but also includes human and social capital such as previous managerial and sectoral experience and access to appropriate professional and personal networks. The undercapitalization of women-owned firms has been associated with their experiences of gender disadvantage within waged work and the labor market. Gendered occupational segregation guides many women toward low skill, poorly paid work (Bradley, 1999). This has negative connotations for any future entrepreneurial careers as evidence indicates that most nascent entrepreneurs utilize waged work-based skills and experience to inform and support careers in self-employment. Hence, the more human, social and financial capital that is accrued in the process of waged work, the greater the potential for personal credibility and enterprise durability (Marlow, 2002; Storey, 1994). If women are not accruing work-based capital which helps to support the development of robust new firms with growth potential, their enterprises are more likely to under perform.

However, a growing number of women are breaking through traditional gender-based occupational and sectoral confines by entering the professions, such as medicine, law and accountancy. According to recent data from the Equal Opportunities Commission in the UK, 40% of women (compared to 60% of men) are now working in professional occupations (Equal Opportunities Commission, 2002). Although a gender gap persists, it is closer than in executive managerial posts for example, where fewer than 10% of company directors are women and 77% of the Financial Times Stock Exchange (FTSE) 100 highest performing companies have no women employed in executive roles (Equal Opportunities Commission, 2002). Regarding the professions, the likelihood is that even more women will be entering such occupations in the future as, for example, more than half of undergraduates currently studying medicine, law and accountancy-based courses and nearly three quarters studying veterinary science are women. There are exceptions to this trend with some entrenched areas such as engineering and computer sciences still retaining their traditional male dominance (Dench et al., 2002).

The shift toward greater participation of women in professional employment has a number of implications for entrepreneurial behavior. Given that the professions demand higher levels of skills and offer better opportunities in terms of training, experience and remuneration, professional women who subsequently become self-employed should be better prepared to overcome the problems of undercapitalization stemming from the disadvantages concerning the influence of feminized waged work upon self-employment. Moreover, the growing number of women entering diverse areas of work as employees or entrepreneurs demands greater recognition of the heterogeneity within this group. Research and indeed, policy initiatives pertaining to female entrepreneurship often view women as a homogenous group struggling at the peripheral edge of the economy and little effort is made to differentiate between groups of women which is a disservice to all those involved. This chapter adds to this discussion with an examination of the experience of a specific group of women entrepreneurs, those of professional self-employed accountants in the UK. To explore the issues raised, the discussion provides a brief overview of female entrepreneurship in the UK, followed by an analytical consideration of the notion of gender and how this underpins our understanding of women's position in contemporary society. Thereafter, the chapter presents some empirical findings from a study of male and female accountants in independent practice and finally, discusses the implications of these results with regard to issues of gender, capitalization and performance.

WOMEN OWNED BUSINESSES AND UNDERCAPITALIZATION

The importance of women as a largely untapped pool of entrepreneurial talent has been widely recognized by economic development agencies in most western economies (OECD, 1998). Yet the popular perception of growth in the number of female entrepreneurs in the UK, a view perhaps influenced by the range of public policy initiatives designed to increase female self-employment, contrasts starkly with the statistical evidence. Over the past decade, the number of self-employed women declined from 857,000 in 1990 to 824,000 in 1999 while the female share of self-employment (26%) has remained static (Labour Force Survey, 1999). Although the proportion of female entrepreneurs in the UK is comparable with other Northern European countries (Holmquist, 1997; Nilsson, 1997), it is considerably lower than in the United States, where the female share of business ownership increased from 5% in 1970 to 38% in 1999 (Brush &

Hisrich, 1999). Estimates suggest that in the United States, 5.4 million women-owned businesses account for 23.8 million employees and $2.3 trillion in sales revenue (Brush & Hisrich, 1999). Perhaps what is more important, there is evidence that women-owned businesses in the United States are moving out of traditionally "female" sectors such as retailing and low-order services and into construction, production and technology-based sectors (Carter & Allen, 1997; Brush & Hisrich, 1999). This too contrasts with the UK, where female entrepreneurship is still predominantly located within the service economy (Marlow, 1997) and even in the "new economy" sectors, initially believed to offer gender-neutral opportunities for entrepreneurship, the number of firms owned by men significantly out number those owned by women (Wilkinson 2001).

Female entrepreneurship in the UK is not merely differentiated by low levels of start-up allied to high levels of sectoral concentration, however. Research investigating female entrepreneurship suggests that women's experience of business ownership differ substantially from that of men (Allen & Truman, 1993; Carter et al., 2001; Goffee & Scase, 1985). An individual's experience of business ownership is intricately related to their abilities in mobilizing the appropriate resources or capital. The type of capital required to start and sustain a successful business includes not only finance, but also human capital derived from the entrepreneur's education, training and business related experience and social capital in the form of access to relevant professional and social networks. When access to economic and social capital is achieved primarily through waged work, women face a range of barriers associated with their gender to gaining such resources. As waged workers, most women are located where, as Mirchandani (citing Ferguson, 1984), notes, "femaleness gets inscribed into jobs which involve little control or power, and these jobs are simultaneously labeled as 'unskilled' work requiring feminine traits" (1999, p. 231). The majority of these feminized jobs are located in the service sector and particularly, in the least valued part of this sector.

It is well documented that the majority of those engaging with self-employment develop enterprises based around skills gained in previous waged work (Wynarczyk et al., 1993). The experiences, skills and training gained as an employee are utilized as the basis for new firm foundation, equally the network of contacts gained in employment are drawn upon—as new customers, suppliers or merely for market credibility purposes (Aldrich, 1989). Accordingly, if self-employment reflects prior employment, women will be disadvantaged in that where prior waged work was low paid, low skilled and of poor status, this becomes translated into low profit and insecure self-employment. Low paid, low skilled work constrains opportunities to amass the financial and human capital necessary to place new firms on a secure footing. Hence, the individual is restricted to areas that do not require substantial levels of initial investment and subsequently, business development is constrained by low levels of investment and knowledge. If this is then added to a disadvantageous location within crowded parts of the service sector, female owned firms are likely to struggle to survive, experience poorer growth and to be higher risks for external funding agencies. When Meager et al. (1994, p. 15) commented upon the over representation of women in poor performing and failing firms, they summed up this argument succinctly, "because they [women] had less financial or human capital than male counterparts, or because they tended to enter sectors with poorer business prospects."

Segregation theorists (Hakim, 1979; Halford & Leonard, 2001) have also demonstrated that as well as being located in feminine ghettos of employment, when women do gain access to work with higher levels of remuneration and status they are concentrated within the lowest levels of the hierarchy. Overall, the manner in which women are segregated and subordinated in waged labor underpins their position in self-employment. Issues such as sectoral concentration, credibility gaps, access to finance and networks, and hence firm performance, are directly related to their subordination within prevailing gender systems and then reinforced by their positioning in waged and domestic labor. Clearly, accruing various forms of capital is crucial for business success, yet access to capital is determined by social structures that are deep rooted and gender based (Breitenbach, 1999).

Further to experiencing gender related challenges in accruing social and financial capital from waged work, research has also indicated that women face particular challenges when seeking funding to establish and then grow their businesses. Limited access to high pay sectors of waged labor both restricts women's opportunities to generate any substantial level of personal savings to invest in new enterprise and places limitations upon their ability to generate credit histories and so, they present a greater risk to formal lenders (Carter & Kolvereid, 1997). The combination of these factors constrains funding opportunities and contributes to women having a propensity to establish firms in poorly performing segments of the service sector. These sectors are cheap to enter but are ones in which they struggle to survive, so reinforcing the negative image of women in self-employment (Carter, Williams, & Reynolds, 1997). Indeed, women use only one third of the starting capital that men do, irrespective of sector, are more likely to rely on limited personal savings and are rarely given access to venture funding (Carter & Rosa, 1998; Green et al., 1999; Marlow & Patton, 2003). This issue is of critical importance as studies have indicated that the long-term growth performance of firms is strongly affected by the resources mobilized at start-up (Carter & Rosa, 1998; Rosa et al., 1996). As a consequence, women's businesses employ fewer core staff, are less likely to have grown substantially in employment (more than twenty employees) after twelve months in business, have a lower sales turnover, and are valued at a lower level than male owned businesses. Men are significantly more likely to own other businesses (19.6% compared with 8.6% for women) and also to have strong growth ambitions in so far as they wanted to expand their businesses "as far as they could" (43%, versus 34% of women) (Rosa et al., 1996). As a consequence of these and other factors, business ventures owned by women tend to underperform across a variety of different business measures (Boden & Nucci, 2000; Cliff, 1998; Lerner et al., 1997; Rosa et al., 1996). Not only is it arguably more difficult for women to start in business, but their growth rates tend not to match those of equivalent male owned firms.

Despite the popular presumption of their stronger networking and interpersonal skills (Wilkinson, 2001), there is some evidence to suggest that women also face challenges in gaining access to networks able to provide resources to support new venture creation and firm growth (Aldrich, 1989; Aldrich et al., 1989). Networks are known to assist in business start-up and growth by providing access to information, advice and finance as well as much needed business contacts (Aldrich, 1989; Shaw, 1997). As a result of their employment experiences, women may not have such resources within their personal networks. Many traditional business networks have been developed by men and there may also be an unwillingness to provide women with access to them. As Brush (1997, p. 22) described "women are less welcome in social networks ... and are left out of some of those loops, meaning they do not have access to as much information. So social structures and the way that women socialize influence the human and social capital endowments with which they start their businesses." On a more positive note, recent research has found that the Internet has provided a new opportunity for women to build their own business networks (Carter et al., 2001). The growing number of virtual networks, such as High-TechWomen.com and DigitalEve.com and an increasing number of web-sites dedicated to providing women with business advice, such as everywoman.co.uk provide firm evidence of women's desire to network and make the most of new technology to help them achieve their business objectives. Nevertheless, while there is much anecdotal evidence to suggest gender differences both in the way networks are constructed and used, this is a subject that has received little rigorous research attention (Carter et al., 2001).

GENDER, WORK, AND SELF-EMPLOYMENT

Over recent years, a growing body of literature has begun to emerge which suggests that female entrepreneurs' experience of business ownership will be influenced and shaped by their gender. To date, however, whilst a rich analytical tradition has been established in sociological theory and related disciplines regarding the notion of "gender," within the study of entrepreneurship, this has not been so evident. While there certainly is a general recognition that gender will intrude into the experience of self-employment, little consideration has been afforded to what is actually meant by the term. Bem (1993), for example, used the term "lenses of gender" to describe the hidden assumptions that produce and reproduce the meaning and salience of gender in society. There are three hidden assumptions: essentialism, androcentrism, and gender polarisation. Essentialism is the assumption that basic differences in orientation and personality between men and women are rooted in biology and nature. Androcentrism is male centredness, the belief that males are more valuable than females and that male experience is both gender neutral and the norm for all people. Assuming that work is full-time, lifelong and contains no breaks for family commitments, or when "he" is used to mean he or she, is an androcentric position. Gender polarization is the assumption that not only are women and men different, but this difference is superimposed in so many ways that a link is forged between sex and virtually every aspect of human experience, for example, modes of dress, social roles, ways of expressing emotion. The means to justify androcentrism or essentialism is through gender polarisation.

Drawing on Bourdieu's (1990, 1991) conceptual framework with respect to gender symbolism, his roots in structuralism lead him to posit that the social order represents hierarchical relations of difference symbolized in binary opposites—male/female, dominant/dominated, strong/weak. The natural attitude to the gender divide draws heavily on tacitly taken for granted assumptions, from the everyday practices in the sexual division of labor and the "sweet rationale" which explain the "necessity" for things being as they are. Women are connoted with negative qualities and the masculine with the positive. This contributes to masculine domination. A person's structural position is also determined by capital—economic, social, cultural (which includes educational qualifications) and symbolic (e.g., feminine beauty or acquiring masculine traits). Both men and women have formal cultural capital in the form of education and qualifications. However, cultural capital may take the form of a particular combination of educational experiences and family or social connections and interactions with key agents. This could be taken as given or achieved through membership of networks. Alternatively, significant qualities might be recognized like "drive," the ability to work long unsociable hours or having good social skills that help build an enterprise. These qualities can be viewed as part of what Bourdieu calls the "habitus," a set of dispositions like attitudes and taste, which people absorb in socialization and contribute toward their practical knowledge and skill in functioning in business. Bourdieu's framework helps us understand how gender hierarchies work, by recognizing the way in which socially constructed ideas of difference, which are neither neutral nor objective, reflect a hierarchical ordering prevalent in society. The recognition of informal characteristics as constituting cultural capital may help in revealing those virtually invisible social practices that remain difficult to detect and combat. The qualities women bring to business ownership may not realize the same value as men's since the dominant ideology and the doxa, or taken for granted assumptions are in the hands of the predominantly male elite who make key decisions on issues such as access to premises, networks, approve loans, place orders etc.

Also important to this debate, is how men and women as business owners "do gender" (West & Zimmerman, 1987). A person is expected to "do gender" in that we conform to behaviors that are either male or female, and act within parameters of the stereotypical behavior associated with such roles; the ease of interaction depends upon such conformity (Ahl, 2002; Oakley, 1972). Conformity to sex roles and identities is not, however, problematic in itself. Rather, it is the value ascribed to such roles that create the problem, in that the masculine is valued above the feminine creating male dominance (Walby, 1987). However, as both Oakley and Ahl argue, gender difference is ubiquitous, it is so "common sense" that it forms a sex role system to which most of us subscribe and rarely challenge. The acceptance of gender difference then underpins a system of inequality for which the basis is largely invisible (Lorber, 1994).

This gender inequality has been evident in the study of entrepreneurship. It has been noted that, in comparison with the volume of academic research which has been undertaken on the small firm sector, the female entrepreneur has been seriously "neglected" by both the mass media and the academic community (Baker et al., 1997, p. 221). For some, the lack of attention paid to women's experience of entrepreneurship is evidence of a wider problem of gender effects being omitted from mainstream research studies into social phenomena. Carter (1993, p. 151), for example, notes that "historically women have been left off the small business research agenda or made invisible by research practices or in other ways written out of the analysis of self-employment." Hamilton (1990) cites an example of how this is done, using Rees and Shah's (1986) analysis of self-employment in the UK. As Hamilton (1990, pp. 6–7) points out, their study "excludes a number of categories of people and then a whole gender in order to obtain sharper results." Among those excluded are "those who are not heads of household (mainly women); those who worked for less than thirty hours a week (mainly women); females (on the basis that 'self-employment is predominantly a male preserve')." Concepts of entrepreneurship are traditionally assumed to be gender neutral, but as Berg (1997, p. 261) points out: "rely in fact on notions of humanity and rationality that are masculinist." Dualities such as the rational-irrational distinction may appear to have no apparent gender bias, but in reality are "thoroughly imbued with gender connotations, one side being socially characterized as masculine, the other as feminine, and the former being socially valorized" (Massey, 1996, p. 113). Shakeshaft and Nowell (1984, pp. 187–188) conclude that this results in the "elevation of the masculine to the level of the universal and the ideal, it is the honoring of men and the male principle above women and the female. This perception creates a belief in male superiority and a value system in which female values, experiences and behaviors are viewed as inferior."

As a consequence of gender ascription it appears that women are characterized as a devalued group and the social and economic activities with which they engage reflect this valuation. However, the picture is not one of unremitting gloom and has not gone totally unchallenged. Feminist pressure groups, since the suffrage movement in the early twentieth century, have worked to draw attention to gender inequality and in the latter part of the last century, governments in advanced economies introduced a raft of legislation and regulation to address gender-based discrimination. Undoubtedly, however, the regulation route to challenging inequality has met with limited success in the UK. For example, nearly 30 years after the enactment of the Sex Discrimination Act (1975), British women still only earn 80% of the male wage and occupations remain clearly segregated on the basis of gender (Equal Opportunities Commission, 2002).

Yet, one area where the gender balance has changed quite notably and incited popular debate within the UK, is that of secondary education. Girls now outperform boys at school in examination attainment; this is impacting upon university entry with more young women now gaining appropriate qualifications to enter high status, highly remunerated professions. This raises the question whether the attainment of professional status might be able to negate the effects of occupational segregation and accompanying subordination. This discussion now considers this argument with regard to the accountancy profession in the UK where currently more than half of undergraduate students studying finance and accountancy related subjects are female. Regarding the manner in which this impacts upon self employment, the Association of Chartered and Certified Accountants (ACCA) found that in 2001, 38% of independent practitioners were female (compared to national rates overall of 26%) and the expectation is that this figure will rise.

To be recognized as a member of the accountancy profession, an individual must possess specific objective, credited and benchmarked qualifications to indicate the attainment of the necessary skills and competencies to practice. As members of an esteemed profession, accountants have the potential to receive high levels of remuneration in terms of salaries and status. Consequently, it may be supposed that entry into such a profession might be one avenue available to women to address waged labor subordination as access to the necessary qualifications are not gender specific, but dependent upon the attainment of objective entry criteria.

However, such an avenue of escape is by no means assured, the professions are part of the wider social and economic environment of work which is shaped by subjective discrimination based upon social characteristics. As has been argued above, gender will critically affect a person's access to, and progress within, waged labor in ways that disadvantage women. Empirical evidence would indicate that the accountancy profession reflects this trend such that women experience gender-based discrimination within their work in terms of location in hierarchies and segregation (Lehman, 1992). Drawing upon evidence from an empirical study of gendered differences in accountancy careers, Pierce-Brown and Richardson (1995, p. 18) found women to be disadvantaged, commenting that "the most notable differences were found in the distribution of the sexes between employment sectors, the position in management hierarchies, levels of remuneration, the motivation behind career moves and the perceived (negative) influence of gender and family circumstances upon career progression."

These findings are confirmed by Barker and Monks' (1998) study of the careers of male and female accountants, which found that women had substantial problems attaining flexibility at work to accommodate family and work commitments. Even those who did conform to normative career patterns still felt they lacked support networks amongst themselves but perceived there to be a strongly entrenched male network which positively assisted men to progress in their careers. The strength of these networks also undermined women's self confidence to go beyond specialist areas into general practice as they felt they were not able to manage the masculine, politicized environment associated with this activity. The combination of the "old boys" network and the constraints women experienced due to family commitments led to over half of this sample of female respondents rejecting the notion that men and women had equal career opportunities. By contrast, only 20% of the male respondents agreed with this statement.

This is not to suggest that the accountancy profession, in particular, can be singled out as overly prejudicial but rather that it is shaped and influenced by the wider economic and social pressures which interrelate to generate female subordination in all spheres. Hence, it remains debatable that by virtue of profession, women might be able to refute such disadvantage in their career paths.

However, it may be that by transferring their professional skills into independent practice, female accountants may be able to avoid career-based discrimination and develop skills and talents in a manner that supports sustainable businesses. Such firms, owned by accredited and qualified professional women should have the potential to grow and certainly should perform equitably with those of male colleagues with comparable qualifications. This paper will consider this argument in more detail using evidence from an exploratory survey of both men and women in independent practice. The survey explores the size and performance of businesses and the type of clients served and services that are undertaken. The data is disaggregated by gender so enables some preliminary findings to be outlined regarding the differing experiences of men and women who chose to engage with self-employment within the profession.

GENDER AND PROFESSIONAL SELF-EMPLOYMENT: THE CASE OF ACCOUNTANCY

The research reported here was part of a broader project that aimed to develop a profile of independent accountancy practices belonging to the Association of Chartered and Certified Accountants (ACCA) (Ram & Carter, 2003). ACCA is one of the largest international accountancy bodies and has more than 250,000 members and students in 160 countries. A postal questionnaire was administered to all ACCA members based in the UK with small-scale independent practices (3,913). In total, 1567 usable responses were received, equating to a usable response rate of 40%. Female responses (173) constituted only 11% of the effective sample.

The results of the survey reflect the recent historical developments of women in the accountancy profession, but also show some surprising parallels with women who have entered self-employment in nonprofessional capacities. Table 8.1, for example, presents details of the age of both male and female self-employed accountants in the sample. While the majority of male respondents were aged over forty, female respondents were significantly more likely to be aged between 30 and 39 (X^2 50.414, df 5, p.000). Table 8.2 shows a significant relationship between gender and years in independent practice, with women more likely to have been a partner in their current practice for less than three years (X^2 51.018, df 6, p .000). The relative youthfulness of women business owners and the younger average age of their businesses have been noted in many studies of gender and enterprise (Kourilsky & Walstad, 1998). Some studies suggest that these factors are indicative of a general trend toward an increased participation of women in entrepreneurial activities as a by-product of their increased participation in the labor market as a whole (Brooksbank, 2000). Goffee and Scase (1985), however, predicted that an overall rise in female entrepreneurship would occur, at least partially as a result of individualized responses to the experience of labor market discrimination or the "glass ceiling" effect. Within the context of accountancy profession, the lower average age of self-employed women may, perhaps, be explained by both factors. A rise in the number of women entering the profession, particularly in recent years, may have led to an overall and concomitant increase in the number of younger self-employed female accountants. However, following the work of Pierce-Brown and Richardson (1995) and Barker and Monks (1998), it may be equally true that dissatisfaction with career progress and flexibility within the large accountancy firms has led a disproportionate number of younger female accountants into professional self-employment. Not surprisingly, given the lower average age of the female respondents, self-employed women were also more likely to have entered into business more recently than were self-employed men.

Table 8.1. Age of Respondents

Age Range	Men		Women	
	Number	%	Number	%
Under 25	1	—	1	—
25–29	14	1.0	4	2.3
30–39	272	19.5	66	38.1
40–49	541	38.8	69	39.8
50–59	423	30.3	29	16.7
Over 60	143	10.2	4	2.3
Total	1394	99.8	173	99.2

Table 8.2. Years as Partner in Present Practice by Sex of Respondent

Years as Partner	Men		Women	
	Number	%	Number	%
0–3 years	256	18.3	58	33.5
4–5 years	150	10.7	27	15.6
6–10 years	276	19.7	46	26.5
11–20 years	494	35.4	37	21.3
21–30 years	139	9.9	4	2.3
More than 31 years	59	4.2	1	—
Total	1394	98.2	173	99.2

Given that many previous research studies have found the performance of women owned businesses to lag behind those owned by men, an important element of the study was to investigate in broad terms the comparative size and performance of practices owned by male and female respondents. The two main indicators of performance used in the study were annual turnover and employment size. Table 8.3 presents details of the financial scale of businesses in the sample as measured by annual turnover. The largest proportion of male owned practices (38%) reported an annual turnover of between £100,000 and £500,000, although 40% reported a lower turnover and 18% reported a turnover of between £500,000 and over £5 million. By contrast, female owned practices reported significantly lower levels of annual turnover (X^2 29.83, df 7, p.000). The largest proportion of women (40%) reported a turnover in the lowest band (less than £50,000 per annum), while only 14% reported a turnover in the higher bands (more than £500,000).

Table 8.3. Business Turnover (Year 2000) in Male- and Female-Owned Practices

Turnover Range	Male Owned		Female Owned	
	Number	%	Number	%
Less than £50,000	327	23.4	70	40.4
£50,000–£100,000	252	18.0	19	10.9
£100,000–£500,000	529	37.9	56	32.3
£500,000–£1 million	119	8.6	18	10.4
£1 million–£3 million	97	6.9	7	4.0
£3 million–£5 million	15	1.0	—	—
More than £5 million	15	1.0	1	—
Total	1394	96.8	173	98.0

It may be argued that the lower average annual turnover reported by women owned practices is a reflection of their relative youth, and that as women-owned businesses become more established their performance, as measured in terms of annual turnover, will steadily equalize to match those of male-owned practices. In order to try to capture the data that might reveal whether this trend was occurring, respondents were asked to give details of annual turnover over the previous three years. If the performance of women-owned firms showed a steady improvement as their businesses became more established, this might be evidence to suggest that female underperformance was less a function of structural gender disadvantage and more a reflection of their relative inexperience as business owners. Table 8.4 presents details of mean annual turnover for three years from 1998, measured in the same bands used in Table 8.3. Women-owned practices reported significantly lower levels of annual turnover than male-owned practices in each of the three years investigated. In the first year, 1998, the mean difference in annual turnover between male-owned and female-owned practices was 0.33. However, rather than the mean difference narrowing in the second year, as women became more experienced as business owners, the mean difference remained the same (0.33) in 1999. The third year's data (2000) did show a narrowing in the mean difference in annual turnover between male-owned and female-owned practices, but the change was only marginal (0.31). Collectively, the three years' data on business turnover is neither indicative of a systematic narrowing of the turnover gap, nor does it provide any support that the performance of women-owned firms improves as a result of longer experience of business ownership.

Table 8.4. Turnover 1998–2000 in Male and Female Owned Practices: Independent Samples *t*-test

Turnover level Banded (1–7)	Group	Mean	St.dev.	t-test	Significance (2-tailed)
Turnover 2000	Men	2.56	1.35	2.861	0.004
	Women	2.25	1.28		
Turnover 1999	Men	2.47	1.37	2.984	0.003
	Women	2.14	1.32		
Turnover 1998	Men	2.39	1.38	2.958	0.003
	Women	2.06	1.33		

Notes: 1. 95% confidence intervals, 2. Turnover bands as in Table 3

A further measure of business size and scale lies in the number of partners and employees within the respondents' practices. Across the whole sample, the majority of practices employed fewer than four full-time people in each of five different job categories. The average number of partners within each practice was 2.12, while each practice also employed on average 1.29 qualified accountants and 2.27 part-qualified accountants. Continuous variable responses were re-coded into six standard SME employment bands (0, 1–4, 5–9, 10–49, 50–99, and 100+) prior to analysis. Table 8.5 shows that mean employment in women-owned practices was lower than that in male-owned practices across all five different job categories. These differences were statistically significant within three of the job categories: partners, part-qualified accountants and clerical/secretarial staff.

Within the context of professional services, more revealing insights into gender derived differences may lie in the type of client base served by the practice and the content of the work that is routinely undertaken on the clients' behalf. In order to investigate the first issue, respondents were asked

Table 8.5. Full-time Employment Size by Sex of Respondent: Independent Samples t-test

Employment Category	Group	Mean	St.dev.	t-test	Significance (2-tailed)
Partners	Men	0.96	0.57	3.035	.002
	Women	0.82	0.51		
Qualified accountants	Men	0.49	0.70	1.679	—
	Women	0.39	0.61		
Part-qualified accountants	Men	0.66	0.87	2.065	.039
	Women	0.51	0.74		
Finance Assistants	Men	0.48	0.75	1.126	—
	Women	0.41	0.67		
Clerical / secretarial	Men	0.65	0.75	2.688	.007
	Women	0.49	0.63		

Notes: 1. 95% confidence intervals, 2. Mean calculated in employment bands 1–6 (0, 1–4, 5–9, 10–49, 50–99, 100+ employees)

to describe their typical client base in terms of employment size, turnover and sector. Table 8.6 shows that male-owned and female-owned practices reported a very similar client size profile, with most depending on micro- and small-sized firms, however women-owned practices were significantly more likely to report more clients within the smallest turnover category (less than £50,000). More than a quarter of women-owned practices, compared with 18% of male-owned practices, reported that their clients mainly had an annual turnover of less than £50,000, and over half of women-owned practices, compared with less than 40% of male-owned practices reported that their clients' turnover was less than £100,000. Table 8.6 also reveals great similarities between male-owned and women-owned practices with regard to the sectoral profile of their clients. Most mainly served clients across a range of all sectors, and although female accountants reported a slightly higher number of service sector clients, this difference was not significant.

In order to investigate job content, the work that is routinely undertaken on behalf of clients, respondents were asked to report the contribution toward overall fee income derived from different types of service work. Again, great similarities were found in both the types of work undertaken and their relative contribution to overall fee income in male-owned and female-owned accountancy practices. However, a more nuanced insight into job content can be seen from comparing the means reported in Table 8.7. Male respondents were slightly more likely to report that management

Table 8.6. Profile of Business Clients by Sex of Respondent

Client Profile	Men Number	%	Women Number	%
Size of business clients is mainly:				
Micro–small firms (0–9 employees)	1059	75.9	124	71.6
Small–medium firms (10–49)	313	22.4	44	25.4
Medium–large firms (50–249)	7	0.5	3	1.7
Large firms (250 +)	—		—	
(X^2 4.64, df 3, p.200)				
Turnover of clients is mainly:				
Up to £50,000	247	17.7	45	26.0
£50,000–£100,000	306	21.9	44	25.4
£100,000–£250,000	332	23.8	32	18.4
£250,000–£500,000	233	16.7	17	9.8
£500,000–£1 million	161	11.5	21	12.1
£1 million–£5 million	61	4.3	6	3.4
Over £5 million	7	0.5	4	2.3
(X^2 21.02, df 7, p.004)				
Sector of clients is mainly:				
Services	432	30.9	58	33.5
Retail, wholesale and repairs	123	8.8	11	6.3
Pubs, hotels and restaurants	26	1.8	2	1.1
Manufacturing	25	1.8	4	2.3
Technology based firms	10	0.7	2	1.1
Public and voluntary organisations	3	0.2	1	0.5
A mix of all sectors	737	52.8	94	54.3
(X^2 6.16, df 7, p.521)				
Total	**1394**		**173**	

consultancy, business advice, representing clients, auditing and VAT returns made a higher contribution toward overall fee income. Given that the client base of male-owned practices was composed of firms with a significantly higher annual turnover, it is unsurprising that the nature of the work undertaken by male-owned practices emphasized this type of service. Female respondents, conversely, were significantly more likely to derive a higher proportion of fee income from personal taxation work.

Table 8.7. Contribution of Services to Fee Income (Job Content): Independent Samples t-test

Services contributing to fee income	Group	Mean	St.dev.	t-test	Significance (2-tailed)
Preparing accounts	Men	0.93	0.26	−1.366	—
	Women	0.95	0.21		
Auditing	Men	0.96	0.56	1.540	—
	Women	0.89	0.60		
Corporate taxation	Men	0.75	0.46	−0.188	—
	Women	0.76	0.44		
VAT returns	Men	0.78	0.46	1.753	—
	Women	0.72	0.45		
Personal taxation	Men	1.02	0.53	−2.174	0.03
	Women	1.11	0.61		
Representing clients	Men	0.42	0.50	1.956	—
	Women	0.35	0.48		
Business advice	Men	0.51	0.53	1.145	—
	Women	0.46	0.51		
Management consultancy	Men	0.31	0.51	0.890	—
	Women	0.27	0.54		
Other services	Men	0.25	0.54	−0.252	—
	Women	0.26	0.63		

Notes: 1. 95% confidence intervals, 2. Mean calculated in bands 1–4 (0, 1 = 1–25%, 2 = 26–50%, 3 = 51–75%, 4 = 76–100%)

CONCLUSIONS

Although, historically, women's experience of the labor market has been largely confined to low wage sectors and occupations, a growing number of women are engaging in high wage, professional careers. Waged work provides an important source of human, social and financial capital for individuals subsequently moving into self-employment. One explanation for the apparent underperformance of women-owned businesses lies in the lower value of their personal capital derived from waged work, which can be subsequently transferred into business ownership. Previous studies of female entrepreneurship have rarely differentiated between women on the basis of their occupational and professional experience. At the outset of this study, it was postulated that women moving into self-employment from professional work careers may have the ability to circumvent many of the undercapitalization issues faced by women without the benefit of professional backgrounds. Not only does access to professional employment depend on the acquisition of higher educational and skill levels, the rewards gleaned from professional employment, in the form of knowledge, finance and networks, constitute important business resources for potential entrepreneurs.

The results of this exploratory study of male-owned and female-owned accountancy practices, however, reveal some surprising similarities to the results of previous, gender-based studies of nonprofessional entrepreneurs. Not only are female accountants in independent practice younger than their male counterparts, their businesses are also newer. Both of these results mirror the findings of studies that have used more generalized samples. This study also revealed female-owned accountancy practices to be smaller than their male-owned counterparts, both in terms of annual turnover and employment size. As both these measures of firm size are often regarded as primary performance indicators, these results are particularly interesting and also mirror those found in previous gender-based studies. Importantly, while some studies have suggested that the performance gap between male-owned and female-owned businesses will close as women gain more experience of business ownership, these results suggest otherwise. The performance gap in terms of annual turnover remained constant over a three-year period, and the study found no evidence of steadily enhanced performance occurring over the period measured. While it is surprising that the performance gap between male-owned and female-owned firms is so starkly apparent even within professional firms, previous studies of the accountancy sector may explain these gender-based differences. As Pierce-Brown and Richardson (1995) and Barker and Monks (1998) found, gender-based differences in employment, remuneration, hierarchy and network access within the accountancy profession not only result in female disadvantage in terms of career experience they also restrict the level and value of personal capital that they can mobilize.

If female accountants moving into independent practice are disadvantaged in their ability to mobilize capital for business start-up, these disadvantages may be compounded within business ownership by client profile and job content. Previous studies of professional practice (Ram & Carter, 2003) suggest that accountants and their clients share similar characteristics: small, independent practices typically serve small, local companies and ethnic minority practices typically serve ethnic minority clients. If practitioner-client similarities also operate along a gender dimension, female-owned accountancy practices may be disadvantaged in as much as they serve similarly small, low-turnover clients. While the gender of clients was not investigated, it is relevant to note that female-owned accountancy practices were more likely to engage in routine, lower value services. Thus, even within the context of professional services, gender-based differences are apparent in the experience of business ownership.

REFERENCES

Ahl, H. (2002). *The making of the female entrepreneur.* Jönköping, Sweden: Jönköping International Business School.

Aldrich, H. (1989). Networking among women entrepreneurs. In O. Hagen, C. Rivchum, & D. Sexton (Eds.), *Women owned businesses* (pp. 103–132). New York: Praeger.

Aldrich, H. Reese, P., & Dubini, P. (1989). Women on the verge of a breakthrough? Networking among entrepreneurs in the United States and Italy. *Entrepreneurship and Regional Development, 1*, 339–356.

Allen, S., & Truman, C. (1993). (Eds.). *Women in business: Perspectives on women entrepreneurs.* London: Routledge.

Baker, N. Aldrich, H., & Liou, N. (1997). Invisible entrepreneurs: the neglect of women business owners by mass media and scholarly journals in the USA. *Entrepreneurship and Regional Development, 9*, 221–238.

Barker, P.C., & Monks K. (1998). Irish women accountants and career progression: A research note. *Accounting, Organizations and Society, 23*, 813–823.

Bem, S. (1993). *The lenses of gender: Transforming the debate on sexual inequality.* New York: New Haven.

Berg, N.G. (1997). Gender, place and entrepreneurship. *Entrepreneurship and Regional Development, 9*, 259–268.

Boden, R.J., & Nucci, A.R. (2000). On the survival prospects of men's and women's new business ventures. *Journal of Business Venturing, 15*(4), 347–362.

Boudieu, P. (1990). La domination masculine. *Actes de la Recherche en Sciences Sociales, 84*, 2–31.

Bourdieu, P. (1991). *Language and symbolic power.* Cambridge: Polity.

Bradley, H. (1999). *Gender and power in the workplace.* Basingstoke: Macmillan.

Breitenbach, E. (1999). Changing gender relations in contemporary Scotland. In G Hassan & C. Warhurst (Eds.),*A different future: A moderniser's guide to Scotland* (pp. 229–238). Glasgow: The Big Issue and Centre for Scottish Public Policy.

Brooksbank, D. (2000). Self-employment and small firms. In S. Carter & D. Jones-Evans (Eds.), *Enterprise and small business: Principles, practice and policy* (pp. 7–31). London: FT Prentice-Hall.

Brush, C. (1992). Research on women business owners: Past trends, a new perspective and future directions. *Entrepreneurship Theory and Practice, 16*(4), 5–30.

Brush, C. (1997). Women owned businesses: Obstacles and opportunities. *Journal of Developmental Entrepreneurship, 2*(1), 1–25.

Brush, C., & Hisrich, R. (1999). Women owned business: Do they matter? In Z. Acs (Ed.), *Are small firms important? Their role and impact* (pp. 111–128). Norwell MA: Kluwer Academic Publishers.

Carter, N., & Kolvereid, L. (1997). *Women starting new businesses: The experience in Norway and the US.* OECD Conference on Women Entrepreneurs in SMEs, Paris.

Carter, N., & Allan, K. (1997). Size determinants of women owned businesses; Choice or barriers to resources? *Entrepreneurship and Regional Development, 9,* 211–220.

Carter, N. Williams, M., & Reynolds, P. (1997). Discrimination among new firms in retail: The influences of initial resources, strategy and gender. *Journal of Business Venturing, 12*(2), 125–146.

Carter, S. (1993). Female business ownership: Current research and possibilities for the future. In S Allen & C. Truman (Eds.), *Women in business: Perspectives on women entrepreneurs.* London: Routledge.

Carter, S., & Rosa, P. (1998). The financing of male and female owned businesses. *Entrepreneurship and Regional Development, 10,* 225–241.

Carter, S. Anderson, S., & Shaw, E. (2001). *Women's business ownership: A review of the academic, popular and Internet literature.* London: Small Business Service Research Report: RR002/01, Department of Trade and Industry.

Cliff, J.E. (1998). Does one size fit all—exploring the relationship between attitudes towards growth, gender and business size. *Journal of Business Venturing, 13*(6), 523–542.

Dench, S. Aston, J. Evans, C. Meager, N. Williams, M., & Willison, R. (2002). *Key indicators of women's position in Britain.* London: HMSO.

Equal Opportunities Commission. (2002). *Men and women at work.* Manchester: Equal Opportunities Commission, www.eoc.org.uk

Fasci, M., & Valdez, J. (1998). A performance contrast of male and female owned small accounting practices. *Journal of Small Business Management, 36*(3), 1–7.

Ferguson, K. (1984). *The feminist case against bureaucracy.* Philadelphia: Temple University Press.

Goffee, R., & Scase, R. (1985). *Women in charge: The experiences of female entrepreneurs.* London: Allen and Unwin.

Green, P. Brush, C. Hart, M., & Saparito, P. (1999). Exploration of the venture capital industry: Is gender an issue. In P.D. Reynolds, W.D. Bygrave, S. Manigart, C.M. Mason, G.D. Meyers, H.J. Sapienza, & K.G. Shaver (Eds.), *Frontiers of entrepreneurship research 1999* (pp. 168–181). Wellesley, MA: Babson College Center for Entrepreneurial Studies.

Hakim, C. (1979). *Occupational segregation by sex.* London: Department of Employment Research Paper 9, HMSO.

Halford, S., & Leonard, P. (2001). *Gender, power and organisations.* Basingstoke: Palgrave.

Hamilton, D. (1990). *An ecological basis for the analysis of gender differences in the pre-disposition to self-employment.* Paper presented to the RENT Research in Entrepreneurship Conference, Cologne.

Holmquist, C. (1997). The other side of the coin or another coin? Women's entrepreneurship as a complement or an alternative? *Entrepreneurship and Regional Development, 9*(3), 179–182.

Kourilsky, M.L., & Walstad, W.B. (1998). Entrepreneurship and female youth: Knowledge, attitudes, gender differences and educational practices. *Journal of Business Venturing, 13*(1), 77–88.

Labour Force Survey. (1999). *Employment spring figures.* www.statistics.gov.uk
Lehman, C. (1992). HERstory in accounting: The first eighty years. *Accounting, Organizations and Society, 17*(3/4), 261–285.
Lerner, M., Brush, C., & Hisrich, R. (1997). Israeli women entrepreneurs: An examination of factors affecting performance. *Journal of Business Venturing, 12*(4), 315–339.
Lorber, J. (1994). *Paradoxes of gender.* New Haven, CT: Yale University Press.
Massey, D. (1996). Masculinity, dualisms and high technology. In N. Duncan (Ed.), *Bodyspace—Destabilizing geographies of gender and sexuality* (pp. 109–126). London: Routledge.
Marlow, S. (1997). Self-employed women—New opportunities, old challenges? *Entrepreneurship and Regional Development, 9*(3), 199–210.
Marlow, S. (2002). Self employed women—A part of or a part from feminist theory? *Entrepreneurship and Innovation, 2*(2), 26–37.
Marlow, S., & Patton, D. (2003, in press). The financing of small businesses—Female experiences and strategies. In M. Davies & S. Fielden (Eds.), *International handbook of women and small business entrepreneurship.* Cheltenham: Edward Elgar.
Meager, N., Court, G., & Moralee, J. (1994). *Self employment and the distribution of income.* Brighton: Report 270, Institute of Manpower Studies.
Mirchandani, K. (1999). Feminist insight into gendered work: New directions in research on women and entrepreneurship. *Gender, Work and Organisations, 6*(4), 224–235.
Moore, D., & Buttner, H. (1997). *Women entrepreneurs: Moving beyond the glass ceiling.* Thousand Oaks, CA: Sage.
Nilsson, P. (1997). Business counselling services directed towards women entrepreneurs—Some legitimacy dilemmas. *Entrepreneurship and Regional Development, 9*(3), 239–257.
Oakley, A. (1972). *Sex, gender and society.* London: Maurice Temple Smith.
OECD. (1998). *Women entrepreneurs in small and medium enterprises.* Paris: Organisation for Economic Co-operation and Development.
Pierce Brown, R., & Richardson, C. (1995). *Consolidating the minority interest: A study of gender differences in the careers of accountants.* Leicester: Leicester Business School Occasional Paper 26, De Montfort University.
Ram, M., & Carter, S. (2003). Paving professional futures: Ethnic minority accountants in the United Kingdom. *International Small Business Journal, 21*(1), 55–72.
Rees, H., & Shah, A. (1986). An empirical analysis of self-employment in the UK. *Journal of Applied Econometrics, 1,* 95–108.
Rosa, P., Carter, S., & Hamilton, D. (1996). Gender as a determinant of small business performance: Insights from a British study. *Small Business Economics, 8,* 463–478.
Shakeshaft, C., & Nowell, I. (1984). Research on themes, concepts and models of organisational behaviour: The influence of gender. *Issues in Education, 2*(3), 186–203.
Shaw, E. (1997). *The impact which social networks have on small service firms.* Unpublished doctoral thesis, University of Glasgow.
Storey, D. (1994). *Understanding the small business sector.* London: Routledge.

Walby, S. (1987). *Patriarchy at work.* London: Polity Press.
West, C., & Zimmerman, D. (1987). Doing gender. *Gender and Society, 1*(12), 125–151.
Wilkinson, H. (2001). *Dot bombshell: Women, e-quality and the new economy.* London: The Industrial Society.
Wynaczyk, P., Watson, R., Storey, D., Short, H., & Keasey, K. (1993). *The managerial labour market in small and medium sized enterprises.* London: Routledge.

CHAPTER 9

IN SEARCH OF A NEW CELTIC TIGER

Female Entrepreneurship in Ireland

Colette Henry and Sarah Kennedy

ABSTRACTS

The Irish economy has been consistently outperforming other EU countries in its GDP, GNP, exports and employment rates. However, the recent economic downturn has led to concerns about Ireland's economic future, and the search for a new "Celtic Tiger" has already begun.

Interestingly, recent studies suggest that women's businesses can make a significant contribution to the economy, with women now setting up successful companies in high-technology, professional services and construction. In the United States today, female entrepreneurs are responsible for 38% of all new businesses. However, in Ireland, this source of new business creation remains virtually untapped. A recent EU study shows that women make up just 15% of Irish entrepreneurs (16% in N. Ireland), the lowest level among the 14 EU countries surveyed.

This chapter investigates how this source of potential new entrepreneurs in Ireland can be best exploited. The research involves a small comparative study of women-led businesses in both the North and South of Ireland, and determines the particular industry sectors where women are most predominant, as well as the main barriers or deterrent factors affecting women's decision to start a business. Semi-structured interviews with existing female entrepreneurs, as well as consultations with representatives of support agencies, forms the basis of the empirical work. The overall objective of the research is to identify elements that might be developed into a model (in terms of policy and support) for promoting female entrepreneurship on the island of Ireland.

INTRODUCTION

Over the past decade, the Irish economy has been consistently outperforming other EU countries in its GDP, GNP, exports and employment rates (Eurostat, 1999). However, the recent economic downturn, reflected in downsizing, job losses and business closures, has led to concerns about Ireland's economic future. While there is currently some debate as to whether or not Ireland is actually in recession (Fitzgerald, 2002), economists' views are mixed with regard to growth forecasts, with conservatism advised in predicting future economic performance levels (Suiter, 2001).

Entrepreneurship is often seen as the answer to economic downturns and rising unemployment rates in most countries (Hisrich & Peters, 1998; Jack & Anderson, 1998). In fact, the importance of new business creation to the economy has been the focus of much attention since the Bolton Report (1971), with the phenomenal growth in the small firms sector witnessed on a European scale (Deakins, 1999; European Observatory for SMEs, 1994). There is, therefore, a need to continually increase the supply of entrepreneurial talent to create and grow new businesses that will generate employment and create wealth for the local economy. Typically, such entrepreneurial talent has been mainly generated from the male section of the population, with significantly more men than women becoming entrepreneurs (GEM, 2001). However, recent U.S.-based studies (Kauffman Center, 2001; Langowitz, 2001) suggest that women-led businesses can also make a significant contribution to the economy. Women are now setting up the so-called *new economy* companies, with success in high-technology, professional services and construction. Female entrepreneurs tend to have strong growth aspirations, are customer-oriented, place greater value on the human capital and cultural aspects of the business, and are geared toward financial performance. Women are also starting new businesses faster than their male counterparts, and in the USA today, female entrepreneurs are responsible for 38% of all new businesses. According to Langowitz (2001), the average business in her survey of the top 100 women-led businesses in Massachusetts reported revenues of $46.1 million in 2000, and employed 319 staff.

In Ireland, however, this source of new business creation remains virtually untapped. A recent European study (OECD Report, as cited in Smyth, 2001) shows that women make up just 15% of Irish entrepreneurs (16% in N. Ireland), the lowest level among the 14 EU countries surveyed. This figure compares poorly with some other EU countries, where female entrepreneurs can account for up to 41% of all new start-ups.

This chapter investigates how this source of potential new entrepreneurs in Ireland can be best exploited. The research samples a small group of women-led/founded businesses in County Louth, in an attempt to quantify the actual level of female entrepreneurship, and to determine the particular industry sectors where women are most predominant. Semi-structured interviews with existing female entrepreneurs, as well as consultations with representatives of agencies and organizations supporting business women, forms the basis of the empirical work. The research also involves a small comparative study with a region north of the Irish border (Newry and Mourne in South Down). The overall objective of the research is to develop a model (in terms of policy and support) for promoting female entrepreneurship on the island of Ireland. A consideration of Ireland's dual economic nature and the impact of the Euro will be among other interesting aspects considered in the study.

FEMALE ENTREPRENEURSHIP

A *female* or *women entrepreneur* can be defined as:

> a woman who has initiated a business, is actively involved in managing it, owns at least 50% of the firm, and has been in operation one year or longer. (Moore & Butter, 1997, p.13)

In most countries, the majority of businesses are not owned or managed by women. Indeed, less than one third of all businesses in Europe are led by females, despite the fact that women make up half the European population (Women's Unit UK, 2001).

The literature overall reports a lack of basic information and statistics on female entrepreneurship. This is mainly due to the fact that in most regions, official statistics relating to the particular gender of business owners do not exist, with most businesses categorized according to sector, location and size. This makes it extremely difficult to determine, with any degree of accuracy, the actual level of female entrepreneurship, and the variations between different regions. However, some general figures are available which broadly indicate the levels of female entrepreneurship in different countries. For example, a recent report from the Observatory of European SMEs (2002) indicated that 22% of all 7,600 entrepreneurs (where the gender of the owner could be established) in their study of 19 countries were women, with Greece (14%), Austria (15%), the UK (16%) and Denmark (16%) having the lowest level of female entrepreneurship. The report also showed that the Netherlands (27%), Luxembourg (27%) and France (30%) had the highest levels of female entrepreneurial activity. In the same study it was also found that female business owners are mainly operating in the retail, business and personal services sectors (24%–29%), with the lowest percentage in transport and communication (11%).

In a similar vein, the GEM (Global Entrepreneurship Monitor) Report (2001) found that men were more than twice as active in entrepreneurship as women, and that this was the case in all but three of the 29 counties included in their survey. The difference in entrepreneurship activity between men and women was not as significant in Italy, New Zealand and Spain, where female entrepreneurship rates were either two-thirds of or almost equal to that of men (GEM, 2001, p.15).

In the UK, women are notably underrepresented among the self-employed. Figures quoted by the ONS Labour Force Survey (as cited in Women's Unit UK, 2001) show that women account for just 27% of entrepreneurship activity. However, there are significant differences between regions, with inner London showing the highest level of female entrepreneurs (36%), and West Yorkshire showing one of the lowest levels with 19% (Women's Unit UK, 2001, p.10).

Interestingly, in terms of Ireland, there would appear to be some controversy over the actual number of female entrepreneurs. Some reports have suggested that only 15% of Ireland's entrepreneurs are women (OECD Report, as cited in Smyth, 2001; Women's Unit, UK, 2001; OECD, 2001), with evidence of considerable variation between regions (Bray, 2001; Sia Group, 2001). However, a recent GEM Report (2002) suggests that the level of female entrepreneurship in Ireland is, in fact, even lower at only 7.5%, a figure, the report states, that compares well with other EU countries (GEM, 2001). The common lack of statistical data notwithstanding, it would appear that differences in defining female entrepreneurs, as well as variations in the types of methodologies used, have led to such confusion over Ireland's stock of women entrepreneurs.

Despite the above, the importance of women as an untapped source of entrepreneurship is now widely accepted (Carter, 2000; GEM, 2001; Kauffman Center, 2001). However, the contribution that women make to the business sector was not fully recognized until the mid 1980s (Watkins & Watkins, 1984) when a number of studies relating to gender-specific barriers (Hisrich & Brush, 1986), motivations for start-up (Goffee & Scase,

1985) and comparisons with male entrepreneurs (Hisrich & O'Cinneide, 1985) started to appear in the literature. More recently, studies on female entrepreneurship have focused on motivation and key success factors (Moore & Buttner, 1997), management style (Davidson & Burke, 2001), policy and support (Women's Unit UK, 2001), and characteristics and challenges (Langowitz, 2001).

Barriers to Start-up

The literature accepts that fact that women entrepreneurs tend to experience different opportunities and problems than their male counterparts (Carter, 2000; CEEDR, 2001; Hisrich & O'Cinneide, 1985). The issue of finance for start-up, development and growth, remains one of the most significant difficulties for female entrepreneurs (EC - Staff Working Paper, 2000), and there would appear to be some anecdotal evidence that women have experienced some discrimination by finance providers in this regard (CEEDR, 2001). Women tend to rely more on self-generated finance than men during the start-up phase, with bank credit only increasing once the businesses has established itself. Bray (2001), in her study of 113 aspiring and established female entrepreneurs in the Louth region of Ireland, reported that the most common difficulties experienced by women in attempting to set-up or develop their business were as follows:

- Lack of finance (65%)
- Isolation of working and taking decisions alone (39%)
- Lack of confidence (42%)
- Lack of skills and training (23%)
- Lack of support from agencies (23%)
  (Figures do not total 100% due to multiple answers)
  (Bray, 2001, p. 10).

Similar difficulties have been reported by others (CEEDR, 2001; Hisrich & O'Cinneide, 1985; Langowitz, 2001; ProWomEn Workshop, 2002; Sia Group, 2001), who, while supporting the above, have also uncovered additional problems. Hisrich and O'Cinneide (1985), for example, have reported a lack of management experience, the absence of guidance, and relatively little experience in hiring outside help, as often overlooked difficulties that women entrepreneurs encounter at the early stages of their business (p. 5). Lack of availability of childcare facilities, and society's attitude toward women entrepreneurs in general, figured strongly in reports by both the CEEDR (2001) and the Sia Group (2001). In this regard, the traditional culture of an unequal distribution of family responsibilities between men and women was highlighted as a continuing area of difficulty for women who attempt to combine an entrepreneurial or management career with having children (Sia Group, 2001, p.4).

Elsewhere, the literature reports that other gender-related barriers, particularly with regard to the freedom of decision making that comes with having one's own business, are continuing to exist beyond the set-up stage for many women entrepreneurs (Brindley & Ritchie, 1999).

Profiling the Female Entrepreneur

It would appear from the literature that, when compared to men, most women enter self-employment with fewer financial assets, less management experience, and relatively underresourced in terms of human capital (Carter, 2000). Despite this, and the many barriers they face at the start up stage, successful women-led businesses would appear to be dispelling many of the long-standing myths about female entrepreneurship. Today's female entrepreneurs are growth and profit oriented, they value human capital and are setting-up and running many of the "new economy" companies (Langowitz, 2001). Despite the undisputed fact that most female entrepreneurs start businesses in the service, craft or nonmechanical sectors, there are women who successfully operate in non-traditional sectors, such as construction and high-tech. They are also highly educated and, while lacking managerial experience from their previous employment, are having to make do with gaining it quickly in their own companies (Langowitz, 2001).

According to Moore and Buttner (1997), the successful female entrepreneur is a women who:

> strongly values her autonomy and freedom, has high self-esteem, has felt the stifling effects of a bureaucratic environment in her earlier career, was competent but did not always fit well into the organization, did not necessarily experience discrimination at work but realized that gender made a difference in the endless game of organizational politics, sought her own business to make work exciting again, was perhaps unaware of her skills and savvy when she left here organization but went for it anyway, and although she experienced doubts, she sought assistance, networks, and with a balanced view and experience of leadership, she tried to manage her people wisely. (as cited in Travers, 1998, p.46)

To some degree, this view has been echoed elsewhere in the literature where the *glass ceiling, social attitudes* and *old boy networks* have been identified as key issues that women still encounter in terms of progressing their careers or attempting to start their own business (Sia Group, 2001).

Support for Female Entrepreneurship

Up until recently, most EU countries had no specific policy pertaining to the promotion of female entrepreneurship. However, despite gender specific statistics in the business sector still being difficult to access, it is clear that things are beginning to change.

In the European Union's multi-annual Programme for Enterprise and Entrepreneurship 2001–2005 (Brussels, 2000), the promotion of entrepreneurship among women emerged as a key action within the broader objective of making the EU "the most competitive and dynamic knowledge-based economy in the world, capable of sustaining economic growth, with more and better jobs and greater social cohesion" (EU Commission Staff Working Paper, 2000).

In the UK, there is a dedicated Women's Unit and this forms part of the government's Cabinet Office. In addition, the Small Business Service (SBS)—the government's main support agency for the small business sector—has developed initiatives to address particular issues faced by women starting their own business. However, in Ireland, dedicated support for the promotion of female entrepreneurship is not quite so apparent. Apart from a few independent women's business networks and the occasional "women into business" support program, there is no national or government-led dedicated support service for female entrepreneurs.

The Irish Context

The situation with regard to female entrepreneurship in Ireland is particularly interesting when considered in a historical context. In the past, Ireland has been viewed as one of the poorest countries in the European Union, with high inflation, high emigration levels, slow growth rates and alarming unemployment rates (Brennan, 2000). Historically, there was no enterprise tradition or culture (Garavan et al., 1997), and there appeared to be limited economic opportunities for the creation of indigenous entrepreneurship overall (GEM, 2000). Ireland's economic policies had deliberately focused on inward foreign direct investment, typically in the high technology sectors. Indeed, it was not until the 1980s that the interest in indigenous start-ups and small firms really increased in Ireland, and government finally realized the importance of promoting entrepreneurship to advance the economy.

As in most other parts of the world, the traditional role of women in Irish society was very much that of homemaker, which typically included sole responsibility for children and other family dependents. Although, throughout Europe, women started to become an active part of the workforce in the 1940s, laws establishing equality only became an issue in the 1970s. In Ireland, the "Marriage Bar"—a law requiring women to retire from employment in the civil service upon marriage (Civil Service Regulations Act, 1956) was not abolished until 1973. However, even then, only widows or married women who were not supported by their husbands could apply for reinstatement to the Civil Service. These requirements have since been held to be discriminatory, but it was not until the late 1990s that the act was repealed (Murdoch's Irish Legal Companion, 2003). During the 1990s, the impact of such legal changes resulted in Irish women joining the labor force at four times the rate of the two previous decades. Indeed, in a 1998 survey, women accounted for almost 38% of all paid employees in Ireland (FAS, 1998, as cited in Brennan, 2000).

Thus, with an extremely poor enterprise tradition and, historically, a very conservative view of women, it is hardly surprising that Ireland has failed to augment its stock of female entrepreneurs. There is currently no particular government policy designed to encourage more women to get involved in entrepreneurship, nor are there any specific supports on offer for female entrepreneurs, despite clear evidence that women experience different types of problems in starting and running their business.

RESEARCH CONDUCTED AND METHODOLOGY USED

This study was designed as part of a larger piece of research which sought to investigate the level and nature of female entrepreneurship on the island of Ireland. This chapter presents the findings from the first part of the research which involved a small-scale, highly qualitative study in both the north and south of Ireland. The methodology used consisted of a series of face-to-face, semi-structured interviews with existing female entrepreneurs, as well as consultations with representatives of support organizations and agencies seeking to promote female entrepreneurship. To facilitate comparative analysis, the authors chose to conduct both the interviews and the consultations in areas close to the north/south Irish border. To this end, female entrepreneurs from Louth (southern Ireland) and Newry and Mourne/South Down (Northern Ireland) were selected at random for interview. A total of 20 business women were interviewed, with ten of these from the Newry and Mourne/South Down region, and ten from the Louth region.

The database for the entrepreneurs was developed with some difficulty, as businesses are not categorized according to gender in either of the two regions under investigation. Hence, the names of female entrepreneurs were provided on an ad-hoc basis by the local support agencies, based on their own particular client lists. The only criteria applied by the researchers in determining the make-up of the sample were that:

- The business of the female entrepreneur was based in one of the two regions under investigation.
- The entrepreneur either owned all of her business, or was the majority share holder.
- Her business had been in operation for a least one year.

The first ten names from the database that proved accessible "subjects" in each of the two regions were thus interviewed accordingly. It should be noted that this study did not seek to examine or compare female entrepreneurs in particular industry sectors, size or turnover categories. However, such criteria will be applied in the wider research program, of which this particular study represents the initial, pilot stage.

The interviews lasted between 30 and 40 minutes each and consisted of 22 questions in total. The first set of questions sought general background data on the entrepreneur's business, including the business type, when it was established, and the number employed. The next set of questions focused on the entrepreneur's own background, and covered issues such as education, work experience and support received. The final set of questions focused on the particular experiences of the interviewee as a female entrepreneur, and sought to investigate the individual's motivation for setting up the business, as well as the particular difficulties she faced both at start-up and on a day-to-day basis. Other issues, such as family responsibilities, management style, and the perceived differences between male and female entrepreneurs were also investigated. Finally, the researchers sought the opinions of the business women on what needed to be done to help aspiring female entrepreneurs.

In addition to interviewing female entrepreneurs, representatives from a number of enterprise support agencies, as well as organizations seeking to promote female entrepreneurship, were consulted. A total of eight such representatives, two from Northern Ireland, five from Southern Ireland and one all-Ireland organization (InterTradeIreland), were contacted. The consultations were conducted through meetings and by telephone. This part of the study sought to answer the following questions:

- How many female entrepreneurs were in their region.
- Whether or not the particular agency/organization has a specific policy for women entrepreneurs and the specific nature of this policy.
- Why there would appear to be such a low number of female entrepreneurs in Ireland.

The organizations that participated in this part of the study were: Louth County Enterprise Board, Louth Leader II Programme; Enterprise Ireland; Dundalk Chamber of Commerce, Women's Business Link; Invest Northern

Ireland. (formerly LEDU); Newry & Mourne Enterprise Agency, and InterTradeIreland—the new all-Ireland business support agency.

RESEARCH FINDINGS

Interviews with the Female Entrepreneurs

The findings from this part of the research are presented below under three headings, each relating to the particular set of questions posed in the interviews.

General Background to the Business

All 20 businesses in this pilot survey had been in operation for at least one year, with the majority (eleven businesses) between two and 15 years old. Seven of the businesses had been in operation for more than 16 years. The mean age of the businesses in the survey was 11.4 years. There was a notable difference between the mean age of the businesses in the North (13.7 years) and those in the South (9.1 years). The businesses surveyed were in a range of industry sectors, as illustrated in Table 9.1.

Table 9.1. Industry Sectors

Industry Sectors	Northern Businesses	Southern Businesses	Total
Food (Processing/Wholesale)	2	1	3
Training/Consultancy	4	1	5
Textiles/Clothing	1	0	1
Chemicals	2	0	2
Design/Illustration	0	1	1
Professional Services*	1	2	3
Art/Crafts	0	4	4
Creche Facility	0	1	1
Total	10	10	20

* Professional service: this category includes legal, technical, and recruitment services.

It was interesting to note that the largest number of businesses in the survey overall was in the training or consultancy sector (five businesses), with the smallest number in textiles/clothing, design and childcare (one business in each sector). From the survey, it appears that the typical business sector for the female entrepreneur in the North of Ireland is training and consultancy, with craft-based businesses being the most popular sector for women in the South.

In terms of employment levels, there was a considerable range between the number of employees in each of the businesses surveyed. The figures for full-time employees, which included the female entrepreneur herself, ranged from as few as one, to as many as 70. The mean number of employees for the businesses in the survey overall was 7.1. However, there was a considerable difference between the employment levels of those businesses in the north and those in the south. The mean number of employees in the northern businesses was 11.3, while the mean number of employees in the southern businesses was only 2.9. Even when the two largest employers on each side of the border (two northern businesses with 70 and 18 employees, and two southern businesses with seven and five employees) were removed from the calculation, the difference in mean employment levels was still noticeable, i.e., 3.1 employees for the northern businesses, and 2.1 for the southern businesses. In almost all cases, the entrepreneurs also worked with part-time staff or associates who were contracted as required.

The researchers were also interested to learn about the level of female employees in the businesses surveyed. These figures ranged from just one female staff member (the business owner herself) to 20 (a meet processing company in the north). Exactly half of the businesses surveyed had just one female employed (the entrepreneur herself), with eight companies employing between two and five female staff. Once again, there was a considerable difference between north and south, with the southern businesses having fewer female employees overall—19 among the ten southern businesses surveyed, compared to 52 among the ten northern business surveyed. Even when the two businesses with the largest number of female employees (13 and 20 in the north, and four and one in the south) are removed from each part of the survey, the total number of female employees in the north (19) is still higher than in the southern part of the survey (14). Overall, it appears that the typical female led business in the north of Ireland employs 5.2 women, while the typical female led business in the south of Ireland employs 1.9 women. These figures become less extreme when the two largest employers are removed from each of the calculations, thus giving female employee rates of 2.4 (north) and 1.8 (south).

In terms of customer base, all but nine (two from the north and seven from the south) of the businesses surveyed were involved in cross border or export trade. However, in most cases, this was not extensive, and the introduction of the euro did not appear to have had a significant impact. While one of the entrepreneurs commented that the introduction of the euro and cross border trade had a positive impact on her business, another entrepreneur (a food processing company in the north) indicated that the euro was making it difficult for her business to compete with imports from the Republic of Ireland and mainland Europe, which resulted in the company having to refocus its strategy more on the domestic market.

Entrepreneurs' Backgrounds

While the study revealed a variety of educational standards among the interviewees, all but two of the entrepreneurs had qualified to at least diploma standard, with ten of those surveyed having a degree or postgraduate qualification. The level of qualifications appeared to be slightly higher in the northern part of the survey, with six of the interviewees indicating that they had been educated to degree or postgraduate level, compared with only four in the south.

With regard to work experience, the survey revealed a wide range of industry sectors in which the female entrepreneurs had worked. Most of the women in this particular survey had gained at least some type of work experience, with only two of those surveyed (both from the south of Ireland) having started their business directly after college. The most typical industry sectors where the women had gained their work experience prior to start-up appeared to be education (three entrepreneurs), followed by training/consultancy (two) and food (two).

Only 13 of those surveyed (eight in the north and five in the south) had worked in an area directly related to the particular industry sector in which they were now operating. This was interesting because all of the interviewees felt their work experience had been extremely useful to them in setting up their businesses.

Experiences of Female Entrepreneurship

In this part of the study, the authors sought to determine what motivated the women to set up their businesses. The responses varied from *experiencing frustration in the work place* (one respondent), to *a lack of good employment opportunities* (6). Two of the women wanted the freedom of working for themselves, two were simply passionate about their particular area of work, and one was not sure why she ended up running her own business. Other reasons quoted were *independence* (2), *luck or accident* (2), and having been *made redundant* (1). Interestingly, three of the women in the survey had either one or both parents who were entrepreneurs and viewed this as a strong influence in their decision to start their own business. "*My father had several businesses, so there was always a spirit of entrepreneurship in the family,*" commented one of the interviewees. Another appeared to be strongly influenced by her mother's entrepreneurial flair *"my mother had a driving school business and she was the first female driving instructor in the region. She was a great inspiration to me."*

Among the many difficulties encountered by the women at the start-up stage of their businesses, accessing finance and managing cashflow seemed to be the most common (eleven respondents). "It was horrendous," commented one of the women, *"I had to sign over practically everything at the beginning."* Not being taken seriously (3) and time management (2) were also mentioned in the interviews as areas of difficulty. Other responses included difficulties with purchasing (one respondent), staffing (2), getting clients (2), and making the decision to give up a secure job (1). Interestingly, two of the interviewees felt that they did not experience any real difficulties at the set-up stage (figures do not equal total number surveyed due to multiple responses), and in one case, this seemed to be due to the particularly low set up costs of the business concerned (a small jewelry design business). Some of the difficulties the entrepreneurs experienced at the set up stage continued to cause problems for them as their businesses got up and running. Finance remained one of the main areas of concern, with time management, administration, staffing, competition and self-motivation representing other problematic areas faced by the women on a day to day basis.

Interestingly, the majority of the women (15) felt that none of the difficulties they encountered was specific to them being female. Of the four interviewees who held the opposite view, two indicated that the difficulties they experienced with accessing finance were directly related to the fact that they were women. *"The attitude of the banks appeared to be very much gender related"* commented one of the entrepreneurs. Another referred to the reluctance of the banks to lend money to women:

> The banks were very hesitant at the beginning and still are. The fact that we were two young girls definitely had an impact on how seriously they viewed our business proposal. The fact that we were also in the design business meant that they viewed us as high risk.

The other two women did not mention a particular difficulty that was gender related, and one indicated that she was not sure whether indeed the difficulties she experienced were gender related or not.

Apart from family and friends, most of the support received by the entrepreneurs at the start-up stage was from their local enterprise agencies, with Invest Northern Ireland in the north, and Louth County Enterprise Board in the south being the agencies most frequently mentioned (80% of interviewees in each area). Local Partnerships, the Craft Council, the Tourist Board, colleagues from previous jobs, fellow entrepreneurs and, in one case, the local female bank manager, were also mentioned as additional sources of support and guidance at the early stage of the business. Interestingly, two of the entrepreneurs felt that the agencies did not advertise their services enough, as they had no idea of the support that was on offer before hand. One entrepreneur commented that, while the agencies were excellent for helping you to get started, they do not offer much support after that:

> Once you have made the decision to start, you really are on your own. Then there seems to be a big gap until you make your first million!

With regard to their particular management style, the women in the survey described themselves as having an *open, direct, honest and personal approach to business*. They also felt that their style was *hands-on, focused, business-oriented and efficient*. Fifteen of the women surveyed (ten in the north, and five in the south) felt that their overall management style was different to that of their male counterparts in the sense that women were less forceful, more relaxed and prepared to think things through before acting. Two of the interviewees in the south did not feel that their style was significantly different to that of their male colleagues, and two were unsure. All 20 interviewees felt that, where their management style differed from their male colleagues, this had a very positive impact on the way they managed their business. However, one of the southern entrepreneurs commented that women seemed to adopt a very pessimistic attitude to making money, and this could be a limiting factor in the development of their business:

> Women seem to worry about not getting enough work, and as a result, are more serious about the financial side of things. Men don't tend to get as stressed out about money.

Another entrepreneur supported this view to some degree with her comment that "*men are not afraid to put a price on their work.*" Finally, one woman strongly recommended that women should be encouraged to exploit their honesty and their softer skills, as these were strong assets when running a business:

> Women are much more open and willing to talk things through. They also readily admit any weaknesses or difficulties they might have, whereas men play power games and always want to be in control. They never admit any weaknesses and are confident all the time.

The entrepreneurs were also asked whether they felt it is more difficult for a women to set up a business than a man. Fourteen of the interviewees (five from the north and nine from the south) did not believe it was any more difficult for a women to start a business. Of the five individuals who felt otherwise, lack of confidence, credibility and a patronizing attitude from others were quoted as the main reasons for their response. One of the interviewees suggested that, while modern business women are *"breaking the glass ceiling, they still have to do the housework."* In contrast, another interviewee commented that she could not understand why anyone would feel that starting a business was any more difficult for a women that it was for a man. In her view, it really depended on the particular women and the business she was setting up.

In terms of family responsibilities, eleven of the women (seven from the north and four from the south) had children dependant on them, either currently or when they were setting up their business. Interestingly, only eight of these felt that family responsibilities had a direct impact on their availability to run their business. In most cases, running the business seemed to become easier once the children had grown up: *"Now that the kids are older it's much easier, but when I first started the business and the kids were a lot younger I had to put in really long hours"* commented one of the women. Further investigation, however, revealed that the women clearly had to juggle their business and family responsibilities in an attempt to fit their activities around their children/family life:

> It's really hard to juggle everything. I've had to make lots of sacrifices along the way.

> At times I felt I couldn't give 100% commitment to the business.

This survey also sought to determine what the women had learnt from their entrepreneurial experience, and what advice they would offer to aspiring female entrepreneurs. Several different pieces of advice were offered, with the following being those most frequently mentioned:

- Be clear on your long-term objectives and stay focused (3)
- Don't be too trusting of others (3)
- Realize the importance of personal relationships/networks and dealing with people (2)
- You must be completely confident about your business idea (2)
- Remember to allow yourself some flexibility - it's your business! (2)
- Practice good credit management (1)
- You have to take risks (1)
  (Figures may not equal the total number surveyed due to multiple answers)

Remaining focused and keeping sight of long-term objectives seemed to be particularly important learning experiences for the women in this survey. This was evidenced by comments such as:

Never loose sight of why it is you are in business and where exactly your company is headed.

Remember why you started up the business in the first place.

Stay focused; concentration is the key.

The final question in the interview sought the entrepreneurs' opinions as to what could be done to help encourage more women into business. The following were the most popular responses.

- Promote realistic female entrepreneurs as role models and highlight their contribution to the business sector (7)
- Provide confidence building programs (4)
- Provide more credit facilities (3)
- Provide coaching and motivation programs (with a holistic perspective—to help woman manage all aspects of their life, not just the business part) (3)
- Offer women-only start your own business programs (they can always join their male counterparts at a later stage once they have gained confidence) (2)
- Encourage networking (2)
- Ensure women understand what is involved (2)
- Better advertising of grants and funding opportunities (2)
- Provide more entrepreneurship education at school to raise awareness (1)
- Offer special financial incentives for women (1)
- Offer opportunities to "shadow" successful entrepreneurs (1)
- Revisit the Make-up of policymaking bodies to ensure that they include both women and entrepreneurs (1)
(Figures may not equal the total number surveyed due to multiple answers.)

From the interviews, there appeared to be a sense that women-owned businesses were not viewed in the same way as those owned by male entrepreneurs, and that there was an imbalance between male and female-led businesses. These sentiments were evidenced by comments such as the following:

> There are so many women in business but, because they are in the types of business that are traditionally owned by women, i.e., hairdressing salons and childcare facilities, etc., they are not seen as equals to their male counterparts. Their businesses are seen as weaker, but their contribution to our entrepreneurial society is just as significant and as worthwhile.

I do not think many women consider business as a possible avenue. The practical concern of financial stability often deters them from further investigation. I think this concern deters more women than it does men. For this reason, it might be essential to create a special case for women starting up in business, with extra financial support or semi-funded workspace.

Soft skills are extremely important and most women have these in abundance. They should promote and use these as much as they can, and stop trying to be a man in a man's world and be confident at being a women in a man's world.

Consultations with Support Agencies/organizations

The consultations with the support agencies and those involved in encouraging entrepreneurship revealed a clear concern about the low level of female entrepreneurship both north and south of the border. In terms of an appreciation of the level of female entrepreneurship activity locally, most of the organizations consulted, with the exception of two, had no specific statistics on the number of female entrepreneurs in their region. This appeared to be due to the fact that their client list/database had not traditionally been gender-specific. However, all of the representatives consulted were aware that the number of women-owned businesses was quite low in their region, despite the fact that they had witnessed increased numbers of women participating in early stage "Start Your Own Business Programmes." Due to their particular focus on women, both the Louth County Enterprise Board (through the Women's Business Officer) and the Louth Women's Business Link had specific client lists of their female members, and hence, were able to provide some figures. The County Enterprise Board had around 70–80 names on their list, and the Women's Business link had around 20 members on theirs. Unfortunately, since one of these organizations (Louth County Enterprise Board) provided support to both aspiring and established female entrepreneurs, and the other had recently expanded its remit to cover both business and career women, neither could offer specific figures for the number of women who had already set up their business, i.e., existing female entrepreneurs. In addition, the potential overlap between these two lists was unclear.

In terms of a specific policy, only three of the organizations consulted—the two women-focused organizations mentioned above and Louth Leader - had a clear documented policy pertaining to women. The main focus of these policies appeared to be represented through the common objective of "assisting and encouraging women with the ongoing development of their careers and their businesses." In the case of Louth Leader, however, the emphasis was on trying to get women out of the home and more involved in training and development, to improve their confidence, skills and employment prospects. While the other organizations consulted had no specific policy on women, in enterprise or otherwise, each of them appeared to be in the process of revisiting their policies or developing new initiatives to encourage more female entrepreneurship. In the North of Ireland, for example, despite not having been involved in women-specific enterprise programs for some time, the Newry & Mourne Enterprise Agency had just started to compile a database of women involved in business in their region, and had around 80 names included in the first draft. Invest Northern Ireland had just completed a thorough review of its policy with regard to women in business, and, through consultation with other regional agencies/organizations, was now beginning to design programs specifically targeted at promoting female entrepreneurship throughout the province. InterTradeIreland, Ireland's new all-island support agency, stated that it was in the process of developing a strategy specifically geared toward female entrepreneurs. It appeared that the agency would be joining forces with Invest Northern Ireland to conduct or commission research on this topic, but this was still at an early stage. The Dundalk Chamber of Commerce had plans to embark on a marketing drive to increase the level of female membership, while Enterprise Ireland was in the process of revisiting their policy on women and had already commissioned research into the reasons behind the low level of female entrepreneurship in the country.

When asked why they thought the level of female entrepreneurship was so low in Ireland, those consulted offered a variety of reasons. The following list is a summary of the reasons given:

- Women tend to have more than their fair share of family responsibilities (i.e., housework, as well as caring for children, elderly/sick parents or relatives)
- Women simply find it more difficult to start a business than men, and tend to struggle more once they set up
- There is a lack of childcare facilities in the region
- Women often lack the necessary confidence to start a business
- Women tend to experience more difficulties than men in accessing finance

In all cases, it was agreed that much more needed to be done by way of specific targeted support initiatives to encourage female entrepreneurship. Whether such initiatives should take the form of women-only or mixed gender programs would appear to be still open to debate. While some commentators, including policy makers, claim that no distinction should be made in terms of gender with regard to supporting entrepreneurship, there are valuable arguments to support the view that aspiring female entrepreneurs could benefit from gender specific support initiatives, at least at the early stages of such support provision (Carter et al., 2002; Puechner, 2002; Sia Group, 2001).

CONCLUSIONS

This chapter has attempted to contribute to the existing literature on female entrepreneurship by investigating the background, characteristics and challenges of today's women business owners in the Louth and Newry & Mourne areas of Ireland. The study conducted by the authors revealed that most of the women surveyed in these border regions choose entrepreneurship as an alternative to traditional employment mainly because of a lack of good employment opportunities in their particular field. Funding, not being taken seriously and time management would appear to be the main difficulties that female entrepreneurs face at both the start-up and development stages of their businesses. However, despite most of the women in the study (14) claiming that it is significantly more difficult for a women to set up a business than it is for a man, it was interesting to note that most of them did not feel any of the difficulties they encountered were specifically related to their gender.

The typical business women in this survey is relatively well educated with valuable work experience, who seeks support from family and friends and received much of her technical/financial start-up support from her local enterprise support agency. While many of the women in the survey have children dependant upon them and still manage to run their business, it was clear from the interviews that, for the most part, women are having to juggle their business activities with their family responsibilities, and that in many cases, this is a source of additional stress.

There were some interesting comments about management style, with most of the women surveyed accepting that they had a different management style to that of their male counterparts. Words such as *softer*, *honest* and *open* were used to describe the typical female entrepreneur's management style, a style that was, overall, felt to have a positive impact on her business.

The study also revealed some interesting differences between northern and southern based female entrepreneurs. For example, the typical northern business woman in the survey had been in business for 13.7 years and employed 11.3 staff, of which 5.2 were female. The typical southern female-owned business was somewhat younger at 9.1 years, with 2.9 employees, of which 1.9 were women. The most common business sector for female entrepreneurs in the north of Ireland was training/consultancy, while the most popular sector in the south was arts and craft.

The consultations with the agencies and support organizations showed a clear appreciation of the difficulties faced by female entrepreneurs in Ireland. The fact that most of the agencies were in the process of reviewing their policies on female entrepreneurship could be viewed as a positive indicator that change was on its way.

The study presented in this chapter represents the first stage of a larger piece of research, and clearly, a significant amount of further investigation is needed before definitive conclusions can be drawn with regard to a model for improving female entrepreneurship levels on the island of Ireland. Despite this, however, the comments from the female entrepreneurs surveyed offer valuable insights into the actual experiences of women business owners on the island and contain advice that could be extremely beneficial to aspiring female entrepreneurs. This information, together with the comments made by the support agencies/organizations, highlights some of the underlying reasons for the low level of female entrepreneurship in Ireland and, in this context, offers a framework within which a model for promoting higher levels of entrepreneurial activity among women can be developed. In addition, the significant differences uncovered between the entrepreneurs on opposite sides of the border also merit further investigation, as does the scope for the mutual economic benefit that might be derived from the sharing of information and experiences.

REFERENCES

Bolton Report. (1971). *Report of the committee of inquiry on small firms* (Bolton Committee). HMSO: London.

Bray, L. (2001). *Research into gender equality in enterprise creation in County Louth.* Louth: Louth Women's Enterprise Project, Louth County Enterprise Board and Louth Leader.

Brennan, N. (2000). *An exploratory study of the financial support available to female tourism entrepreneurs.* Unpublished B.Sc (Management) thesis, Dublin Institute of Technology.

Brindley, C., & Ritchie, B. (1999, November). *Female entrepreneurship: Risk perspectiveness, opportunities and challenges.* Paper presented at the Institute of Small Business Affairs Conference, Manchester Metropolitan University.

Carter, N., Brush, C., Gatewood, E., Greene, P., & Hart, M. (2002, November). *Does enhancing women's financial sophistication promote entrepreneurial success?* Proceedings of the Promoting Female Entrepreneurship Research Forum, Dundalk Institute of Technology, Ireland.

Carter, S. (2000). Improving the numbers and performance of women-owned businesses: Some implications for training and advisory services. *Journal of Education and Training, 42*(4/5), 326–334.

CEEDR. (2001). *Young, women, ethnic minority and co-entrepreneurs—Final report.* Middlesex: Middlesex University.

Davidson, M.J., & Burke, R.J. (Eds.). (2001). *Women in management: Current research issues.* London: Chapman Publishing.

Deakins, D. (1999). *Entrepreneurship and small firms* (2nd ed.). London: McGraw-Hill.

EC—European Commission. (2000). *Benchmarking enterprise policy, first results from the scoreboard.* Staff Working Document, Brussels.

European Observatory for SMEs. (1994). *Second annual report.* EIM Small Business Consultancy, The Netherlands.

EU Report. (2000). *Towards enterprise Europe—Work programme for enterprise policy 2000–2005.* Commission Staff Working Paper, Brussels.

Eurostat. (1999). *European commission's report.* Luxembourg: Office for Official Publications of the EC.

FAS. (1998). *Women in the Irish labour force.* Dublin: Department of Enterprise and Employment.

Fitzgerald, G. (2002, November 30). From prudence to politics and back again for McCreevy. *Irish Times,* p. 16.

Garavan, T., O'Cinneide, B., & Fleming, P. (1997). *Enterprise and business start-ups in Ireland, Vol. 1: An overview.* Dublin: Oak Tree Press.

GEM—Global entrepreneurship monitor report. (2001). Babson College, Kauffman Centre for Entrepreneurship, USA, and London School of Economics, UK.

GEM—Global entrepreneurship monitor report. (2002). Babson College, Kauffman Centre for Entrepreneurship, USA, and London School of Economics, UK.

Goffee, R., & Scase, R. (1985). *Women in charge: The experience of female entrepreneurs.* London: Allen & Unwin.

Hisrich, R., & Brush, C. (1986). *The woman entrepreneur: Starting, financing and managing a successful new business.* Lexington, MA: Books, Lexington Books.

Hisrich, R.D., & O'Cinneide, B. (1985). *The Irish entrepreneur: Characteristics, problems and future success* (Working paper). Tulsa, OK: University of Tulsa.

Hisrich, R.D., & Peters, M.P. (1998). *Entrepreneurship* (4th ed.). Boston: Irwin McGraw-Hill.

Jack, S.L., & Anderson, A.R. (1998). *Entrepreneurship education within the condition of entreprenology.* Proceedings of the Conference on Enterprise and Learning, Aberdeen.

Kauffman Center. (2001). *Report on women entrepreneurs: Unlocking the potential to create opportunity, jobs and wealth.* Kauffman Center for Entrepreneurial Leadership, Missouri.

Langowitz, N. (2001). *The top women-led businesses in Massachusetts.* Babson Park, MA: Center for Women's Leadership, Babson College.

Moore, D.P., & Buttner, H. (1997). *Women entrepreneurs: Moving beyond the glass ceiling.* Thousand Oaks, CA: Sage.

Observatory of European SMEs. (2002). *Highlights from the 2001 survey.* Luxembourg: No. 1, European Commission Enterprise Publications.

OECD Report (for DG Enterprise). (2001). *Female entrepreneurship indicator: Benchmarking enterprise policy—Results from the 2001 scoreboard.* Brussels: Commission Staff Working Document.

ProWomEn Project. (2002, February). *Findings from the 1st ProWomEn workshop on problem awareness of female entrepreneurship*. Ireland: Dundalk Institute of Technology.

Puechner, P. (2002, November). European best practices: Preliminary results from the ProWomEn thematic network. *Proceedings of the Promoting Female Entrepreneurship Research Forum*. Ireland: Dundalk Institute of Technology.

Sia Group. (2001). *Distillation of findings from report to enterprise Ireland policy and planning on developing women in enterprise*. Dublin: Unpublished report, SIA Group.

Smyth, J. (2001, December 10). EU study shows women make up just 15% of Irish entrepreneurs. *Irish Times*, p. 16.

Suiter, J. (2001, November 21). Trade revival next year should stimulate economy. *Irish Times*, p. 20.

Watkins, J., & Watkins, D. (1984). The female entrepreneur: Background and determinants of business choice—some British data. *International Small Business Journal, 2*(4), 21–31.

Women's Unit UK & Ministry of Industry, Employment and Communications (Sweden). (2001). *Women as entrepreneurs in Sweden and the UK*. London: Cabinet Office.

CHAPTER 10

WOMEN BUSINESS OWNERS AND MANAGERS IN POLAND

Richard T. Bliss, Lidija Polutnik and Ewa Lisowska

ABSTRACT

As managers, business owners, and entrepreneurs, women have played an important role in Poland's transition to a market economy. This paper uses data from a survey of approximately 1,900 Polish women managers and business owners to make comparisons between the two groups along a variety of demographic, social, and economic dimensions. Significant differences are reported and discussed in the context of recent social, political, cultural, and economic changes in Poland. Our results provide valuable insights into the status of women managers and business owners, and should be of interest to policymakers and practitioners in Poland and all transitioning economies.

INTRODUCTION

During the 1990s, Poland made significant progress in its transition to a market economy. After the "shock therapy" of the 1990 Balcerowicz Plan—which initially caused the economy to contract—the country saw nine straight years of annual GDP growth in excess of 4% and steadily falling

New Perspectives on Women Entrepreneurs, pages 225–241
Copyright © 2003 by Information Age Publishing
All rights of reproduction in any form reserved.

inflation and unemployment. Poland is viewed by many as the economic success story of Eastern Europe, joining the OECD in 1996, and NATO in 1999. Although macroeconomic conditions deteriorated in 2000 and 2001, Poland is part of the recently approved 10-nation European Union (EU) expansion.

As in many transitions economies, this economic progress was primarily due to growth in the private sector and a large increase in the number of small and medium-sized enterprises (SMEs). Poland's private sector accounted for almost 70% of 1999 GDP, up from just 18% in 1989, while the percentage of the work force employed by the private sector grew from 33% to 71% over the over the same period (The Economist Intelligence Unit, 2000).

Polish women played a major role in the economic transition as managers, business owners, and entrepreneurs, in spite of little formal support and often in the face of significant obstacles. Having suffered disproportionately under socialism, they continued to face both subtle and overt discrimination during the 1990s in their quest to be part of Poland's economic progress. There is extensive academic research on differences between entrepreneurs, business owners, and corporate managers along numerous dimensions. However, little of this work is focused on transition economies or women. This paper compares women business owners and corporate managers in Poland using survey data collected in 2000. Data on a variety of demographic, social, and economic dimensions is used to compare the business owners to women corporate managers in Poland, and to explore how the two groups differ and the factors behind these differences.

We believe this research is important for several reasons. Women are already an integral part of Poland's work force and their role in the ongoing economic transition will become more important due to several factors. These include continued social and cultural changes that make it more acceptable for women to start and run companies, an increase in the number of women studying business and economics, and continued growth in Poland's private sector. These factors highlight the need for solid empirical research on women managers and business owners in Poland and we believe this paper is an important contribution in this area.

The next section of this paper reviews Poland's recent economic transition, highlighting the crucial role of private enterprise in this transformation and its impact on women. The third section more closely examines the existing research on Polish women managers, entrepreneurs and business owners, and describes the data used in this paper. Our results and discussion are presented in the fourth section, and the fifth section concludes.

ECONOMIC TRANSITION, PRIVATE ENTERPRISE AND WOMEN IN POLAND

Economic Transition

By numerous benchmarks, Poland has made a surprisingly rapid transition to a market economy. After the initial shock of the Balcerowicz Plan, which caused a 29% *decrease* in GDP and a 37% drop in industrial production between 1989 and 1991, Poland's GDP growth averaged 5.0% between 1992 and 2000. Official unemployment, which peaked at 16.4% in 1993, fell to 10.7% in 1997 before rising to 14.4% in 2001 and inflation, which hit 555% in 1990, was down to 12.6% by the fourth quarter of 1999 (The Economist Intelligence Unit, 1997, 2000). Foreign direct investment (FDI) in Poland averaged $6.5 billion annually between 1996 and 2000, more than in the Czech Republic, Hungary, Slovakia and Slovenia *combined* (The Economist Intelligence Unit, 2002, p. 8). These achievements drew international recognition as Poland joined the OECD in 1996, NATO in 1999, and is targeting EU entry for 2004.

Private Enterprise

To understand the role of private enterprise in Poland's transition to a market economy, the starting point must be clear. A key tenet of socialist economic theory is economies of scale made possible by the production of standardized products. Consumer choice and product differentiation—antitheses to the concept of socialist equality—were considered wasteful. The resultant centrally planned economy featured huge, state-run monopolies that served both economic and political purposes. By 1980, 90% of the productive property in Poland was state-owned and 70% of workers were employed in large firms (more than 1,000 employees), while just 0.5% worked in small firms (between 10 and 100 employees). In the West by comparison, 20% were employed at large firms and 35% at small firms (The Economist Intelligence Unit, 2002, p. 8). The impact of such conditions on private enterprise was clear. Brunner (1993, p. 506) points out that 40 years of this approach had "...stifled the actualization of their economies' entrepreneurial potential."

In the transition to capitalism, the biggest challenge is developing efficient firms that can operate profitably in competitive, customer-driven markets. In theory, this can be accomplished by privatizing state-owned entities (SOEs). Brunner (1993, p. 508) argues that such a strategy is doomed to failure because it does not "...create the economic organization, characterized by industrial diversification, a high degree of turbulence, localized inter-firm networks, and informational properties conducive to entrepreneurial activities."

In Poland, the explosion in small businesses came after socialism fell in 1989. Although the number of SOEs declined from approximately 8,000 to 3,500 between 1990 and 1997, the number of new commercial companies in Poland grew from 30,000 to more than 100,000 in the same period (Central Statistical Office of Poland, as cited in Koen (1998), p. 31). By 1999, the private sector accounted for 69% of GDP and fully 80% of gross profits, up from 41% and 33% respectively in 1995 (Central Statistical Office (GUS) 2000a, p. 360).

Women in Poland's Economy

Polish women did not share equally in the country's economic gains. The plight of women in Poland stands in stark contrast to socialism's professed tenets. Under the "General Equality Principle" of the 1952 Constitution, Polish women and men had the same rights in their political, social, and economic lives. At the same time, gender-specific legislation precluded certain careers for women and ensured they bore primary responsibility for domestic duties. These laws excluded women from highly paid occupations, imposed workplace restrictions on pregnant women, and offered maternity leave and unpaid childcare leave only to women (Simpson, 1998, pp. 19–20).[1] It can be argued that these mandates strengthened Polish families at the expense of equality for women. The lack of a developed service sector and the traditional division of tasks between genders ensured that even women with full-time jobs were responsible for the majority of the housework. A 1999 UNICEF report (Women in Transition, 1999, p. 40) estimates the total workload of Eastern European women "...averaged close to 70 hours per week, about 15 hours more than the workload of women in Western Europe." By 1989, women held "...the lowest paying, and often most monotonous and unsafe jobs concentrated in the textile, food, and pottery industries, the clothing trade, and education and health services. Thus, the average woman earns only 65% of the average man's wages" (Bishop, 1990, p. 17).

When the political and economic landscape shifted at the end of 1989, things only got worse. Arguably, while necessary, shock therapy in Poland was initially devastating to the economy. Negative GDP growth in 1990 and 1991 were 11.6% and 7.0% respectively with annual inflation of 251% and 585% over the same period.[2] Unemployment, virtually unknown as late as 1989, quickly grew and was a major social problem by 1994, when 3.1 million people representing 16.4% of the labor force were out of work. The numbers for women were even more discouraging. In 1995, the unemployment rate for women was estimated at 14.4% versus just 12.1% for men, a gap that persisted and grew in 1999, when 18.1% of the female and 13.0% of the male workforce were without work (Central Statistical Office (GUS) 2000b, p. 144).

Ironically, the competition brought on by the move to a free market contributed to these disparities. SOEs, where women had made the most inroads prior to 1990, were the least efficient organizations and subject to mass dismissals. These losses were countered by private sector employment growth. In the first half of 1995, 228,000 lost SOE jobs in Poland were more than offset by the net addition of 308,000 private sector positions (Mroczkowski, 1997, p. 85). But, many private employers avoided hiring women due to the more costly benefits associated with lengthy maternity leave, sick-child leave, and other "pro-family" policies. Regulations protecting women's rights in the workplace were typically ignored, and newspaper advertisements for open positions often specified that only males of a certain age should apply. Although Poland was making great strides on a macroeconomic level, women were falling further behind.

In spite of both overt and subtle discrimination, Polish women made progress in the 1990s as the perceived role of women in society changed, albeit slowly. In a 1998 survey, 71% of Polish women said "... that society holds a professional career woman in higher regard than either a homemaker or a woman who tries to juggle both roles, compared with 48% in 1993." In another survey, "... 31% of men polled last year said they do laundry, iron and wash dishes in a family, compared with 15% in 1993" (Dow Jones & Company, Inc., 1998, p. 1). Between 1992 and 1999, almost one million women were hired into the private sector. At the beginning of 2000, there were approximately 884,000 "Senior officials and managers" in Poland, fully one-third of them women (Central Statistical Office (GUS), 1999, p. 71; Central Statistical Office (GUS), 2000a, p. 20). Growth rates for women as business owners and employers were remarkable; e.g., the number of women employers grew 63.8% between 1992 and 1999 versus 20.4% growth in male employers over the same period (Central Statistical Office [GUS], 2000a, pp. XXXVIII–XL). There were still more male than female Polish entrepreneurs, but the growth rates for women were much higher.

In summary, the era of socialism and the early years of Poland's economic transition were not good for women. They suffered discrimination and were underrepresented in well-paid positions, improperly trained for careers in the new economy, and penalized disproportionately during hard economic times. In spite of this, Polish women made significant progress as managers, business owners, and entrepreneurs and by 2000, represented a large and rapidly growing segment of the country's private sector.

LITERATURE REVIEW AND DATA

Literature Review

This section briefly reviews the existing research relevant to this paper. We first discuss prior work on business owners and entrepreneurs in Central Europe, highlighting the research that focuses on Poland and women. The balance of the literature review looks at existing research on differences between managers, business owners and entrepreneurs.

The subject of new venture creation in transition economies has been studied extensively. Peng (2001, p. 106) examines the wealth creation process in transition economies from Central Europe to East Asia, concluding that the common element is that "In essence, startup firms create an alternative organizational form that challenges and may eventually destroy the state sector." Russell (1996) presents a new framework for entrepreneurial development in Eastern Europe using the concept of "Complex Adaptive Systems." Scase (1997) argues there is a key distinction between entrepreneurship and proprietorship in Eastern Europe and that the motivations and actions of the two groups differ considerably. He suggests that more research is needed to determine the type of ventures with the potential to transform economies rather than just provide a living to their owners.

Dandridge and Dziedziczak (1992) and Arendarski, Mroczkowski, and Sood (1994) both discuss challenges to private sector growth in Poland after the fall of socialism. The former believe that transforming a "Polish workforce accustomed to taking orders and not taking risks..." is the biggest hurdle, and argue that only training and experience can overcome this (Dandridge & Dziedziczak, 1992, p. 107). Arendarski et al. (1994, p. 50) believe the Polish government must recognize the strategic importance of small business development and fashion "...policies that will enable this sector to survive difficult times so it can lead the economic development of the nation." Kolvereid and Obloj (1994) and Zapalska (1997) survey Polish entrepreneurs and conclude this government support is missing. Mroczkowski (1997, p. 90) blames the fact "...that governmental policies have not been focused on promoting private sector development..." on Poland's trade unions, and the political power they wield.

More recently, Godkin, Cyrson, and Valentine (2000) use personal interviews with 207 Polish entrepreneurs to examine the problems they faced. To the authors' surprise, there were few differences in the problems faced by urban versus rural entrepreneurs or startup versus established businesses. The biggest difference in perceptions of business problems was between men and women. In a study of "latent entrepreneurship" across nations, Blanchflower, Oswald, and Stutzer (2001) rank Poland first among 20 countries in entrepreneurial spirit.

The problems encountered by female business owners around the world and in Eastern Europe have been the focus of several studies. Carter, Anderson, and Shaw (2001) present an excellent review of the existing research on women's business ownership around the world while Jalbert (2000) discusses the important role of women entrepreneurs in the global economy. Hisrich and Fulop (1994) surveyed 50 female Hungarian entrepreneurs about the difficulties they encountered in starting up their businesses. The three most common problems cited were: (1) obtaining credit, (2) weak collateral position, and (3) demands of the company on family life. Additional "female only" factors included: (1) fewer mentors, (2) lack of respect for women in business, and (3) insufficient business training. Izyumov and Razumnova (2000) survey the status of female entrepreneurs in Russia, with a focus on their training needs.

Zapalska (1997), Mroczkowski (1997), and Lisowska (1996) all focus specifically on women entrepreneurs in Poland. Zapalska uses a telephone survey to explore differences between men and women in (a) their motivation for starting a new venture, (b) the types of businesses they select, and (c) their objectives in becoming entrepreneurs, finding significant differences between men and women with respect to the objectives for their ventures and what they perceived as critical success factors.

Mroczkowski (1997) reviews government statistics and numerous prior studies in examining the experiences of male and female entrepreneurs in Poland. He concludes that women in Poland have not made the same progress as men in the private sector. However, rather than attributing this solely to gender discrimination—which Mroczkowski argues is no worse in Poland than in Western Europe—he cites a lack of training and education and the difficulty women face in juggling their professional and family obligations. In fact when asked directly if they had been subject to gender discrimination, 91% of Polish women business owners surveyed said no, although it can be argued that the education and career/family hurdles are vestiges of earlier discrimination (Mroczkowski, 1997, p. 87). Lisowska (1996), suggests that Polish women face three types of barriers to participation in the private sector: (1) social and stereotypical, (2) educational, and (3) economic. Lisowska argues the first applies only to women, while the second and third impact women more harshly than men, concluding training programs promoting self-employment for women are the best means to overcome these barriers.

There is considerable research comparing the characteristics, ethics, leadership styles, etc., of entrepreneurs/owners and managers. Brockhaus (1980) found no difference in the risk-taking propensity of new entrepreneurs and corporate managers, although this result has been challenged.[3] Birley and Norburn (1987) compare the Venture 100—the nation's top entrepreneurs—to senior executives at Fortune 500 companies. They conclude the "...entrepreneurs were younger, better educated, had more international experience, and worked harder than their corporate colleagues" (Birley & Norburn, 1987, p. 351). There was no difference when entrepreneurs and executives were asked to rank the characteristics most important to success; both groups agreed the keys were "...results, people, creativity, and integrity" (Birley & Norburn, 1987, p. 359). Ohe, Honjo, and MacMillan (1990) survey entrepreneurs and corporate managers in Japan, finding the former are older and less educated than their managerial colleagues and change jobs more often. These results contrast with those in Birley and Norburn (1987), implying that cultural, societal, and economic differences between the U.S. and Japan may be factors. Ohe, et al., also find that entrepreneurs prefer an entrepreneurial decision style and extrinsic rewards.[4]

Fagenson (1993) assesses the personal value systems of male and female entrepreneurs and managers, finding few gender differences, but contrasting value systems for managers and entrepreneurs. The most important terminal values for entrepreneurs include self-respect, freedom, a sense of accomplishment, and an exciting life, while managers ranked friendship, wisdom, salvation and pleasure highest. Entrepreneurs ranked being honest, ambitious, capable, independent, courageous, imaginative, and logical as the most important characteristics in achieving these terminal values. Managers felt the keys to achieving their goals were being loving, compassionate, forgiving, helpful, and self-controlled. Fagenson (1993, p. 410) concludes that "...knowing whether an individual is an entrepreneur or a manager appears to be a better indicator of his/her values than knowing whether an individual is male or female." Bucar and Hisrich (2001, p. 78) examine the ethics of managers and entrepreneurs, finding enough differences between the groups to conclude "...that entrepreneurs are more prone to hold ethical attitudes." They attribute this to the entrepreneur's higher equity stake and risk, and the expectation people will act more ethically when dealing with their own property.

In a study of Russian entrepreneurs and managers, Ardichvili (2001) finds significant differences in their leadership styles. Entrepreneurs are more likely to use charismatic and inspirational techniques, while managers rely on passive, laissez-faire leadership behavior. Russian entrepreneurs also use performance-based incentives as motivation more often than managers. Holt (1997) compares Chinese entrepreneurs and managers and finds sharp differences between their value systems. Holt (1997, p. 484) suggests these differences are serious enough to create the possibility of China "...facing an extremely difficult transition period toward a constrained market economy with overtones of a possible ideological backlash." In fact, he concludes Chinese entrepreneurs have values more similar to American entrepreneurs than Chinese managers.

In summary, there is considerable research on the importance of new enterprise growth in transition economies and a few studies into the role of women entrepreneurs in these countries. There are also numerous studies comparing corporate managers, business owners, and entrepreneurs in different cultures. However, there is little research on female managers in Central and Eastern Europe, and no empirical studies comparing them to business owners. This paper is an attempt to bridge this gap. The next section describes the data used in our analysis, and then discusses the results.

DATA AND RESULTS

Data

The data used in this paper was taken from a survey of approximately 1,900 female managers and business owners conducted in January 2000 under the auspices of the International Forum for Women at the Warsaw School of Economics, Babson College, and Project FIRMA 2000, a Warsaw-based business development effort funded by the United States Agency for International Development (USAID). The results presented are based on the final sample of 1,635 Polish women managers and 207 women business owners and are broken into three broad categories:

1. Demographics/Education/Personal
2. Industry/Firm Characteristics
3. Professional Experience/Managerial Style

Demographics/Education/Personal

Our results focus on the significant differences between the managers and owners/entrepreneurs. We first consider the demographic, educational and personal characteristics of the two groups of women. The managers' average age is 45.2 years versus 43.8 for the owners, a small but statistically significant difference. However, a closer look at the data shown in Figure 10.1 reveals some interesting differences. Fifty-three percent of the owners are under 45 years old versus just 42% of the managers. This is offset by the 15% of the managers over 55 years old, compared to just 10% of the owners. Although the means are the same, a significantly larger proportion of the owners are under 45.

There is little difference in where the owners and managers reside. Just over half of each group lives in cities with a population of more than 200,000, and about 41% in cities between 50,000 and 200,000. Finally, the

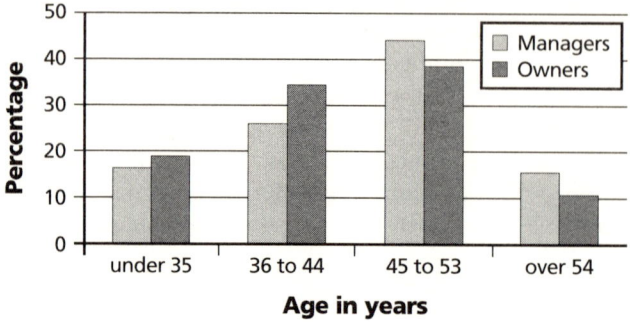

Figure 10.1. Age of respondents

same percentage, about 7.5%, of owners and managers reside in "villages" of less than 50,000.

The women managers in our sample have more formal education than the owners. Seventy-three percent of managers hold university or postgraduate degrees versus just 61% of the owners. Managers were more than twice as likely as owners to have studied economics or management (46% versus 23%), while many more owners/entrepreneurs than managers listed "no formal education" as their academic field (24% versus 6%).

The managers appear to have placed more focus on their careers (and less on family issues) than the owners/entrepreneurs. The managers are more likely to be single (14% versus 6%) and childless (21% versus 12%). Of those women with children, the owners have more responsibility as 46% of them are currently supporting two or more children versus 36% for the managers. The overall number of children is not different across the women in the two groups; about 37% have one child, 50% two children, and 13% three or more. Their commitment to career is also evident in the proportion of women in each group that are the primary wage earner in their household and the hours they work. More managers than owners claim this role (46% versus 35%), although this result is biased by the fact that a larger proportion of managers are unmarried. The average hours worked per week—50.8 for the managers and 53.6 for the owners—is significantly higher for the owners. The difference is primarily due to the higher proportion of owners working more than 60 hours per week (17% versus 7%).

Industry/Firm Characteristics

There are significant differences in the type, size, and age of the businesses where the managers and owners work. The largest number of owner/entrepreneurs is in the Trade and Repairs (36%) and Production (32%) industry segments. While a similar proportion of managers work in the Production industry (31%), there is only half the proportion of managers working for Trade and Repair firms (17%). Managers are more likely than owners/entrepreneurs to be found in the Financial Services industry (11% versus 0.5%) and Construction (10% versus 5%). The capital and regulatory requirements of the Financial Services and Construction industries may be significant barriers to small business owners and entrepreneurs.

State-owned enterprises represent 14% of the companies in our manager sample. Almost half (48%) of the managers work for public corporations; only 11% of the owned businesses are public. As expected, there is a much larger proportion of private companies among the owners/entrepreneurs sampled (85% versus 23%).

The women owners' businesses are significantly smaller—both in revenues and number of employees—than the firms where the managers are employed. Two-thirds of the women-owned businesses have sales less than 10 million Polish zloty (approximately $2.5 million), while this is true for only 35% of the firms employing the managers. Surprisingly, the same proportion of firms from each group fell into the largest revenue category; approximately 9% of each group were companies with sales of more than $250 million. The mean (median) number of employees at the manager companies is 419 (60). This is very different than the owner firms, where the mean (median) number of employees is 47 (9). Clearly, the owner firms are much smaller. There is a much larger proportion of very small firms—defined as five or fewer employees—among the owner businesses (34% versus 3%) and fully 93% of the women-owned companies have 50 or fewer employees (versus 42% for the firms employing the surveyed managers).

The woman owners have businesses considerably younger than their management counterparts. The average manager company was established in 1975 compared to the 1989 founding date for the owner/entrepreneur businesses. This 14-year difference is significant and in fact, 78% of the women owners started their companies after the fall of socialism in 1990, a finding that holds for approximately half of the manager firms. At the other end of the spectrum, only two women-owned firms (1%) were started prior to 1945 versus 8% for the manager companies.

Professional Experience/Managerial Style

The women were surveyed on the total length of their professional careers, their time in managerial positions, and the tenure of their current position. The managers had more total career time on average, with mean (median) results of 22.5 years (24 years). The owners/entrepreneurs averaged 20.4 years of professional experience, with a median of 20 years. These results are driven by significantly fewer managers in the 11–20 year category (25% versus 34% for owners) and significantly more managers with more than 31 years of experience (20% versus 10% for owners). The mean gap in professional experience (2.1 years) is greater than the average age gap between managers and owners (1.4 years). One possibility—borne out by the above-reported data on marriage and children—is that the owners have taken more time out of the workforce for family obligations.

We find similar differences in the groups based on time in managerial positions. The mean (median) values are 13.5 (12) years and 11.9 (10) years for the managers and owners respectively. However, when the question is tenure in current position, the owners' average (median) response is 8.1 years (8 years) versus a mean (median) value of 7 years (6 years) for the managers. So despite shorter professional and managerial experiences, the owners have spent more time in their current position. This is in spite of the fact that the owner firms are significantly younger than those companies employing the managers.

There is little difference in the salary component of compensation between managers and owners. Respondents did not provide actual salary data, but rather selected among a choice of ranges as shown Figure 10.2. There are fewer owners in the $1,500–$2,250 range and significantly more in the highest bracket (7.7% versus 2.1% for the managers). Owners earn the highest salaries by a margin of three-to-one over managers, but in every other category, their proportions are comparable. The owners are working slightly more hours per week, but it does not appear that as a group they are earning significantly more in salary than their managerial counterparts.[5]

When asked about fringe benefits, there were several significant—but not unexpected—differences between owners and managers. Managers were much more likely to receive cash bonuses than owners (43.9% versus

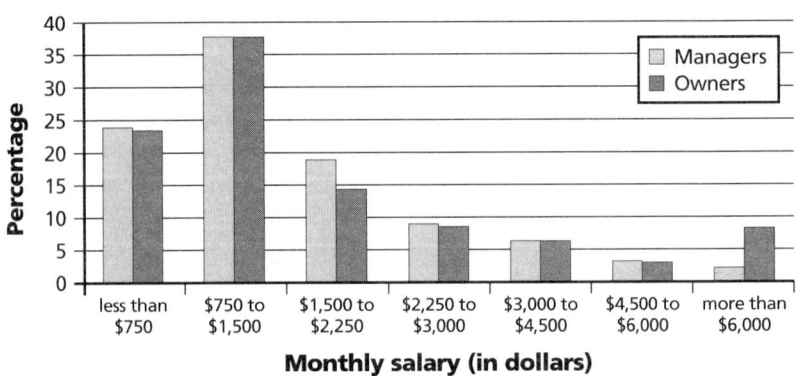

Figure 10.2. Current salary data (assumes an exchange rate of 4.0 zloty/US$).

9.3%), while owners participated in profit-sharing at a much higher rate (25.9% versus 9.9%). Owners were also much more likely to have a company car (38.0% versus 12.3%), an indication that automobiles, which are still relatively expensive in Eastern Europe (and therefore convey more status), have not yet become common managerial perquisites in Poland.

Respondents were asked to what extent their overall compensation met their expectations. Since the owners have control over their salary and benefits, it might be expected that they were more satisfied. However, there is no significant difference between the two groups; nearly identical percentages said their compensation met their expectations to a "large extent" (32% for managers and 32.8% for owners) or to "some extent" (48.5% for managers and 50.0% for owners). For both groups, more than 80% of the respondents seem generally satisfied with their compensation.

We asked the Polish women what percentage of their subordinates were also women. The managers had women subordinates much more frequently than the owners. The average (median) percentage of women among subordinates was 67% (70%) for the managers, but just 46% (40%) for the owners. Approximately twice as many managers as owners had only women working for them (26.1% versus 14.6%). There is no evidence that Polish women business owners make any attempt to "hire their own."

There are interesting differences in the factors owners and managers feel are responsible for their career success. While both groups rate Communication and Interpersonal Skills highest, approximately twice the proportion of managers as owners (51.6% versus 26.9%) felt that Professional Experience was an important factor. Other factors perceived as significantly more important to managers included Professional Image (65.0% versus 38.2%) and Mentor Relationships (21.7% versus 11.0%). Owners rated the Support of Family Members (41.8% versus 24.0%) and the Ability to Change Life Patterns (47.3% versus 29.8%) as more important success factors than managers. Owners were also much more likely to attribute their success to Luck or Coincidence than managers (30.7% versus 13.9%). This is an interesting result as many surveys in the West have ascribed entrepreneurial success primarily to hard work and persistence.

SUMMARY AND CONCLUSIONS

This paper compares women managers and business owners in Poland. Using data from a survey of approximately 1,900 women, we analyze responses across three broad categories:

1. Demographics/Education/Personal
2. Industry/Firm Characteristics
3. Professional Experience/Managerial Style

The business owners and managers in our sample are comparable in age and size of the city where they reside. The idea that private sector ownership in a transition economy is mainly for the young is not supported by our data. The business owners have less formal education than the managers and appear to be more focused on family obligations. Women business owners are more likely to be married and to have children and less likely to be their family's primary wage earner. One conclusion from these results is that women business owners have less financial responsibility and use their own firms to provide flexibility that allows them to spend more time on their personal lives. This is partially contradicted by the finding that women business owners work more hours than managers on average (although this result is driven by a small proportion of owners that work more than 60 hours per week).

The owner businesses are significantly smaller than the firms employing the managers in our sample, both in terms of revenues and employees. The business owners are twice as likely as managers to be in the Trade and Repair industry, while managers are more often found in the Financial Services and Construction industries. The latter two industries have significant capital requirements, which may make them less attractive for entrepreneurs. Over three-fourths of the women owners' firms were founded after the fall of socialism in 1990 and the owner firms are significantly younger than the companies employing the managers. This is not surprising since most of the economic growth in Poland since 1990 is attributable to new, private sector enterprises.

Managers have more total professional and managerial experience than owners, but a shorter tenure in their current position, possible evidence of upward mobility for women managers in Poland. The salary distributions of the two groups were very similar; the main difference being significantly more owners than managers in the highest income bracket. Managers more often received cash bonuses as fringe benefits, while owners were more likely to have profit sharing and get a company automobile. Both groups were quite satisfied with their overall compensation, a surprising result since owners have much more destiny over what and how they are paid.

Of particular interest is the finding that women managers have a significantly higher percentage of female subordinates than women business owners. In the United States, women entrepreneurs and business owners are more likely to hire other women. This clearly does not seem to be the case in Poland, although it is not entirely clear why. One possibility is the status of all workers under socialism, which evolved into an "us versus them" mentality against state-owned enterprises. This is much different than in the United States, where perceived inequities between men and women have been analyzed for decades and may be part of the reason American women business owners "hire their own."

Women business owners cited the support of family members and the ability to change life patterns as important success factors more frequently than managers, again supporting the hypothesis that the owners are more focused on family activities. Surprisingly, the owners also were significantly more likely than managers to attribute their career success to luck or coincidence. This is at odds with the perception that entrepreneurial success is the product of hard work and persistence.

Since political and economic reform began in Poland over a decade ago, the country has made great strides in its transition to a free market. For a number of historical, cultural, and political reasons, women have not benefitted as much as men from this economic advancement. At the same time, women have made progress as both managers and owners and have always been an important part of the Polish workforce. Their role will be even more critical in the future as Poland's entry to the EU creates demand for motivated and trained managers and entrepreneurs. To facilitate this, and to guide policy makers and the women themselves, solid empirical data on the current status of Polish women managers and business owners is needed. Our hope is that this paper makes a contribution to this effort.

ACKNOWLEDGMENT

The authors gratefully acknowledge the support of the Babson College Board of Research, and the assistance of June Lavelle and her staff at FIRMA2000 in Warsaw. Finally, we thank the participants at the *Polish Women Managers 2000* conference in Warsaw.

NOTES

1. Some of these barriers were lifted in 1996, but some remain, e.g., in 2001, women were still banned from working in mines. Child care leave for men has been available since 1994, but is rarely used.
2. EBRD data as cited at: http://www.info.usaid.gov/regions/eni/seed/
3. Numerous other researchers explore this issue, reaching conflicting conclusions. In a recent paper, Stewart and Roth (2001) review the literature and use rigorous methodology to conclude there are differences in risk-taking propensity between entrepreneurs and managers.
4. Entrepreneurial decision-making is characterized by speed, flexibility, and a willingness to take risks. Extrinsic rewards include recognition and the chance to show ability over personal satisfaction and financial remuneration.

5. Recall that owner firms are significantly smaller than the companies employing our sample managers. Extensive research has shown that salary is highly correlated with firm size, which means that the owners would be earning more on a size-adjusted basis.

REFERENCES

Ardichvili, A. (2001). Leadership styles of Russian entrepreneurs and managers. *Journal of Developmental Entrepreneurship, 6*(2), 169–187.

Arendarski, A., Mroczkowski, T., & Sood, J. (1994). A study of the redevelopment of private enterprise in Poland: Conditions and policies for continuing growth. *Journal of Small Business Management, 32*, 40–51.

Birley, S., & Norburn, D. (1987). Owners and managers: The venture 100 versus the fortune 500. *Journal of Business Venturing, 2*(4), 351–363.

Bishop, B.S. (1990). From women's rights to feminist politics: The developing struggle for women's liberation in Poland. *Monthly Review, 42*(6), 15–20.

Blanchflower, D.G., Oswald, A., & Stutzer; A. (2001). Latent entrepreneurship across nations. *European Economic Review, 54*(4), 680–691.

Brockhaus, R.H. (1980). Risk taking propensity of entrepreneurs. *Academy of Management Journal, 23*(3), 509–520.

Brunner, H.P. (1993). Entrepreneurship in Eastern Europe: Neither magic nor mirage. A preliminary investigation. *Journal of Economic Issues, 27*(2), 505–513.

Bucar, B., & Hisrich, R.D. (2001). Ethics of business managers vs. entrepreneurs. *Journal of Developmental Entrepreneurship, 6*(1), 59–82.

Carter, S., Anderson, S., & Shaw, E. (2001). *Women's business ownership: A review of the academic, popular, and Internet literature.* Glasgow: University of Strathclyde Report to the Small Business Service.

Central Statistical Office (GUS). (2000a). *Labor force survey in Poland, I Quarter, 2000.* Warsaw.

Central Statistical Office (GUS). (2000b). *Concise statistical yearbook of Poland, 2000.* Warsaw.

Central Statistical Office (GUS). (1999). *Structure of wages and salaries by occupation in October 1999.* Warsaw.

Dandridge, T.C., & Dziedziczak, I. (1992). New private enterprise in the new Poland: Heritage of the past and challenges for the future. *Journal of Small Business Management, 30*(2), 104–109.

Dow Jones & Company, Inc. (1998, June 2). *The Wall Street Journal Europe*, p. 1.

Economist Intelligence Unit. (2002). *Business Europe, 42*(2), 8, London.

Economist Intelligence Unit. (2000). *Country profile 2000: Poland*, London.

Economist Intelligence Unit. (1997). *Country profile1996–97: Poland*, London.

Fagenson, E.A. (1993). Personal value systems of men and women entrepreneurs versus managers. *Journal of Business Venturing, 8*(5), 409–430.

Godkin, L., Cyrson, E., & Valentine, S.R. (2000). Entrepreneurship in Wielkopolska: Problems and prospects in Poland. *International Journal of Management, 17*(1), 68–81.

Hisrich, R., & Gyula, F. (1994). The role of women entrepreneurs in Hungary's transition economy. *International Studies of Management & Organizations, 24*(4), 100–118.

Holt, D.H. (1997). A comparative study of values among Chinese and US entrepreneurs: Pragmatic convergence between contrasting cultures. *Journal of Business Venturing, 12*(6), 483–505.

Izyumov, A., & Razumnova, I. (2000). Women entrepreneurs in Russia: Learning to survive the market. *Journal of Developmental Entrepreneurship, 15*(1), 1–19.

Jalbert, S.E. (2000). *Women entrepreneurs in the global economy,* (Accessed on March 17) www.cipe.org/pdf/jalbert.pdf .

Koen, V. (1998). Poland: Privatisation as the key to efficiency. *The OECD Observer, 213,* 30–31.

Kolvereid, L., & Obloj, K. (1994). Entrepreneurship in emerging versus mature economies: An exploratory survey. *International Small Business Journal, 12*(4), 14–27.

Lisowska, E. (1996). Barriers to a wider participation by women in private sector growth in Poland. *Women & Business, 2–3,* 64–67.

Mroczkowski, T. (1997). Women as employees and entrepreneurs in the Polish transformation. *Industrial Relations Journal, 28*(2), 83–91.

Ohe, T., Honjo, S., & MacMillan, I.C. (1990). Japanese entrepreneurs and corporate managers: A comparison. *Journal of Business Venturing, 5*(3), 163–176.

Peng, M.W. (2001). How entrepreneurs create wealth in transition economies. *The Academy of Management Executive, 15*(1), 95–110.

Russell, R.D. (1996). The emergence of entrepreneurship in Eastern Europe: A self-organizing perspective. *International Journal of Commerce & Management, 6*(1–2), 21–37.

Scase, R. (1997). The role of small businesses in the economic transformation of Eastern Europe: Real but relatively unimportant? *International Small Business Journal, 16*(1), 13–21.

Simpson, P. (1998). *Polish women in the transition 1990–1996: Political and economic changes* (Working paper). Bloomington, IN: Russian & East European Institute, Indiana University.

Stewart, W.H., & Roth, P.L. (2001). Risk propensity differences between entrepreneurs and managers: A meta-analysis review. *Journal of Applied Psychology, 86*(1), 145–153.

UNICEF. (1999). *Women in transition.* Florence: Regional Monitoring Report, No 6.

Zapalska, A. (1997). A profile of woman entrepreneurs and enterprises in Poland. *Journal of Small Business Management, 35*(4), 76–83.

CHAPTER 11

FEMALE ENTREPRENEURSHIP IN POST SOVIET COUNTRIES

Friederike Welter, David Smallbone, Elena Aculai,
Nina Isakova, and Natalja Schakirova

ABSTRACT

The process of transformation toward market economies deprived a majority of women in the former Soviet states of their paid jobs, as well as most of the social securities provided under socialism. In this context, female entrepreneurship is important not only as a solution to growing unemployment but also in order to take advantage of the potential contribution of women entrepreneurs to economic and social transition. The paper is based on an ongoing collaborative research project dealing with female entrepreneurship in the Ukraine, Moldova and Uzbekistan, all represent economies where entrepreneurship in all sections of society is at a relatively low level. The first part of the paper introduces an institutional theory-based viewpoint to analyze female entrepreneurship in transition countries. This is followed by a presentation of results from the literature-based review, supplemented with preliminary survey evidence concerning the nature of female entrepreneurship in these countries. The paper concludes with a discussion of the distinctive contexts and roles of female entrepreneurs in post socialist countries, relating this to the Soviet legacy.

INTRODUCTION

The Context

The process of transformation toward market economies deprived a majority of women in the former Soviet states of their paid jobs, as well as most of the social securities provided under socialism. On the other hand, the needs of women to earn additional income have grown during the transition period. In Western economies self-employment and small business ownership appear as one means for women to gain greater economic and social independence, enabling them to combine family and work. However, even in mature market economies the level of female entrepreneurship is typically considerably below that of the male population (Carter, 2000), which represents an untapped source of potential talent as far as economic development is concerned, as well as raising issues of social exclusion in some cases. In a transition context it would appear that starting and running a business for oneself, or becoming self-employed, might be the only possibility left for women to overcome the increasing discrimination in the labor market during the transition period and to contribute to the alleviation of poverty (Moghadam, 1992).

Empirical evidence shows that in Slovenia, for example female entrepreneurs are typically better educated than their male counterparts and have more business experience before starting their own business, while they are less and less involved in paid employment and experience growing unemployment (Glas & Petrin, 1998; Lokar, 2000). In Moldova, the level of registered female unemployment to all registered unemployed decreased from 63% in the early 1990s to 53% in 1996, while female participation in small businesses grew (Subashi & Rusanov, 1998), where some link between the two may be inferred.

In this context, female entrepreneurship is important for transition economies not only as a solution to growing unemployment but also in order to take advantage of the potential contribution of women entrepreneurs to economic and social transition. Relevant studies on women in transition countries mainly focus either on sociological questions neglecting their economic role (e.g., Bútorová & Bútora, 1996), on labor market aspects without paying (much) attention to female entrepreneurship and self-employment (e.g., Degtjar, 2000; Hübner et al., 1993; Lapidus, 1992; Lokar, 2000) or on the development of private businesses, discussing the sex of entrepreneurs as one variable amongst many (e.g., Gray & Whiston, 1999). This latter study in the Ukraine found that women-owned businesses accounted for 43% of all small and medium enterprises and 13% of large companies as an important part of the total business community (Gray & Whiston, 1999). Other research on women entrepreneurs in Russia and Ukraine (Babayeva & Chirikova, 1996; Ivaschenko, 1994) and Hungary (Koncz, 2000) revealed gender differences with respect to the motivation, business sectors, business characteristics and strategies. These results confirm the overall picture that emerges from Western research, namely that: women businesses are typically smaller than their male counterparts, tending to dominate in sectors which have low barriers of entry in terms of human and financial capital, but high turnover rates (e.g., Brush, 1990; OECD, 2000). All this leaves women business potentially more vulnerable, which might be aggravated in an uncertain or even hostile transition environment where the institutional infrastructure is still poor.

An important research question for female entrepreneurship in transition countries concerns the extent to which any distinctive characteristics of women-owned businesses that are observed, may be attributable to gender-related factors, such as the position of women in the economy and society, or instead to the overall business environment. Research in mature market economies apparently confirms a mixture of structural, sociological and individual explanations for differences between female and male entrepreneurs (Brush & Hisrich, 1999; Loscocco et al., 1991; McManus, 2001). However, part of the differences are also a result of widely heterogeneous forms of female entrepreneurship, which covers small and micro business, street trade, co-entrepreneurial activities in their husband's business, home-based self-employment or subsistence business in an attempt to combine family and income.

Previous research on female entrepreneurs in transition countries has concentrated on the characteristics of women entrepreneurs, but most of these studies neglect both the heterogeneity of female entrepreneurship and the influence of the role attributed to women in society on the nature and extent of their involvement in entrepreneurship. Society as it manifests itself in cultural norms, traditions and religion might result in presuppositions concerning the roles ascribed to men and women (Chell & Baines, 1998). This in turn could influence the routes for women into entrepreneurship as well as the extent of female entrepreneurship, the form their entrepreneurial activities take and also their success. Research on young entrepreneurs in transition economies revealed that female entrepreneurs in NIS countries were more likely to pursue a business with their husband/ friend or father as partners or guardians, while in Central European countries it was apparently easier for women to act as entrepreneurs on their own (Roberts & Tholen, 1999). Although this might be partly a result of differing business environments at different stages of market development, it certainly also reflects gender specific roles with respect to the role of women and the overall entrepreneurial image in NIS countries.

Therefore, when researching female entrepreneurs in transition economies it is important to recognize the differing cultural background between, and even within, countries as well as varying historical paths and the current role of women in society. Female entrepreneurship in transition countries such as Ukraine and Moldova might differ from that in Central Asian countries, because here traditional cultural values survived throughout the Soviet period and gained importance during the transition period (Tabyshalieva, 2000). Regional differences could aggravate constraints on female entrepreneurship not only where the business environment and the access to external resources and support are concerned, but also with respect to the role of women when traditional clan and patriarchal family structures restrict female roles.

RESEARCH METHODOLOGY AND STRUCTURE OF THE PAPER

The paper is based on an ongoing collaborative research project (INTAS 00-843, financed by the EU), dealing with female entrepreneurship in the Ukraine, Moldova and Uzbekistan. These countries were selected for investigation for a number of reasons. All represent economies where entrepreneurship in all sections of society is at a relatively low level. By focusing on the nature and extent of female entrepreneurship, we aim to provide new insights into the involvement of women entrepreneurs in transition. The investigation involves identifying the barriers and enabling factors, as well as female entrepreneurial strategies, thereby contributing to a deeper understanding of their current and potential contribution to economic and social development in these countries. At the same time, differences in country size and cultural traditions lead to some expectations that there are differences in the opportunities for women's involvement in entrepreneurial activity.

Our project combines literature-based and empirical research into the nature and extent of female entrepreneurship in selected transition economies. The lack of gender-specific statistical data rendered an empirical survey necessary in order to obtain data on female entrepreneurs in Ukraine, Moldova and Uzbekistan. Surveys of female entrepreneurs and a control group of male entrepreneurs were undertaken in the summer of 2002. In Ukraine, a total of 297 female and 81 male entrepreneurs were surveyed; in Uzbekistan and Moldova the figures were 200/60 and 218/63 respectively. Case studies with selected female entrepreneurs are also being undertaken, in order to contribute to developing a typology of female entrepreneurship under transition conditions, and offer additional insights into the entrepreneurship process.

In this context the paper considers female entrepreneurship in Ukraine, Moldova and Uzbekistan. The first part introduces an institutional theory-based viewpoint to analyze female entrepreneurship in transition countries. This is followed by a presentation of results from the literature-based review, supplemented with preliminary survey evidence concerning the nature of female entrepreneurship in these countries. The paper concludes with a discussion of the distinctive contexts and roles of female entrepreneurs in post socialist countries, relating this to the Soviet legacy.

THE ROLE OF THE ENVIRONMENT IN DEFINING FEMALE ENTREPRENEURSHIP

An Institutional Viewpoint

The institutional and legal contexts play an important role for entrepreneurship under transition conditions, influencing its nature and extent as well as its potential economic contribution. Empirical evidence indicates that the dominant feature influencing the nature and pace of entrepreneurship especially in transition countries is the external environment (Peng & Heath, 1996; Peng, 2000). With regard to female entrepreneurship, this also refers to public attitudes, which could restrict their participation in the labor market, with implications for female entrepreneurial activities through putting a higher value on housebound roles.

In this context, institutional theory appears to be an appropriate interpretative framework (Hoskisson et al. 2000; Peng 2000), drawing attention to external political, economic and societal influences on individual behavior. North (1990, p. 3, 1995) understands institutions as the incentive structure of a society, defining them more specifically as "the rules of the game in a society or, more formally ... the humanly devised constraints that shape human interaction." Institutions assist in reducing uncertainty and risk for individual behavior as well as the transaction costs connected with entrepreneurship. They "define what actors can do, what is expected from them, or they must do, and what is advantageous for them. In this way, they give stability and predictability to economic interaction" (Dallago, 2000, p. 305).

Formal institutions include political and economy-related rules and organizations while informal institutions contain uncodified attitudes which are embedded in a society, regulating individual behavior. Raiser (1997) distinguishes between conventions (i.e., societal solutions to collective choice problems), social norms which reflect one's desire to be accepted in society and where breaches are without consequences, and self-enforcing moral norms or values. As North (1990, p. 37) put it: "They [the informal institutions] come from socially transmitted information and are part of the heritage that we call culture." North (1995) also draws attention to the path-dependent behavior of informal institutions, which are deeply rooted in society. While formal institutions may be easily modified and transformed, informal institutions such as norms of behavior and values are more persistent, which leads to an incompatible institutional framework fostering institutional distrust.

Applying this concept to (female) entrepreneurship, institutions set boundaries for enterprise behavior. While informal institutions are the culturally accepted basis for legitimating entrepreneurship, formal institutions provide the regulatory frame (Wade-Benzoni et al., 2002). In other words, formal institutions create opportunity fields for entrepreneurship; informal institutions determine the collective and individual perception of entrepreneurial opportunities. Fundamental rules such as private property rights are the basis for any entrepreneurial activity while the day-to-day economic and political decisions as well as non-written rules, which are defined through applying laws, determine the actual scope for the behavior of entrepreneurs and their actions.

How Do Institutions Influence Female Entrepreneurship?

With regard to female entrepreneurship, the question arises if (and if so, how?) the institutional environment in transition economies restricts their access to entrepreneurship. Gender-specific formal institutions refer first of all to the overall constitution ensuring equal opportunities for women and men. While gender equality is inscribed constitutionally in most countries, its application in a particular economy or society might still involve discrimination against women in practice. Open discrimination is one aspect, especially where wage gaps are concerned, but also, where traditional attitudes of society forbid women to carry out certain activities. In addition, hidden constraints, expressing themselves through the institutional environment, and reflected in policies and legal regulations might play an even more important role in restricting women entrepreneurship. More specific formal institutions apply to labor market rules giving equal access to employment positions, family policies such as specific tax regulations or the overall infrastructure for child care. Moreover, social and tax policies could influence women entrepreneurship, for example, with respect to the level of social security, which is an important factor for potential women entrepreneurs, who might consider business ownership in some cases, as a means of improving household income.

Examples of gender-specific informal institutions include religion and traditions, which can lead to specific influences on the behavior of women thus shaping their standing in society and their economic function. The image of an entrepreneur which could differ across countries implicitly reflects the traditional values of a society. Busenitz et al. (2000) speak of a "normative dimension" which measures the degree to which a society admires entrepreneurial activities. In this regard, empirical studies have shown that most Western cultures still appear to portray the entrepreneurial role as more masculine than feminine (Fagenson & Marcus, 1991). In transition countries, this takes an additional dimension, because gender roles have been revised during the transformation period (Zhurzhenko, 1999).

Moreover, women entrepreneurship depends not only on the availability of market opportunities. It is also influenced to a large extent by the value that society attributes to women in employment. This can contribute to labor market discrimination, which in turn may contribute to women being pushed into self employment/business ownership (Holst, 2001; Munz, 1997), and the value attributed to the family. The latter includes attitudes toward gender-specific role distributions, which might leave potential women entrepreneurs little time to pursue economic opportunities. It also refers to the role of the extended family as, for example, in African countries where (women) entrepreneurs who are successful are expected to assist their extended family and clan, although this argument can also be applied to African entrepreneurs regardless of gender (Rocksloh-Papendieck, 1988). The informal institutions reflected here influence the responsibilities, tasks and the workload that women entrepreneurs would have to cope with as well as any assistance from their milieu they might expect when setting up their own enterprise (e.g., Lauterbach et al., 1994).

Thus, with regard to women entrepreneurs, formal institutions mainly influence the nature and extent of female entrepreneurship. Cultural norms and values (Leitbilder) help to shape the way into entrepreneurship and more specifically women's intention to set up a business. Informal institutions gain importance in those cases where formal constraints fail or are absent. For example, in an unstable and weakly structured environment, networks and contacts often play a key role in helping entrepreneurs to mobilize resources, and to cope with the constraints imposed by highly bureaucratic structures and often unfriendly officials (Ledeneva, 1998). This points to the importance of social capital in the form of personal trust, which is embedded in informal institutions in influencing initial entry into entrepreneurship, as well as for consequent business development and growth. Moreover, the social context inherited from the former socialist period appears to affect both the attitudes and behavior of entrepreneurs and the attitudes of society at large toward entrepreneurship, drawing attention to the constraining effect of path-dependency in the sense of legacies from the past on entrepreneurial behavior. Regarding female entrepreneurship, this refers to ongoing traditional gender relations that persisted even during Soviet times, despite an ideological commitment to promote emancipation through labor participation of women (Kerblay, 1977).

In addition, inadequate formal institutions in the transition process can block the adaptation of informal constraints inherited from centrally-planned economies (Mummert 1995, 1999), thereby reinforcing "socialist" norms and contributing to unproductive and informal entrepreneurship. Here, Leipold (1999) identifies a "syndrome of mistrust" in transition economies, thus referring to the important role that trust plays in shaping enterprise behavior. Trust determines ways into entrepreneurship, and the forms that it takes, as well as entrepreneurial behavior. However, it is necessary to distinguish between the different forms and levels of trust and mistrust. Institutional mistrust frequently occurs during the early stages of transition particularly, and where economic, political and societal reforms are lagging behind (Raiser, 1997; Rose-Ackerman, 2001; Smallbone & Welter, 2001a), while personal trust continues to play an important role for entrepreneurship and in facilitating the adaptation to a market economy. In this context, gender could represent an additional dimension, in that the evolving institutional framework might constrain women's formal integration into the emerging market economy due to redefined and changed gender roles, thus restricting their access to external resources and organizations that are needed in order to realize a venture.

FEMALE ENTREPRENEURS IN THE UKRAINE, MOLDOVA, AND UZBEKISTAN

Ukraine

In the Ukraine, women make up 54% of the population and an estimated four fifths of economically active women are either employed or seeking employment (Dovzhenko & Golubeva 1998, p. 5). An estimated 40% of employed women have higher education or have studied in specialized secondary education institutions, which is 5% higher than men with these same qualifications (Dovzhenko, 1998). Some experts believe that women in the Ukraine face more constraints in the labor market compared to men, which is reflected in higher unemployment rates, lower salaries, a poor child care system (Kiev International Institute of Sociology, 2000), and, in recent years of transition, limited opportunities to obtain a higher education diploma or professional training free of charge.

According to Zhurzhenko (2001b), despite certain changes in the labor market and employment structures, the segregation of the Soviet gender order is still in place, both vertically (as reflected in the professional hierarchy) and horizontally (as manifested in an uneven distribution of men/women labor across industries). Women are still employed mainly in non-production institutions with lower salary levels compared to production enterprises. Moreover, female employees still tend to occupy lower positions and jobs with lower salary levels in state-owned enterprises and institutions than men.

On the whole, the number of employees in state-owned enterprises decreased by 5.3% (totaling 7.3 million people) in the year 2000, while the number of private sector employees increased by 1.1% (totaling 14 million people). The share of self-employed people also increased from 23.8% in 1999 to 25.6% in 2000. At the same time, paid employment decreased by 1.7%. The level of official unemployment reportedly increased continuously from 1991 onwards, which especially hit women. While in 1991 there were 5,700 officially unemployed women, in 2000 this had risen to 746,500. As official data neglects hidden unemployment, such as unpaid leave, the level will be much higher in practice. According to the International Labour Organisation, the actual unemployment in the Ukraine in 2000 has reached 14.7%, which is three times the official level. Moreover, the State Employment Service reports that people who have lost their jobs because of enterprise restructuring or liquidation are less inclined to register as unemployed. The same holds true for graduates and young people with a secondary education.

In this context, female self-employment and entrepreneurship have an important potential role in job generation. Women-owned and controlled businesses account for a considerable part of the small business sector. According to a recent survey (Gray & Whiston, 1999), 50% of all enterprises without employees were women-owned, although the proportion is less in the case of larger enterprises: 27% in the case of those with 1–5 employees; 30% for those employing less than 50. Studies confirm that some of the characteristics for women-owned business in the Ukraine are similar to those in Western economies, but there are also differences. Women tend to run small businesses mainly in the retail, wholesale trade and catering sectors, while in large enterprises, women-owned businesses dominate in the area of mining and manufacturing, two strategic industries in the country (Kiev International Institute of Sociology 2000).

Our survey evidence, which is specifically focused on small firms, suggests that women are involved in a wide range of activities. In business, women fill gaps in personal and professional services, which were sectors that were underdeveloped during the Soviet period. More than half of our sample of women entrepreneurs work in service sectors, including a wide variety of consumer- and business-oriented services, such as dress makers, hair dressers, catering in the streets, realtors, medical services, child care services, educational services, audit and consulting. With regard to trade businesses, women also constitute a significant part of the "shuttle" traders who travel to Poland, China and Turkey to import and sell a wide range of consumer goods that were otherwise missing in the Ukrainian domestic market, although they are now facing increasing competition from new supermarkets in cities such as Kiev, at least. Small scale privatization was another route for women into business, as many small shops, hair dressing shops, restaurants and pharmacies, for example, were managed in the Soviet times by women. Typically, these types of private businesses operate completely or partially in the shadow economy and are very small enterprises. For example, our survey suggests that most women entrepreneurs either own firms without employees (8%) or those with less than 10 employees (61%).

In a situation where the overall level of entrepreneurship is at a very low level, the engagement of women in entrepreneurial activity is making an important contribution to the overall level of entrepreneurship in the economy. Although underrepresented in the business owning population, the contribution of women to the emerging service sector is an important one in a post-Soviet economy. It can also be argued that their accumulated capital, knowledge and experience is adding to what is a scarce human capital base of resources relevant to private sector development.

Market reforms provided new opportunities for those with some capital resources, personal professional expertise and skills, together with an interest in engaging in entrepreneurial activities and the chance to be gainfully and independently employed. Independence is the most important reason given by surveyed women for starting a business in the Ukraine (25%), as well as by men (27%), although the push of unemployment is more commonly reported by women (18%, 11% men). Significantly, few women or men (7% for both groups) referred to the pull of market opportunities, although men were much more likely to refer to opportunities presented in terms of available resources (21% men, 6% women).

In comparison to the early years of economic reforms particularly, the absence of a state social security system encouraged women to start up enterprises to provide some income for themselves and their families. The Ukraine is typical of post-Soviet economies in this respect, although it must be recognized that individuals can change as a result of their learning experiences. The influence of "push" factors at start-up does not preclude the development of more opportunity driven entrepreneurship at a later stage. This is reflected in the data in Table 11.1 which gives the most important business aims of women and men in the last 12 months prior to the survey in the Ukraine. Although women were more likely to state income goals such as "providing a living for their families" as their main business aim as well as being more survival oriented, a large share of both women and men indicated "growth" as their main goal.

At the macro level, female entrepreneurs can be seen to be contributing to job generation, particularly for other women, thereby performing a wider social role in terms of inclusion and partly compensating for any discrimina-

Table 11.1. Most Important Business Aim in Ukraine by Gender

	Women	Men
Growth	46.9%	67.9%
Survival	31.0%	14.8%
Providing living for family	12.6%	4.9%
Increasing personal/household/family income	5.4%	9.9%
Total	297	81

Own survey—Respondents were asked to state three business aims for the last 12 months in order of priority. This table reports data for the most important aim. Data do not add up to 100% because two minor aims (reducing shadow turnover, preparing for selling business) were left out.

tion against women in the labor market. In addition, providing job opportunities for women can help to fight the problem of women trafficking in the country, which is recognized as one of the most urgent social issues in the Ukraine. Finally, female entrepreneurs who started businesses in the 1990s serve as role models for the younger generations, demonstrating new employment (self-employment) opportunities. In a broader context, a successful woman is more likely to provide better care for her children and her family (in those cases where marriage and family are among a woman's ambitions), which doubtless leads to a more comfortable social and psychological environment in the country and greater social stability.

Moldova

Women account for more than half of the population in Moldova, although their share in the economically active population decreased from 51% in the mid-1980s to 44%, compared with 49% for men. Since transition began, the level of registered female unemployment increased to more than 60% of registered unemployment. On average, women experience longer periods of unemployment once they have lost their jobs; they are also more reluctant to leave a job on their own initiative, which is reflected in statistical data showing that comparatively more women became unemployed on the grounds of a firm's reorganization than in the case of men.

Official statistics on private enterprises do not offer gender specific data. However, previous research on small and medium enterprises shows women-owned and women-managed businesses in Moldova accounting for more than one third of all small enterprises (Aculai, 1999; Welter et al., 2000; Smallbone et al., 1999), which is a higher proportion than in many western countries. According to these studies, and our own survey, women-owned businesses are mainly set up in sectors such as services and trade where female employment dominates, reflecting the previous working experience of new business owners, as well as low barriers to entry. Women entrepreneurs in Moldova are typically involved to some extent in the informal economy. They either set up small home-based enterprises that are partly or wholly illegal and/or employ unregistered labor, which in some cases can involve other family members. In this regard, our survey results show that 23% of female respondents estimated that 25–50% of business income was earned in the shadow economy, in businesses such as theirs[1] with another 12% stating that the share amounted to between 75% and 100%. Women also typically own micro enterprises which make it easier for them to hide their activities. This is reflected in the fact, that more than two thirds of surveyed enterprises without employees earned all of their income in the shadow economy.

The pressure for women employees to accept part-time and temporary jobs, most of which are in the informal economy, is associated with their sense of responsibility to provide an income for their families. Women also predominate among work emigrants, who work illegally abroad; anecdotal evidence suggests that the total overall number of these emigrant workers amounts to between 700–800,000. They emigrate illegally to South European countries, such as Greece, Italy, Spain or Portugal, in order to work as unregistered household help, or waitresses.

As far as education is concerned, our survey showed little difference overall between men and women, with 62% educated to university level, compared with 65% of men. Interestingly, women entrepreneurs in services and trade were often better educated than their counterparts in manufacturing and construction. This overall high education level points to discrimination in the labor market, which forces women to look for different employment possibilities, but it may also reflect the role that higher education might play in contributing to boosting women's self-confidence. On the other hand, fewer female entrepreneurs have previous management experience than men (48% women; 56% men), but significantly more women (19%; 14% men) have previously worked in small private firms before setting up their own venture, reflecting their tendency to have worked in micro enterprises and/or shadow economy firms.

A comparison of the motives given for starting an enterprise by men and women from our survey, supports the proposition that women are more likely to be driven by the need to generate income for their household to survive, as well as to increase their feeling of self-fulfilment, which was more commonly reported than in the case of men. The need to earn income for families also is reflected in Table 11.2 which reports the most important business aim as stated by our respondents and where women are more likely than men to mention income goals as their priority business aim. Again, as in the Ukraine, "growth" predominates for both women and men, which in the case of women appears to indicate a shift toward more opportunity driven entrepreneurship since setting up their venture.

Table 11.2. Most Important Business Aim in Moldova by Gender

	Women	Men
Growth	48.6%	55.6%
Survival	26.6%	25.4%
Providing living for family	16.1%	15.9%
Increasing personal/household/family income	6.9%	3.2%
Total	218	63

Own survey—Respondents were asked to state three business aims for the last 12 months in order of priority. This table reports data for the most important aim. Data do not add up to 100% because two minor aims (reducing shadow turnover, preparing for selling business) were left out.

At the macro level, female entrepreneurs in Moldova are contributing to the process of economic transformation through setting up businesses in activities that are new to the economy, even if they mainly operate informally. Female entrepreneurs also create employment possibilities for themselves and others, with previous research demonstrating that female entrepreneurs prefer permanent employment, thus also contributing to solving the unemployment problem (Welter et al., 2000). Our survey results from Moldova also demonstrate that women mainly employ female workers. While the average employment figure in 2001 amounted to 7.8 persons per enterprise, the average figure for female employees was 5.8 persons.

Moldovan women appear to be less career oriented than men, placing more emphasis on family relationships, which is partly due to the Soviet heritage, where men had higher incomes, and partly due to patriarchal traditions. In this context, our respondents were asked to evaluate different aspects of their aptitude toward business, using a scale developed by Jerschina et al. (1996). Preliminary analysis of their answers suggests that, in comparison to men, Moldovan women are less risk oriented and more inclined to plan their future activities. The transition process added to this attitude, increasing the workload of women at home and their family responsibilities. Nowadays, most women entrepreneurs in Moldova would not set up business without the approval of their family. Especially during the process of venture creation, women often need material assistance and advice from husbands, fathers or male friends. This can often lead to women-owned enterprises, where the female entrepreneurs only execute simple administration tasks, while the male partner deals with all major business problems. In other words, women are not always the key decision makers in businesses that they own.

In this context, our survey also shows that in comparison to men, women are less likely to be supported by their partner, even if the latter approve of the business activity. For example, only 49% of surveyed women entrepreneurs reported that their spouse approved and supported their business, compared with 57% of male respondents; 5.4% of women indicated a negative or neutral attitude of their spouse toward their business activity, compared to less than 2% of men. This male-female contrast is also reflected in the distribution of household duties, since 17% of surveyed female entrepreneurs suggested that their partner and/or family could contribute more in this respect, compared with none of the men. Thus, while female entrepreneurs are playing an important role in economic development in Moldova, facilitating the transition process on the microeconomic level, there is evidence to suggest that their current societal role is affecting the nature and extent of their entrepreneurial activities.

Uzbekistan

In Uzbekistan, the situation of women during the Soviet period improved compared with the pre-Soviet times, when Uzbek women had to live according to the rules of "shariah," which prohibited Muslim women from working outside their house. Once the transition started, the share of economically active women again decreased, albeit slightly, amounting to 44% in the year 2000, compared with 56% for men. At the beginning of the 1990s, 47% of all women were economically active, with 18% working in administration and management. Official data shows a considerably larger share of unemployed women (62%) than men (38%). A survey conducted by the State Department of Statistics indicates a high motivation to work on behalf of women, the majority of whom prefer either part-time employment or flexible hours (UNDP, 1998), which is associated with the decreasing number of state preschool institutions during the transition process. Moreover, the rising unemployment rate often pushes women into low-paid and low-valued economic activities. Women who lose their jobs are generally less inclined to register as unemployed, but instead shift at least partly to informal economic activities. However, this is only partly reflected in our survey data where a large share of female entrepreneurs (43%) claimed that businesses such as theirs are not involved in the informal economy at all, while 28% estimated that businesses such as theirs earn between 25% and 50% of their income informally.

Female entrepreneurship largely operates in narrow segments of the market in Uzbekistan. Businesswomen have mainly occupied economic niches that are related to "traditionally female" types of activity, such as trade catering, healthcare and consumer services, or traditional handicrafts. Women are also represented in the manufacturing sector, although in this case their role is typically restricted to internal management issues. Female managers in large companies and women running small enterprises in intermediary, medical, advertising services or trade constitute only a small part of women in business. The majority of Uzbek female entrepreneurs across all age groups work as shuttle traders and street vendors, including a considerable share of women with higher education, former scientists and government employees in education or healthcare, many of whom took up business because salaries in government institutions were either low or not paid on time (Maksudova, 2000). Rural women mainly earn additional income by either selling surplus from their land, or turning to traditional and home-based economic activities, such as silk embroidery and carpet weaving. Incomes received from these activities play an increasingly important role in the family budget.

While female entrepreneurs contribute to the process of transition at both the microeconomic and macroeconomic levels, their function as social role models is even more important in a society, where cultural norms and values strongly influence the nature of female entrepreneurship. Business remains a predominantly "male territory," requiring so-called "male" qualities, such as strength and assertiveness. An additional factor is that in Uzbekistan, transition has been associated with the "Uzbekisation" of society, which refers to the revival of patriarchal values and Islamic norms. In rural areas particularly, traditional values did not change much during the Soviet period, but after the start of transition, they have gained importance across all layers of society in core and periphery regions alike. Akiner (1997, p. 287) describes this as reestablishing the "concept of male guardianship" in public and private life, which is a trend with enormous potential consequences for female entrepreneurship.

Traditional Uzbek society has always attributed high importance to family and marriage, which typically involves female subordination. A commonly recognized "good" daughter-in-law gets up at six o'clock in the morning, cleans the house, makes breakfast, then wakes up the rest of the family. When the family sits for meals, she must pour tea, look for anything needed at the table be in place and quickly bring what is missing. In case the wife has learned handicrafts, she may earn money but her earnings will not influence her status in the family, as they are handed over to the mother-in-law who is responsible for family finances. In traditional Uzbek society, divorce and other forms of protest caused by husband's violence or mother-in-law's pressure are subject to public condemnation. Sociological surveys have shown that this subordination serves as a major obstacle for taking independent decisions on issues related to their own destinies. The woman does not decide herself when and whom to marry, what profession to choose, how many children to have, and what career to build (Tokhtakodjaeva, 2001).

In this context, the revival of Islamic values restricts the activities of women, especially in those Uzbek regions such as the Ferghana valley, where men enforce Islamic values on women, despite the fact that the current government is determined to control any political Islamic movement (Tazmini, 2001). All this is reflected in the early marriage age, large numbers of children and extended family sizes across several generations (UNDP, 1998). Current research on the image of women in the mass media demonstrates that both radio and television portray Uzbek girls as timid and modest, having excellent housewife qualities, and answering to their parents, especially their fathers (Tokhtakhodjaeva, undated). The collapse of the social and health systems following the transition to a market-based economy added to the societal pressure on women to stay at home, in order to care for elderly or sick family members and children. Women also disappeared from public life. For example, the share of female politicians decreased from 35% at the beginning of the transformation process to a mere 6% in 1994 (Tokhtakhodjaeva, 1998). In addition, specific territorial community structures (so-called Mahallas, cf. Geiss, 2001), which nowadays are self-governed neighborhood communities acknowledged by the Uzbek state, play an important role in supervising women's public and private behavior.

All this results (at best) in a neutral attitude of society toward female entrepreneurship. It also poses conflicting roles for women in Uzbekistan where entrepreneurship is one way to gain independence, as our survey data demonstrate. The main motives for starting a business between genders show that women first of all strive for independence when setting up their business (42%; 20% men), followed by "push" motives such as unemployment (18%; 5% men), while income reasons played a less important role for women (30%; 43% men). Men, by contrast, were significantly more likely to report being motivated by a desire to have their own businesses (52% men; 16.5% women) and to have taken advantage of the availability of suitable resources (40% men; 20.5% women). Women were also less likely to have started a business in response to market opportunities than men (7.5% women; 15% men). Interestingly, today's business aims do not reflect female entrepreneurship as mainly necessity driven, thus (as in Ukraine and Moldova) indicating a change of motivations and learning experiences since setting up a business (Table 11.3). While income goals still play a more important role for women compared to men, a large share of both groups is growth-oriented.

Table 11.3. Most Important Business Aim in Uzbekistan by Gender

	Women	*Men*
Growth	70.0%	76.7%
Survival	7.0%	11.7%
Providing living for family	11.5%	8.3%
Increasing personal/household/family income	10.0%	3.3%
Total	200	60

Own survey—Respondents were asked to state three business aims for the last 12 months in order of priority. This table reports data for the most important aim. Data do not add up to 100% because two minor aims (reducing shadow turnover, preparing for selling business) were left out.

While the economic reality requires their increased entrepreneurial engagement, the specific cultural traditions in Uzbekistan re-enforce the traditional role of women in society. However, since 1995 the state has adopted a number of protectionist measures regarding women[2] to strengthen and raise their rights and to rendering support to the women's movement. Active government measures, which are aimed at supporting the development of small and medium-sized businesses in the country, assisted women in setting up small businesses, although the recent shift toward an import-substitution policy tends to drive small (female) traders and female entrepreneurs relying on imported raw materials out of business. Moreover, the ongoing redistribution of state ownership has concentrated the overwhelming majority of income-generating resources in men's hands, while the privatization process hardly benefitted women. This was because typically women did not possess sufficient resources to allow them to become owners of large or even medium property. The reforms of agricultural enterprises and their privatization also took place without women's participation. As a consequence, very few women could participate in privatization and create their own firms or farms. Thus, despite all efforts and the fact that the Constitution of the Republic of Uzbekistan decrees equal rights for women and men, progress has been slow, thereby restricting the nature and extent of female entrepreneurship.

THE DISTINCTIVENESS OF FEMALE ROLES IN POST SOVIET COUNTRIES

The Soviet Gender Order: A Historical Perspective

Soviet legacies have set the basis for developments during the transition period. Thus, any attempt at understanding the distinctiveness of female entrepreneurship in post socialist countries needs to consider the gender policies and gender order dominant under the previous regimes. Marriage and family responsibilities were perceived as the main social goal of a woman during the Tsarist period and women were deprived of any political and economic independence in society.

The revolution of 1917 attempted to change this patriarchal gender. The first years of Soviet power witnessed a boom in policies and practices with respect to equal rights for men and women, albeit limited geographically to large industrial cities and socially to working class and professionals ("intelligentsia"). An important social development, with a long-lasting effect on the status of women, was the policy of "illiteracy liquidation," which covered women as well as men. This campaign allowed women to become a notable part of the workforce, enlarging their place in the labor market. According to the socialist ideologists women were supposed to have equal rights with men and to be actively participating in the "construction" of a socialist state. This policy was consistently pursued for almost two decades, although in traditional societies such as in Uzbekistan, which relied on strong patriarchal traditions and which were previously dominated by Islamic laws such as the Shariah, women always appeared to be under a double pressure, to work for the state on the one hand and to execute the duties of a mother, wife and daughter-in-law, on the other (Tokhtakodjaeva, 2000).

However, even in the other Soviet republics the period of the proclaimed equality of rights was short. Already by the 1930s a shift toward the "double burden" responsibilities for women had taken place. The state placed a dual responsibility on women for performing the roles of successful worker and successful mother (Aivazova, 1998), while at the same time men were looked upon as agents of political, economic and social changes and progress. In families, the patriarchal order prevailed with women being in charge of family budgets, household activities, bringing up children and serving their husbands.

The war years between 1941 and 1945 and the postwar period aggravated this double burden: women had to work even harder to replace men who were serving in the army, and then substituting for men who were lost in the War. A more active participation of women in social and economic activities was also accompanied by a certain feminization of education. The number of female students increased during the postwar period, although this was mainly a result of a decrease in the male population. The increase in the number of women with higher levels of education had little influence on perceptions or on the actual distribution of male and female roles in society. Gender roles stereotypes continued to define the household as a female sphere and work as essentially a male sphere of activity (Turetskaya, 2001). In traditional societies, such as the Soviet Central Asian republics, the essentially top-down emancipation process failed to involve women from all layers of society. Although the Soviet system partly created a women's nomenclature, it failed to overcome the traditional attitude toward women. This particularly affected young women and girls whose rights were limited to a considerable extent by the family context (Tokhta-khodjaeva, 2001). In Uzbekistan for example, girls were still expected to obey to the eldest person in the family and/or their husband, and these values were particularly pronounced in the countryside.

Apart from the women's double burden responsibilities, the traditional gender order was accompanied by discriminating policies in the labor market. Throughout the Soviet period, men occupied the leading positions in politics, economy and society, while women were perceived as "second class" employees. The average income of female employees was typically lower than that of their male counterparts; women were also the last to be hired and the first to be fired. Even in industries with a high percentage of female employment, such as light industry, food processing, teaching and medicine, men would be typically responsible for supervision and decision making while women had auxiliary roles (Zhurzhenko, 2001a). The gender order remained intact until the beginning of the "perestroika" period in 1985, when feminist ideas began to emerge. However, feminism and feminist ideas are not widely recognized in the post socialist societies (e.g., Bruno, 1997; Lipovskaya, 1997; Pavlychko, 1997). Both men and women appear skeptical about the need to change the existing gender order, as indicated by Meshcherkina (2000, p. 115) in her study on business people in Russia. Men in politics and positions of authority do not take gender studies and feminist organizations seriously, although they may be slow to admit this publicly. As far as women are concerned, anecdotal evidence indicates that while the majority will admit that their life is hard and tedious, few appear to blame the existing gender order.

Female Roles in the Transition Context

This specific context and background in transition countries have generated distinctive post Soviet female roles, thus influencing the characteristics and patterns of female entrepreneurship. Even though modern societies theoretically offer a broad range of gender role models, post Soviet societies tend to emphasize a housewife identity for women (Zhurzhenko, 2001a). This predominance of traditional gender roles goes hand in hand with a "renaissance of patriarchy" (Zhurzhenko, 1999, p. 246), which can be observed in most post Soviet societies. This is not surprising in the Uzbek context because in Central Asia cultural values emphasizing family relations survived throughout the Soviet period, gaining momentum since the transition started (Tabyshalieva, 2000). However, there is a similar trend in the European post Soviet countries such as the Ukraine or Moldova, reflected in "widely held public assumptions that business is a masculine occupation" (Zhurzhenko, 1999, p. 246).

This trend is due to the inherited gender order. Fajth (2000, p. 90) describes many achievements of the Soviet period as superficial and the underlying process as authoritarian rather than rights-based. Despite an ideological commitment to promoting emancipation through the participation of women in the labor market (Kerblay, 1977), women still faced conflicting roles in economy and society. Although the Soviet state sought to redefine the role of women in society, in order to utilize their economic potential, the preferred Soviet role model was still the worker-mother whose duties were to work, produce children and run the household, while the state assisted them in meeting their competing role demands by providing the legal and institutional framework that included benefits for working mothers, job protection and childcare systems (Ashwin, 2000; Zhurzhenko, 2001a). Even though the Soviet state partly socialized the male role to provide for the family, traditional gender relations persisted (Kiblitskaya, 2000a). Bruno (1997), for example, referred to the distinctive styles of female entrepreneurship in post Soviet countries because of the effect of womens' experiences during the Soviet period in organizing their household consumption. This left women during the transition period with broad experiences in managing shortages through a complicated system of bartering goods and favors and cultivating informal knowledge and information networks.

Albeit theoretically based on concepts of equality, in practice, the Soviet system discriminated against women, who experienced a glass ceiling in politics and economy. Despite its commitment to working women, the state tacitly acknowledged and supported the male dominance in the public sphere (Ashwin, 2000). Men held most leading positions in politics and in state enterprises, which resulted in women being omitted from the Soviet nomenclature, "parallel circuits" in state firms and other high level networks, which have previously been suggested to be important influences on the development of entrepreneurship during the transition period (Smallbone & Welter, 2001b). As a result, at the beginning of the transition process, women consequently had fewer opportunities to enter entrepreneurship through privatizing large state firms or through setting up small spin-off firms from larger state enterprises.

However, during the transition period, the economic and social roles of women underwent an enormous change, leading to conflicts between family needs, women's responsibilities and their individual wishes. With respect to women's roles the Soviet state left a "paradoxical legacy..." with "strong and independent women who nevertheless ended up doing all the housework" (Ashwin, 2000, p. 18). While the Soviet working-mother contract is responsible for the ongoing interest of women in work, the responsibilities of motherhood became redefined. Following the destruction of the state social welfare and childcare system, post Soviet governments transferred motherhood and family responsibilities back into the private sphere, which post Soviet societies were quick to accept.

Theoretically, the contemporary revival of patriarchal values should have given post Soviet women the choice of staying at home, provided that men were willing and able to fulfil the "breadwinner" role (Kiblitskaya, 2000b). However, widespread and rising female unemployment, combined with growing labor market discrimination forced more and more women into business ownership, in order to be able to support their families. This happened especially in the early years of transformation and in countries where reforms did not progress quickly. Moreover, although post Soviet women look for emotional, practical and financial support from their spouses, they also value the independence that any paid work gives them. Despite the fact that this type of activity is typically restricted to low-value and low-growth activities (at least from a macroeconomic point of view), it helps to strengthen women's economic status, especially where they operate in "female market niches" (Zhurzhenko, 2001a, p. 44).

Regional variations add another dimension to the distinctiveness of female roles in transition economies. On the one hand, core-periphery differences are connected with the institutional environment, where access to the external resources needed for businesses and support is easier in core regions because of the quicker path of institutional transition. However, it also reflects differences in the level of effective demand, which affects the opportunities for entrepreneurship, including the participation of females. On the other hand, core-periphery differences also reflect cultural traditions, which can vary within countries, as well as between them. In Uzbekistan, for example, 70% of the population lives in rural areas which are characterized by strong clan and patriarchal family structures, thereby dictating a distinctive role for women and limiting their entrepreneurial opportunities (Chakimowa, 1999). This often results in women taking up activities that are suitable for being home-based, which is also part-time and low income, with relatively low growth opportunities.

Another factor influencing female roles is *religion*. Most post Soviet societies experienced a return of religious influences, in the form of either the Orthodox Church or Islam. A revival of religious values might impose strict rules on women, which could result in conflicting economic and societal roles, when women are (implicitly) forced to adhere to these regulations. This appears to be problematic for female entrepreneurship especially in Central Asian regions, where Islamic ideas have gained political ground during the transition years, allowing Uzbek fundamentalists, for example, to extend the religious order of Islam to women's rights, affecting their personal attire and their public appearance (Ilkhamov, 2001). This partly built on the legacy from the pre-Soviet period, where the social status of a Muslim woman and her mode of life was shaped by the sexual segregation that is prescribed by the shariah. Although Muslim women could earn income through home crafts, mastership and literacy teaching, this was required to be home-based and only males could work outside home (Tokhtakhodjaeva, 2000, p. 30).

All this contributes to the prevailing forms of female entrepreneurship in transition countries, a large part of which involve home-based or marginal subsistence activities in an attempt to combine family and income. In addition, women often entered entrepreneurship through small scale privatization of shops, restaurants, pharmacies, at least in those cases where they could transfer their management position from Soviet time into ownership. A large share of de-novo female-owned enterprises were set up in sectors, which were underdeveloped during the Soviet time, while female "shuttle" traders import and sell consumer goods or raw materials missing in the domestic market. Thus, transition contributed to the emergence of female entrepreneurs despite the contradictory attitudes of post-Soviet societies toward (independently) working women.

At the same time, anecdotal evidence suggests that generational change is associated with a challenge to the existing social order, including gender roles, especially as more and more women may take up entrepreneurship as one way of sustaining their (economic) autonomy. Similarly, anecdotal evidence also suggests that "necessity push" into enterprise activity does not preclude (women) business owners acquiring those attributes associated with more opportunity driven entrepreneurship over time, such as the identification of new market opportunities, innovation and creativity, and the ability to adapt to rapidly changing external conditions. As a consequence, one must be cautious about overgeneralizing the characteristics and behavior patterns of female entrepreneurs in post-Soviet economies, and more detailed analysis of our survey and case study data may enable us to identify more variation and subgroups within the female business-owning population. In this context, female entrepreneurship could play an important role in modernizing (post Soviet) societies and changing public attitudes toward women which in turn will enable governments to make better use of the economic potential of female entrepreneurs.

ACKNOWLEDGMENT

This paper is based on an ongoing collaborative research project INTAS 00-853, which is financed by the European Union.

NOTES

1. The question asked respondents to estimate the percentage of sales turnover generated from the shadow economy in businesses such as theirs, in order to avoid requesting them to admit they were actually operating illegally themselves.
2. Decree by the President of the Republic of Uzbekistan of 1995 "'On Measures for Raising the Role of Women in the State and Public Development in the Republic of Uzbekistan."

REFERENCES

Aculai, E. (1999). *The contribution of small businesses to regional economic development in Ukraine, Moldova, and Belarus.* Chisinau: National Report for INTAS-UA-95-266.

Akiner, S. (1997). Between tradition and modernity: The dilemma facing contemporary Central Asian women. In M. Buckley (Ed.), *Post-Soviet women: From the Baltic to Central Asia* (pp. 261–304). Cambridge: Cambridge University Press.

Ashwin, S. (2000). Introduction: Gender, state and society in Soviet and post-Soviet Russia. In S. Ashwin (Ed.), *Gender, state and society in Soviet and post-Soviet Russia* (pp. 1–29). London: Routledge.

Aivazova, S. (1998). *Russian women in labyrinth of equality of rights.* Moscow. (In Russian)

Babayeva, L., & Chirikova, A. (1996). Women in business. *Sotsiologicheskie issledovanya, 4,* 75–80 (in Russian).

Bruno, M. (1997). Women and the culture of entrepreneurship. In M. Buckley (Ed.), *Post-Soviet women: From the Baltic to Central Asia* (pp. 56–74). Cambridge: Cambridge University Press.

Brush, C., & Hisrich, R. (1999). Women-owned businesses: Why do they matter? In Z.J. Acs (Ed.), *Are small firms important? Their role and impact* (pp. 111–128). Dordrecht: Kluwer.

Brush, C. (1990). Women and enterprise creation. In OECD (Eds.), *Enterprising women* (pp. 37–55). Paris, OECD.

Busenitz, L.W., Gómez, C., & Spencer, J.W. (2000). Country institutional profiles: Unlocking entrepreneurial phenomena. *Academy of Management Journal, 43*(5), 994–1003.

Bútorová, Z. & Bútora, M. (Eds.). (1996). *She and he in Slovakia: Gender issues in public opinion*. Bratislava.

Carter, S. (2000). Gender and enterprise. In S. Carter & D.J. Jones Evans (Eds.), *Enterprise and small business: Principles, practice and policy* (pp.166–181). *Financial Times*, Pearson Education. Prentice-Hall.

Chakimowa, M. (1999). Wo stehen die usbekischen Frauen heute? *Wostok-Spezial, 1*, 60–63.

Chell, E., & Baines, S. (1998). Does gender affect business performance? *Entrepreneurship and Regional Development, 10*(2), 117–135.

Dallago, B. (2000). The organisational and productive impact of the economic system: The case of smes. *Small Business Economics, 15*, 303–319.

Degtjar, L. (2000). Transformation process and the situation of women. *Voprosy ekonomiki, 3*, 66–73 (in Russian).

Dovzhenko, V. (1998). The situation of women at the labor market under social and economic transformation. In *The now days problems of women at the labor market and possible decisions* (pp. 196–205). Kiev: Ministry of Family and Youth Affairs of Ukraine, Ukrainian Social Research Institute, International Bureau of Labour.

Dovzhenko, V., & Golubeva, I. (Eds.). (1998). *The democracy development issues and equal rights maintenance for women and men in Ukraine within transformation period.* Kiev: Ministry for Family and Youth of Ukraine, Ukrainian Institute for Social Research.

Fagenson, E.A., & Marcus, E.C. (1991). Perceptions of the sex-role stereotypic characteristics of entrepreneurs. *Entrepreneurship Theory and Practice, 15*, 33–47.

Fajth, G. (2000). Women in transition: Themes of the UNICEF MONEE project. In M. Lazreg (Ed.), *Making the transition work for women in Europe and Central Asia* (pp. 89–101). World Bank Discussion Paper No. 411. Washington, DC: World Bank.

Geiss, P.G. (2001). Mahallah and kinship relations. A study on residential communal commitment structures in Central Asia of the 19th century. *Central Asian Survey, 20*(1), 97–106.

Glas, M., & Petrin, T. (1998, May 20–24). *Entrepreneurship: New challenges for Slovene women*. Paper presented at the 1998 Babson-Kauffman Foundation Entrepreneurship Research Conference. Gent.

Gray, T., & Whiston, W. (1999). *A survey of business in Ukraine*. Washington, DC: Management Systems International and Development Alternative Inc. in collaboration with the Kiev International Institute of Sociology.

Holst, E. (2001). *Institutionelle Determinanten der Erwerbsarbeit: Zur Notwendigkeit einer Gender-Perspektive in den Wirtschaftswissenschaften*. DIW Diskussionspapier, 237. Berlin, DIW.

Hoskisson, R.E., Eden, L., Lau, C.M., & Wright, M. (2000). Strategy in emerging economies. *Academy of Management Journal, 43*(3), 249–267.

Hübner, S., F. Maier, & Rudolph, H. (1993). Women's employment in central and eastern Europe: Status and prospects. In G. Fischer & G. Standing (Eds.), *Structural change in Central and Eastern Europe: Labour market and social policy implications* (pp. 213–240). Paris: OECD.

Ilkhamov, A. (2001). Impoverishment of the masses in the transition period: Signs of an emerging "new poor" identity in Uzbekistan. *Central Asian Survey, 20*(1), 33–54.

Isakova, N. (2000, November 23–24). *Female business in a transition economy.* Paper presented to RENT XIV (Research in Entrepreneurship and Small Business 14th Conference), Prague, Czech Republic.

Ivaschenko, O. (1994). On the development of female entrepreneurship in Ukraine. *Filosofskaya i sotsiologicheskaya mysl, 1–2,* 250–253 (in Russian).

Jerschina, J. et al. (1996, May). *Political stabilisation and foreign investment risk in Russia and 11 countries of Eastern and Central Europe. A comparative analysis of political and economic attitudes on the basis of cross-national surveys.* Paper presented to the WAPOR Annual Conference.

Kerblay, B. (1977). *La Société Soviétique Contemporaine.* Paris: Armand Colin.

Kiblitskaya, M. (2000a). Russia's female breadwinners: The changing subjective experience. In S. Ashwin (Ed.), *Gender, state and society in Soviet and post-Soviet Russia* (pp. 55–70). London: Routledge.

Kiblitskaya, M. (2000b). "Once we were kings". Male experiences of loss of status in post-communist Russia. In S. Ashwin (Ed.), *Gender, state and society in Soviet and post-Soviet Russia* (pp. 90–104). London: Routledge.

Kiev International Institute of Sociology. (Ed.). (1999). *Problems of women in Ukraine under the period of transition (1999), Survey report.* Unpublished report. Kiev: Author.

Kiev International Institute of Sociology. (2000). *Women and entrepreneurship in Ukraine.* Newbiznet project, USAID. Unpublished report. Kiev: Author.

Koncz, K. (2000). Transitional period and labor market characteristics in Hungary. In M. Lazreg (Ed.), *Making the transition work for women in Europe and Central Asia* (pp. 26–41). World Bank Discussion Paper No. 411. Washington, DC: World Bank.

Lapidus, G. (1992). Gender and restructuring: The impact of perestroika on Soviet women. In V.M. Moghadam (Ed.), *Privatization and democratization in Central and Eastern Europe and the Soviet Union: The gender dimension* (pp. 37–43). Helsinki: WIDER.

Lauterbach, J., Huinink, J., & Becker, R. (1994). Erwerbsbeteiligung und Berufschancen von Frauen: Theoretische Ansätze, methodische Verfahren und empirische Ergebnisse aus der Lebensverlaufsperspektive. In P. Beckmann & G. Engelbrech (Eds.), *Arbeitsmarkt für Frauen 2000—Ein Schritt vor oder ein Schritt zurück? Kompendium zur Erwerbstätigkeit von Frauen* (pp. 175–208). BeitrAB 179. Nürnberg, Institut für Arbeitsmarkt- und Berufsforschung.

Ledeneva, A.V. (1998). *Russia's economy of favours: Blat, networking and informal exchange.* Cambridge: Cambridge University Press.

Leipold, H. (1999). Institutionenbildung in der Transformation. In H.-H. Höhmann (Ed.), *Spontaner oder gestalteter Prozeß? Die Rolle des Staates in der Wirtschaftstransformation* (pp. 133–151). Schriftenreihe des BiOst, 38. Baden-Baden, Nomos.

Lipovskaya, O. (1997). Women's groups in Russia. In M. Buckley (Ed.), *Post-Soviet women: From the Baltic to Central Asia* (pp. 186–199). Cambridge: Cambridge University Press.

Lokar, S. (2000). Gender aspects of employment and unemployment in central and eastern Europe. In M. Lazreg (Ed.), *Making the transition work for women in Europe and Central Asia* (pp. 12–25). World Bank Discussion Paper No. 411. Washington, DC: World Bank.

Loscocco, K.A., Robinson, J., Hall, R.H., & Allen, J.K. (1991). Gender and small business success: An inquiry into women's relative disadvantage. *Social Forces, 70*(1), 65–85.

Maksudova, C.M. (2000). *Marketing research of women's role in small business.* Master's thesis. Tashkent: State Economic University.

McManus, P.A. (2001). Women's participation in self-employment in western industrialized nations. *International Journal of Sociology, 31*(2), 70–97.

Meshcherkina, E. (2000). New Russian men: Masculinity regained? In S. Ashwin (Ed.), *Gender, state and society in Soviet and post-Soviet Russia* (pp.105–117). London: Routledge.

Moghadam, V.M. (1992). Gender and restructuring: A global perspective. In V.M. Moghadam (Ed.), *Privatization and cemocratization in Central and Eastern Europe and the Soviet Union: The gender dimension* (9–23). Helsinki: WIDER.

Mummert, U. (1995). *Informelle Institutionen in ökonomischen Transformationsprozessen.* Contributiones Jenenses, 2. Baden-Baden: Nomos Verlag.

Mummert, U. (1999). *Informal institutions and institutional policy—Shedding light on the myth of institutional conflict.* Diskussionsbeitrag 02-99. Jena: Max-Planck Institute for Research into Economic Systems.

Munz, S. (1997). Frauenerwerbstätigkeit im Spannungsfeld veränderter Lebensentwürfe und Wohlfahrtsstaatlicher Regelungen. *Ifo-Schnelldienst, 23,* 21–35.

North, D.C. (1990). *Institutions, institutional change and economic performance.* Cambridge: Cambridge University Press.

North, D.C. (1995). Structural changes of institutions and the process of transformation. *Prague Economic Papers, 4*(3), 229–234.

OECD. (2000). *The OECD small and medium enterprise outlook.* Paris: OECD.

Pavlychko, O. (1997). Progress on hold: The conservative faces of women in Ukraine. In M. Buckley (Ed.), *Post-Soviet women: From the Baltic to Central Asia* (pp. 219–234). Cambridge: Cambridge University Press.

Peng, M. (2000). *Business strategies in transition economies.* Thousand Oaks, London, New Delhi: Sage.

Peng, M., & Heath, P.S. (1996). The growth of the firm in planned economies in transition: Institutions, organizations, and strategic choice. *Academy of Management Review, 21*(2), 492–528.

Raiser, M. (1997). *Informal institutions, social capital and economic transition: Reflections on a neglected dimension.* EBRD Working Paper, 25. London: EBRD.

Roberts, K., & Tholen, J. (1999). Junge Unternehmer in den neuen Marktgesellschaften Mittel- und Osteuropas. In D. Bögenhold (Ed.), *Unternehmensgründungen und Dezentralität - Eine Renaissance der beruflichen Selbständigkeit?* (pp. 257–278). Opladen: Westdeutscher Verlag.

Rocksloh-Papendieck, B. (1988). *Frauenarbeit am Straßenrand: Kenkeyküchen in Ghana.* Arbeiten aus dem Institut für Afrikakunde, 55. Deutsches Überseeinstitut, Hamburg.

Rose-Ackermann, S. (2001). Trust and honesty in post-socialist societies. *Kyklos*, *54*(2/3), 415–444.
Smallbone, D., Welter, F., Isakova, N., Klochko, Yu., Aculai, E., & Slonimski, A. (1999). *The support needs of small enterprises in Ukraine, Belarus and Moldova: Developing a policy agenda.* CEEDR, Middlesex University, Enfield.
Smallbone, D., & Welter, F. (2001a). The role of government in SME development in transition countries. *International Small Business Journal, 19*(4), 63–77.
Smallbone, D., & Welter, F. (2001b). The distinctiveness of entrepreneurship in transition economies. *Small Business Economics, 16*(4), 249–262.
Subashi, B., & Rusanov, A. (1998). *Transformation of labour market and potential increase in employment in the Republic of Moldova.* Chisinau (in Russian).
Tabyshalieva, A. (2000). Revival of traditions in post-Soviet Central Asia. In M. Lazreg (Ed.), *Making the transition work for women in Europe and Central Asia* (pp. 51–57). World Bank Discussion Paper No. 411. Washington, DC: World Bank.
Tazmini, G. (2001). The Islamic revival in central Asia: A potent force or a misconception? *Central Asian Survey, 20*(1), 63–83.
Tokhtatkhodjaeva, M. (1998). *Gender issues in Uzbekistan.* First Draft. Committed by UNFPA. Tashkent. Internet. http://www.undp.uz/GID/eng/UZBEKISTAN/GENERAL/RESEARCH/gender_wrc.html.
Tokhtakhodjaeva, M. (N.D.). *Traditional stereotypes and women's problems over the period of transition* (Survey of media in Uzbekistan). Internet: http/www.undp.uz/GID/eng/UZBEKISTAN/GENERAL/RESEARCH/uzngo_res.html.
Tokhtakhodjaeva, M. (2000). *Between Communist slogans and Islamic laws.* Tashkent.
Tokhtakhodjaeva, M. (2001). *Tired with the past.* Tashkent.
Turetskaya, G.V. (2001). Business activity of women and family. *Sotsiologicheskie issledovania, 2,* 67–73. (In Russian).
UNDP. (Ed.). (1998). *Report on the status of women in Uzbekistan.* Tashkent: UNDP.
Wade-Benzoni, K.A. et al. (2002). Barriers to resolution in ideologically based negotiations: The role of values and institutions. *Academy of Management Review, 27*(1), 41–57.
Welter, F., Smallbone, D., Aculai, E., Subashi, B., & Rodionova, N. (2000). *Employment, SMEs and labour markets in Moldova.* National report for project Intas-97-1805. Essen: RWI.
Zhurzhenko, T. (1999). Gender and identity formation in post-Socialist Ukraine: The case of women in the shuttle business. In R. Bridgman, S. Cole, & H. Howard-Bobiwash (Eds.), *Feminist fields: Ethnographic insights* (pp. 243–263). Ontario: Broadview Press.
Zhurzhenko, T. (2001a). Free market ideology and new women's identities in post-socialist Ukraine. *The European Journal of Women's Studies, 8*(1), 29–49.
Zhurzhenko, T. (2001b). *Social reproduction and gender policy in the Ukraine.* Kharkiv. (in Russian).

ABOUT THE CONTRIBUTORS

Elena Aculai is a senior research officer at the National Institute of Economy and Information of the Ministry of Economy of the Republic of Moldova. She is also a consultant for the "Agdias-Prim" Credit Union. Dr. Aculai has been acting as a research group director at the Academy of Sciences of Moldova for many years. Her research interests include small private business development especially during the start-up period; business management, business-planning and financial analysis; development of industry. Dr. Aculai has been involved in a number of international projects on small business development in the states with transitional economies in Eastern Europe and Asia.

Leona Achtenhagen is a Research Fellow at Jönköping International Business School in Sweden. In addition, she is affiliated to the EXIST High Technology Entrepreneurship Postgraduate Program at the University of Bamberg in Germany. She received her Ph.D. in Business Administration from the University of St. Gallen in Switzerland. Her research interests include early-stage and innovative organizing practices, organizational growth, open source software development, and discourses on entrepreneurship. She teaches mainly in the areas of international and strategic management, as well as organization theory.

Barbara Bird is Associate Professor of Management and chair of the Management Department in the Kogod School of Business, American University in Washington, DC. She serves as editor of Entrepreneurship Theory and Practice and on the editorial board of Academy of Management Learning and Education. She has published in various journals and is author of Entrepreneurial Behavior. She is founding newsletter editor for and a past Chair of the Entrepreneurship Division of the Academy of Management. She consults to the Advanced Technology Program in the Department of Commerce where she reviews commercialization plans for emergent technologies. Her research interests include women entrepreneurs, entrepreneurial competency, and various forms of entrepreneurial cognition including vision, opportunity perceptions, and practical intelligence. She is currently researching business ownership in the U.S. printing industry.

Richard T. Bliss is an Associate Professor of Finance at Babson College in Wellesley, Massachusetts. His research interests are in the areas of corporate finance, transition economics, venture capital in emerging markets, and behavioral finance. His work has been published in *The Journal of Financial Economics, The Journal of Small Business Management, Derivatives Quarterly,* and *Venture Capital: An International Journal of Entrepreneurial Finance,* among others. He earned B.A. and B.S. degrees with honors from Rutgers University in New Brunswick, New Jersey, and M.B.A., M.A., and Ph.D. degrees from Indiana University in Bloomington, Indiana.

Joe Bogue is a Lecturer with the Department of Food Business and Development at University College Cork. His research interests include the management of new product development (NPD), increasing the competitiveness of the Irish Food Sector through NPD, consumer behaviour, and the marketing of novel foods. His research focuses on market-oriented NPD. He received his Ph.D. from the University of Newcastle-upon-Tyne, United Kingdom. His Ph.D. research is an analysis of market-oriented NPD within the food industry. Prior to joining University College Cork he worked in strategic marketing and management within the food sector.

Candida G. Brush is an Associate Professor of Strategy and Policy, Director of the Council for Women's Entrepreneurship and Leadership (CWEL), and Research Director for the Entrepreneurial Management Institute at Boston University. She was a Research Affiliate to Jonkoping International Business School, Jonkoping, Sweden. Her research investigates the influence of gender in business start-up, and resource acquisition and strategies of in emerging ventures. Most recently with four other researchers, she was funded by the Kauffman Center for Entrepreneurial Leadership, U.S. Small Business Administration, the National Women's Business Council and ESBI (Sweden) to investigate women's access to equity capital, for research referred to as the Diana Project. A book, Women and Wealth Creation: Uncovering the Myths (Prentice Hall-Financial Times) is forthcoming in 2003. She has published Journal of Business Venturing, Strategic

Management Journal, Entrepreneurship Theory and Practice, Journal of Management, Venture Capital Journal, Academy of Management Executive, Journal of Small Business Management, and Journal of Business Research. She has authored papers for the Organization for Economic Cooperation and Development (OECD) and International Labour Organization (ILO). She is the 2001 recipient of the Entrepreneurship Mentor Award, given by the National Academy of Management Entrepreneurship Division and co-authored a paper receiving the SBIDA best conceptual paper for 2002.

Nancy M. Carter is the Richard M. Schulze Endowed Chair in Entrepreneurship at the University of St. Thomas, Minneapolis Minnesota. Professor Carter directs the M.B.A. entrepreneurship program at St. Thomas and works closely with government and private sector initiatives promoting women entrepreneurs. Dr. Carter serves on the International Board of Advisors, Jonkoping International Business School, Sweden, and the Board of Directors of the Women's Business Research Center, Washington, D.C. Her research interests include the emergence of organizations with a special emphasis on women- and minority-owned initiatives, and the founding strategies of new businesses. Her research on women and minorities entrepreneurs is funded by awards from the National Science Foundation, the U.S. Small Business Administration, the National Business Women's Council and the Kauffman Center for Entrepreneurial Leadership. She co-founded the Entrepreneurial Research Consortium, the organizing group for the Panel Study of Entrepreneurial Dynamics (PSED), and the Diana Project, a research group focusing on women and high growth ventures. She received her Ph.D. in Business Administration from the University of Nebraska, an M.A. in Mass Communications from California State University, and a B.A. in Journalism from the University of Nebraska.

Sara Carter is currently on internal secondment from the Department of Marketing to the Hunter Centre for Entrepreneurship at the University of Strathclyde. Professor Sara Carter has undertaken several research studies of gender and enterprise, funded by organisations such as the Economic and Social Research Council, Department of Trade and Industry Small Business Service, Scottish Enterprise and the Centre for Women's Business Research, Washington DC. Sara Carter is co-author (with Tom Cannon) of 'Women as Entrepreneurs' (1992) Academic Press, London and co-editor (with Dylan Jones-Evans) of 'Enterprise and Small Business: Principles, Practice and Policy' (2000) FT Prentice Hall, London.

Richael Connolly holds a Bachelor of Commerce from the National University of Ireland, University College Cork, (UCC) where she is currently a research Masters student in strategic management and entrepreneurship. Her research interests focus on new venture start-up behaviours, the impact of contextual factors on these behaviours, success factors and barriers of starting a new venture for the recent graduate entrepreneur and the importance of practical experience from employment for these graduate entrepreneurs. In addition to her academic pursuits, Richael has won the UCC Entrepreneurship Award and the Enterprise Ireland Postgraduate Student Entrepreneurship Award.

Patricia Greene holds the Ewing Marion Kauffman Chair in Entrepreneurial Leadership in the Henry R. Bloch School of Business and Public Administration, University of Missouri–Kansas City. Dr. Greene earned a Ph.D. from the University of Texas at Austin, an MBA from the University of Nevada, Las Vegas, and a BS from The Pennsylvania State University. She currently teaches courses in new venture creation and entrepreneurial consulting while her previous teaching experience includes marketing, finance, organizational theory, and organization management. Her research focuses on the identification, acquisition, and combination of entrepreneurial resources and minority entrepreneurship has been published in a variety of academic and trade journals. She is a founding member of the Diana Project dedicated to research on the growth of women owned businesses. Her previous industry experience lies primarily in the health care sector.

Margaret J. Greer is an Assistant Professor of Sociology at National University in Sacramento CA. Her research interests focus on systems of inequality expressed through gender, race, social class, and the organization of the labor force.

Colette Henry is Head of the Department of Business Studies at Dundalk Institute of Technology, and Head of the Institute's Centre for Entrepreneurship Research. Prior to joining the Business School, Colette spent a number of years designing and delivering entrepreneurship training and support programmes as part of her role as the Institute's Industrial Services Officer. She has also worked in the private sector, both at home and abroad, in a sales and marketing capacity. Colette is an approved business mentor with; a member of the Institute of Business Advisers; a former Board Member of TII (Technology Innovation Information) in Luxembourg, and manager of DKIT's ProWomEn project—the EU initiative researching the barriers to female entrepreneurship. She has been involved in several EU consultancy and research projects concerning innovation, entrepreneurship and technology transfer. Her current role focuses mainly on entrepreneurship research projects as well as the supervision of

Masters/PhD Research students. Colette has published several papers in the area of Entrepreneurship, more specifically the effectiveness of Entrepreneurship Education and Training, and has just completed a specialist research monograph with two colleagues at Queen's University for Ashgate Publications in the UK.

Nina Isakova holds a scientific degree of Candidate of Sciences in Economics from the National Academy of Sciences Ukraine. Currently she is a senior researcher at the Center for Scientific and Technological Potential and Science History Studies at the National Academy of Sciences Ukraine. She does research on small business and entrepreneurship in transition economies, science and technology policy and innovation. Her recent work focuses on female entrepreneurship. In addition to her academic pursuits, N. Isakova was a co-founder of a private consulting center in Kiev, VENTURE center (1993-1998) and has had work experience at USAID-funded NEWBIZNET project in Kiev as Deputy Director in Small and Medium Enterprise Policy (1997-1998).

Sarah Kennedy is a researcher with Dundalk Institute of Technology investigating the "rise and fall" of the dot.com businesses. The core part of her research work, which she is completing as part of her Masters degree, involves a comparative study of internet businesses in both Ireland and the USA. Sarah holds a B.A. honour degree in Accounting and Finance.

Nan Langowitz is the Faculty Director of the Center for Women's Leadership and an Associate Professor of Management at Babson College. At the Center for Women's Leadership, Professor Langowitz works with Babson faculty on research related to advancing women in business, entrepreneurship, and nonprofit management, oversees the Women's Leadership Program, which offers enhanced leadership training and mentoring opportunities to high-potential MBA and undergraduate women, and develops educational programming for students, alumni, and the business community. In the classroom, Professor Langowitz teaches competitive strategy and the management of innovation. She was previously a design team member and Director of Babson's innovative Intermediate Management Core curriculum, for which Babson received the Pew Leadership Award and the TIAA-CREF Hesburgh Award. Professor Langowitz is the author of numerous journal articles, research studies and cases and her academic background includes a DBA from Harvard Business School, an MBA from New York University and a B.A. from Cornell University.

Ewa Lisowska is an Associate Professor of women's entrepreneurship at the Warsaw School of Economics (Poland). She received her Ph.D. in economic science from this School in 1986. Her recent research interests include business startups by women, women's management style as well as barriers of entrepreneurship in Poland and other countries in transition. Publication included several book chapters, dozens of articles in academic journals and conference proceedings, and two books: "Polish Women in the Business World" (editor together with Professor Ewa Maslyk-Musial) and "Entrepreneurship of Women in Poland and other countries of Central and Eastern Europe" (2001). She has edited the journal "Women & Business" since 1993 (in Polish and English). In addition to her academic pursuits, Dr. Lisowska has founded a non-governmental association–the International Forum for Women (1993) which of she is the president.

Susan Marlow is Principal Lecturer in Human Resource Management at Leicester Business School, De Montfort University where she teaches both undergraduate and post graduate students. Susan Marlow has extensive experience of both research and consultancy in the small firm sector, having also published extensively in academic journals and the wider media, and has also held a number of research awards to investigate issues of ethnic entrepreneurship, female self-employment and employee relations in smaller firms.

Claudia Morgan is a Ph.D. candidate at the Heller School for Social Policy and Management at Brandeis University. She has an M.A. in Social Policy and Women's Studies from Brandeis and a B.A. in Philosophy from Brown University. Claudia was an NIH Social Sciences Research Training Fellow in 1992-94; she has substantial experience in social service program design and human resources management. She is now writing her dissertation on the social objectives and experience of a U.S. federal program for women's self-employment.

Catherine W. Ng is an Assistant Professor in the Department of Management of the Hong Kong Polytechnic University. Her doctoral degree is in Women's Studies from the University of Kent at Canterbury. Her research interests include women and work, women and political participation, and women in management. She has published on topics such as state feminism, women-friendly HRM, work-family conflicts, women and disabled tokens and equal employment opportunities. She is also active in women's, political and community groups, and has served as a co-opted member of the Equal Opportunities Commission in Hong Kong.

Evelyn G.H. Ng is an Honorary Research Fellow at the Centre of Asian Studies, University of Hong Kong. She has an M.A. in Language Studies from the University of Hong Kong and an M.A. in Women's Studies from the University Melbourne. She has recently published in the *Asian Journal of Women's Studies* and the *Asian Journal of Public Administration.* Her research interests include women and work, women and the family, and women in politics. She is a member of the working committee of the Women's Studies Research Centre, University of Hong Kong, which organizes seminars to bring together local scholars in Hong Kong and academic visitors from abroad. She is the current Chair of the Hong Kong Federation of Women's Centres, a grassroots organization.

Bill O'Gorman is a lecturer in the Department of Management and Marketing at University College Cork (UCC), Ireland. Prior to joining UCC Bill worked at senior management level in industry for over twenty-five years. In 1992 he founded and managed his own electronic sub-contract company. In 1993 he received his MSc in Organisation Behaviour from Trinity College Dublin. Bill lectures in Enterprise Management, Small Business Ventures Development, Organisation Development, Manufacturing Systems, and Quality Management. His area of research is entrepreneurship and enterprise development, which includes measuring the impact of multi-national corporations (MNCs) on nascent and sustainable entrepreneurs and their organisations. He also supervises postgraduate Masters students who are researching (i) graduate entrepreneurship and (ii) the impact of policy and policy makers on the development of entrepreneurial activities in rural and urban areas. Bill is the organiser of the annual Management and Marketing Doctoral Colloquium at UCC and was also the organizer of the successful SME Policy Futures Seminar at UCC. Bill also works with the President's Office furthering the entrepreneurial agenda and enhancing the enterprise spirit and culture at UCC. As part of this role he is academic mentor to the students' entrepreneurship society, E-Soc. He is also an academic director of, Technology Transfer Initiative (TTI), which develops closer practical links between industry sectors and the university. He is a director of the South Eastern Business Innovation Centre (SEBIC), which is responsible for nurturing micro-industries and nascent entrepreneurs in the South East region of Ireland. He is also a member of the government's Department of Enterprise, Trade and Employment, round table group for SME development. Most recently Bill has been responsible for the development of the Family Business Management programs at UCC.

Lidija Polutnik is an Associate Professor of Economics at Babson College in Wellesley, Massachusetts. Dr. Polutnik conducts research in strategic cost management, labor economics and public finance where she is examining the role of institutions in countries in transition. Her work has appeared in numerous academic journals including: *The European Accounting Review, Advances in Management Accounting, Journal of Cost Management, Journal of Corporate Accounting and Finance, Industrial Relations Journal,* and *Comparative Economic Studies Journal.* Dr. Polutnik has earned B.S. from University of

Maribor in Slovenia, M.A. from Ohio University and Ph.D. from Georgia State University.

David Smallbone is Professor of Small and Medium Enterprises at Middlesex University and Head of the Centre for Enterprise and Economic Development Research (CEEDR), which is one of the larger specialist SME research centres in the UK. He is also Vice President of the Institute of Small Business Affairs (ISBA) and a member of the Executive Committee of the European Council for Small Business. David has 15 years of experience of SME research on a variety of topics, focusing particularly on applied policy issues, on which he has published widely. David's current research interests include entrepreneurship and SME development in transition and emerging market economies; black and minority enterprise; entrepreneurship and small business development in rural areas; innovation and innovation policy relating to small firms; social enterprise; growth processes in small firms; and strategic management processes in small firms. Professor Smallbone also works part-time as a policy consultant to the OECD.

Natalja Ju. Shakirowa is deputy director for international relationships in the Business Women Association of Uzbekistan which was set up by women entrepreneurs in the early 1990s. She holds a scientific degree of Doctor of Philosophy. Dr. Shakirowa's main areas of interest deal with business trainings for women start-ups, women entrepreneurs in small enterprises and re-training unemployed women in handicraft professions. She has broad international experiences in how to prepare women for entrepreneurial activities.

Friederike Welter is senior researcher in the Rhine-Westfalia Institute for Economic Research (RWI) which is a renowned economic policy institute in Germany, and a lecturer at the University of Lüneburg. She holds a scientific degree of Dr. habil in economics and business administration. For more than 10 years, she has been involved in SME research projects both on behalf of German ministries and international organisations. In addition, she works as a consultant for the German government. Her main research interests, on which she has published widely, are SME development in general, strategic processes in SMEs and new ventures, (female) entrepreneurship and support policies, and entrepreneurship in the emerging market economies in post-Soviet countries in Eastern Europe and Central Asia.

Mary Williams is a Professor in the Managing Information Systems/Decision Sciences department at Widener University. Her recent publications have appeared in the *Journal of Business Venturing, The Quarterly Review of*

Economics and Finance, the Journal of Management and Governance, and *The Tax Advisor.* As Research Director of Wharton's Enterprising Families Initiative her current research is in the field of entrepreneurship and family business with publications in *Family Business Review, Advances in Entrepreneurship, The Journal of Family and Economic Issues,* and *Research in Entrepreneurship and Management* (forthcoming). She received her Ph.D. in Economics from Temple University.